D1265309

Challenger

Mickey Thompson
with Griffith Borgeson

Challenger

Mickey Thompson's Own

Story of His Life of Speed

Prentice-Hall, Inc., Englewood Cliffs, New Jersey

Contents

v

A Few Clues About Mickey

MICKEY THOMPSON IS ONE OF THE MOST FANTASTIC MEN OF OUR age, a legend in his own time. He is an outlaw, but a creative one, with a strong sense of responsibility to his fellow man and his own peculiar code of high ideals. His accomplishments stagger the imagination and so do his stamina, courage, vision, skill and, above all, his determination. He is one human being in two billion. Perhaps five out of that two billion have his drive. It's a shattering thing to witness.

I had the fortune to observe Mickey for many years, while he was obscure and when he began to discover his destiny . . . and then seized it by the throat and directed it where *he* wanted it to go.

When the chips really were down I had the fortune to be the person closest to him, next to Judy and Fritz, in that order. I watched him deal with crushing obstacles—economic, technical, human and emotional—and, incredulously at first, saw him doggedly and confidently overcome each one.

Eventually I came to know that whatever Mickey wants Mickey gets; that there is no personal challenge remotely within the limits of reason which he will not conquer or go down fighting in the attempt to conquer. He is almost pathologically incapable of quitting.

Eventually I realized that *Challenger*, as he called his Land Speed Record machine, had a deeper meaning. *Challenger* is Mickey's middle name; challenge is the pure essence of his life. In his compulsive, violently propelled way he eternally lives the words of the poet who said, "I am the master of my fate, I am the captain of my soul." Mickey acknowledges just one superior force and that is the Divine Force that he believes moves the universe, *is* the universe.

Mickey is entirely capable of writing the story of his life unaided, and of doing a fine job of it. But he would never have the time and he *never* looks back. When he's most involved in the present he's living, mentally, in countless sectors of the future. He foresaw this volume in 1959 when he said to me,

"You know, one of these days they're going to want to publish the story of my life. You're the guy I want to help me put it into words. No hurry. Just whenever the time is right and you're ready. But you're the guy."

We both knew that Mickey was right and that is when he began saving up anecdotes for me and I began ferreting out and spending long interview hours with almost every human being who has played an important part in his life. Only in this way could Mickey's bizarre past be reconstructed, while he continued to manipulate the future. Still, Mickey himself is the major source for the contents of this book. It is *his* story, as he has told it to me and has lived it in my presence. Others helped to fill in forgotten facts and figures . . . and to provide insight into Mickey which he, himself, does not have, can't be bothered with.

Not long ago I made arrangements at the California Institute of Technology for him to be given a series of psychological tests which measure scientific and technical aptitude.

"Maaaaan," Mickey said, "don't ask me to do that. It would just show up what a fake I am."

"OK, Mickey," I said. "Forget it and believe what you want. I know you're acting a part all the time. But so do we all. You just do it bigger and better than most. I know you can blow up an engine out of misjudgement and tell the press it was a planned, scientific test to destruction. But everybody makes justifications, rationalizations like that. Maybe you're just more honest with yourself.

"But don't try to tell me that this fantastic long record of yours for consistently outstanding achievement is some sort of sleight of hand. I think you're afraid that the Caltech tests would prove that you're a genius, if only an erratic, disorganized, undisciplined sort. You'd hate that. It would set you apart from the just plain guys that you like to be one of. It would seem to give you an unfair advantage over them and that might really wreck your life.

"So you're right. Go on thinking that you're just a hard-working backyard mechanic and go on saying, 'Shucks, what I have done anyone can do.' And maybe you're right there too. Maybe one form of genius *is* no more than sheer, overwhelming determination, which anybody supposedly can psych himself into having."

When Mickey read back over the finished manuscript of *Challenger*, he had only one complaint—that he seemed to do an awful lot of bragging in the story. I don't think so but if anyone does, let him put the full blame on me. It is true that Mickey has a strong sense of humility which makes it impossible for him to do justice to his own achievements. It somehow lives side by side with a monumental ego without which these achievements could not have been even contemplated. Consider:

While still in high school he was a consistent top performer in dry lakes racing.

He is one of the greatest creative and competitive figures in the history of drag racing.

He conceived, designed and built the first slingshot dragster, the configuration which soon totally dominated the sport and still does.

He pioneered two-engine and four-engine configurations for record machines.

He made history in the Mexican Road Race.

He has broken practically all major FIA International records for acceleration and did this in machines which he conceived, designed and built.

He conceived, designed, built and drove the fastest *automobile* in history. With it he broke four of the six major FIA records for ultimate speed.

He conceived the unprecedented tire design which made this accomplishment possible.

He has driven over 350 miles at average speeds in excess of 300 MPH and over 140 miles in excess of 350 MPH.

He invaded the Indianapolis 500 Mile Race and by virtue of his own unorthodox ideas, the first year and single-handedly, he created a massive revolution in the engineering of the classic American oval-track racing machine.

He currently holds 186 records which are FIA International, plus USAC American National. It has been impossible to keep track of his drag racing records. They are countless.

These are some of the reasons why Mickey is a legend in his own time. That legend will grow and in a generation or two the perspective of history will enable Mickey Thompson to be recognized as one of the giants of a fabulous, ended era.

Griffith Borgeson

Challenger

1

I WAS BORN ON DECEMBER 7, 1928 IN SAN FERNANDO, CALIFORNIA, A sleepy village about thirty miles from Los Angeles, itself still little more than a big cow town.

Later I came to think of the year of my birth as having a very special meaning. It was the year of the triumph and death of the idol of my youth, a man who always will be my greatest hero. His name was Frank Lockhart. Like many, many other technical geniuses, he was entirely self-trained and had to fight his way to the top against huge obstacles, including terrible poverty. His ambition was to be the world's fastest man on wheels and to bring the World's Land Speed Record back to America.

Lockhart's chief competitor and the holder of the LSR was Britain's Sir Malcolm Campbell, a millionaire, who set the big record at 206 MPH in a vehicle almost the size of a locomotive. Lockhart, in a tiny machine which he designed and built himself, was doing about 220 MPH when a tire blew out, putting an end to his campaign for the LSR and to his life. As a kid I kept one scrapbook and it was devoted to Lockhart. I had sense enough not to tell people that he was the star I steered my little life by. When I was grown I learned to be even more quiet about wanting to be the fastest man alive. It took just one weak smile that said, "You poor, simpering idiot," to teach me that.

The name on my birth certificate is Marion Lee Thompson, Junior. My Dad was working as a construction boss on the Pacoima Dam when I was born and when he first came to see me he brought a friend with him, a big Irish contractor. I had long, flaming red hair and the friend's first comment was, "There's a Mick if I ever saw one!" That's been my name ever since.

Everyone says I was an extremely happy baby and that I remained a happy child until I almost died when I was fifteen. I had every reason to be happy. I had the world's best parents, and my sister Colleen (she came along three years after me) and I seemed to get everything we wanted or needed even though the family income was on the humble side.

My mother is of Holland Dutch descent and her maiden name was Geneva Mischler. When she married Dad she weighed eighty-six pounds, was four feet ten and a half inches tall and wore a size one shoe. She was beautiful then and she still is very beautiful. She is one of those people with an absolutely even temperament—permanently warm, gentle, kind and loving. She was very ill when we children were young and she spent two years in a tubercular sanitarium. This seemed to increase her love for the whole world and she became a professional nurse. In addition to being the essence of gentleness she is very cultured and refined. Too bad I take after her so little.

My Dad also is one in several million but his temperament is the opposite of hers . . . or at least that's the impression that he makes with great success. On the outside at least he's one of the roughest, toughest, sternest, hardest men you could ever meet.

Dad comes from Irish stock, was born in Arkansas but calls Joplin, Missouri his home town. His father, Francis George Washington Thompson, was a legendary frontier type. He was a lawman, a marshal, and at least locally he had the reputation of being the strongest man in America. There's no end of tales of his prowess, like the time some upstart rode a mule into his front garden and he picked up mule and rider bodily and heaved them both into the street where they belonged.

Granddad Thompson was a blacksmith and machinist by trade and was famous for being able to make anything with his gifted hands, from a violin to a threshing machine. If mechanical aptitude is hereditary I get mine from him, through my dad, who is a chip off that tough, talented old block.

Dad was an independent boy and I guess that life with his father wasn't easy. He preferred to leave home and schooling at the age of twelve to go to work in coal mines. Along the line he picked up a great deal of mechanical skill so that in 1925 when he and Mom drove to California in a 1917 Ford, inching their way over board roads through the southwest desert, he was able to rebuild their Model T every night, shimming wheel bearings with pieces cut from tin cans and shimming engine bearings with bacon rind and belt leather. He just senses how to do things. He's built two nice homes without a lick of help except for Mom pitching in. Whether it's plumbing, plastering, masonry, carpentry or electricity he has never needed any help at all.

While working in the southern California oil fields and on big, heavy-construction projects Dad studied at nights and prepared himself to be a law enforcement officer. He joined the Alhambra police force and rapidly worked his way up to become head of the detective division. He served on the Alhambra force for twenty-seven years and believe me he's right when he says nowadays, "It's hard to be a policeman's son."

As I've said, Dad gives the impression of being one of the world's hardest men—which he is. I once met a nephew of the old frontier marshal, Wyatt Earp, and he would tell of paying family visits to the old man before he died. Earp was in his seventies, as I recall, but no one could bear to meet his steady gaze. His fierce, cold blue eyes still burned holes through everyone.

Well, for lots of people Dad's eyes are just like that and he has everything to go with them. A six-foot-one burly frame, fists like hams and a voice of steady, hard command. In a father-of-the-year contest he'd probably finish dead last. But for Colleen and me, his kids, he was like a god and always will be.

Inside, under the stern, wrathful exterior that the world sees, Dad is one of the gentlest, softest men in the world. During the Depression the part of his job that he hated most was arresting men who couldn't find employment and who had broken the law in order to feed their families. "I'll help you," he'd say. "I'll do everything I can to help you, as long as you just don't lie to me." And he would. He helped I don't know how many. But only God could help them if they ever betrayed his trust.

Dad never was tender with me but he was the best friend I ever had. Until I reached kindergarten age, we were almost inseparable. Mom was sick and he took me with him everywhere, except to work. He took me on all his social and business calls, errands and trips. When I was tiny he took me hunting and fishing and taught me the ropes. He taught me to box; to defend myself. He taught me to ride a bike and when I was six I was on his lap, learning to drive. He was California State Pistol Champion and he taught both Colleen and me to handle weapons expertly, and Mom too. He gloried in his family in his own tough way.

My parents say that I never cried as a baby. I don't know about that, but I do know that Dad *trained* both Colleen and me *never* to cry, and we didn't. "It does no good," he'd say. "It doesn't help you to endure anything and it doesn't help to get it over with." I think that he hated crying or tears as signs of weakness but I've seen the tears run down his cheeks from emotion, from sentiment. I'm just the same way.

Now that I've been around the world a while as an adult and now that I have known what it is to be a parent, there are some things about my parents that I never will understand and always will marvel at. One, there *never* was a harsh word in our home. NEVER. The harmony and the unshakable, all-pervading love was fantastic. There *never* was a raised voice. The love felt for each of us toward the rest, and the respect for human dignity felt for each of us toward the rest, made a harsh or loud word unthinkable. No one said that it had to be so. That's just the way it was because that's the way my parents were and are.

Another thing. We kids were never told no; never were told you can do this and you can't do that. By some gentle, immensely sympathetic and wise method, our parents made known to us the standards of behavior they believed in. Because our parents were so good and perfect we never questioned their values and these values became our own without any direct, obvious teaching. I recall that one of the most painful incidents when we were teenagers was when Dad reminded Colleen to help Mom with the dishes. Colleen was heartbroken to think that she had had to be reminded to be thoughtful.

In spite of all his sternness, Dad was very affectionate. He did not cuddle me much as a boy, precisely because I was a boy and he was building a boy. But he would cuddle Colleen and Mom and today he cuddles Mom on his lap like the pampered, loved darling she has always been to him. And he and I still kiss upon meeting and we're proud of it. We're not worried about our manhood.

Throughout my life Dad has stood by me as few fathers ever have. But it wasn't all easy or pleasant for him or for me. The time came when it became clear that I was such a scholastic flop that I'd never be able to begin the medical education which my parents had dreamed of and which had held a lot of appeal for me, too. Let me say I have changed since then and feel it is now imperative that all kids have a good education. But, the time came when my direction in life became fixed beyond anyone's power to control or influence it. Cars, fast cars, were to be my life and I knew this with every cell and fiber of my being.

For my mother this was a grave disappointment but she bore it with a mother's resilient, unquestioning faith in her offspring. For my Dad there were other complications. It's hard to be a hot rodder's father, above all when the father is a respected upholder of the law and when his ability to maintain his most important life's work—his family—depends upon his maintaining that position.

Still, he almost never said no.

2

LIKE MILLIONS OF KIDS, I LOVED TO TINKER WITH MECHANISMS AS FAR back as I can remember. Dad encouraged this and was always lugging home old radios, broken alarm clocks and things for me to tear into. I wasn't interested in the playthings that fascinated other kids my age. I found them childish and preferred the company of older kids and grownups. The back yard was my domain, littered with mechanical junk and riddled with the tunnels and caves I loved to dig. I didn't like to have a lot of kids hanging around, but I always had some little girl friend who admired my junk and played according to my rules. Having a little sister may have set the tone for that.

Colleen and I always were very close and I always felt intensely protective toward her. By the time she was old enough for school, Mom and Dad had explained the facts of life to me according to their constant rule—never underestimate the understanding of a child. We lived in a fairly rough neighborhood, about a mile from school, and although I always was in a rush to get there early to play I would never leave the house without Colleen. Again, no one had to tell me. I would take her across the big boulevard, walk her to within half a block of the playground and then run on ahead so as not to be seen performing such an unmanly task. Later I made no bones about being her protector and until she got married—to a wonderful guy that I approved of—I kept her admirers in a permanent state of terror, which she didn't always appreciate.

Mom's said that when I first began going to school I was given an IQ test and that I scored 146. This meant that I was smart, and it gave my parents and teachers high hopes for a while. But the trouble was that the only subjects that interested me were math, manual skills and athletics. Everything else was a complete bore and I just couldn't give it my attention. When I did apply myself, as in math, I still antagonized teachers by refusing to solve problems the long way if I could find a short cut. I had no patience with unnecessarily tedious procedures when there was a more efficient way to reach the same goal. I had contempt for rigid systems and never tried to hide it. Between this and sheer lack of application in most courses I managed a heartily mediocre academic career.

What did interest me was cars and whatever could be applied to cars. By the age of eleven I had settled into a pattern of feverish activity and work, which has only increased with the years. I took a heavy part in sports, always rushing home either to work on projects or to work at jobs that would provide money for projects. I mowed lawns, did general yard work, washed dishes, sold newspapers. Once I decided there was easy money to be made shining shoes and set up a stand on Main Street in Alhambra. I didn't realize that this was very bad for Dad's stature in the community, but he didn't say no. Instead, through friends, he just saw to it that I was discouraged and demoralized right out of my budding little empire. That was his way.

I was twelve when I built my first set of wheels, a coaster. Over in the Fremont district about four miles from home was Castle Hill, which kids from miles around would roll down in their homemade coasters. I thought that this would be great sport and hammered together a vehicle. I didn't have money for new wheels and had to take worn out ones and wire old garden hose around their rims. I can still hear the *thump, thump, thump* that the joints made as they slapped against the pavement.

Well, the first time I went down Castle Hill it was a fine sensation. But it all went sour when I had to push the coaster back up that long, long grade. Vehicles should *go*, I told myself—not have to be shoved along by brute force. I went back three more times before I gave up the whole thing as ridiculous. Then I went to work on the Mark II model.

For twenty-five cents I got a starter motor off a junked car. There was a service station nearby where I used to hang around. I'd do odd jobs and the owner was kind to me. New storage batteries cost about three dollars at that time but junk batteries cost twelve cents each. I was given the run of the junk pile providing I eventually brought the junk back.

So I learned to test batteries, find cells that still had a little life in them, saw old batteries apart and build useable ones out of the useable cells. I experimented with gear ratios and soon had a motor–driven car. Then I built a free-wheeling clutch device so that when I backed off, the motor wasn't a drag on the car. Then I found that the more cells I could get in series the better the little car would run. I finally wound up with eighteen volts pouring into a six-volt motor and I could really whistle over the three blocks from Tubby's Station to my house and back. That was about the limit of the battery and, with all that voltage, the motors didn't last long. Anyway, that was my first car and, you might say, the beginning of my career of speed.

I had to have more reliability and flexibility and was eager to push on to honest-to-goodness gasoline engines. So I traded junk for an Olson 23 model aircraft engine, traded that for a scale-model midget racer and traded that for an old one-lunger from a Maytag washing machine. I installed it in the coaster but it didn't have enough fractional horsepower to pull the load. So I yanked it down, overhauled it, milled the head and opened up the ports and was in business. But my machine was still a toy; kid stuff. I was ready for the real thing.

This was 1943 and I found a 1927 Chevrolet coupe for sale for seven and a half dollars. Pieces of it were strewn all over a back lot. It had been sitting for years without spark plugs and the pistons were rusted to the cylinder walls. I told Dad about it and about how badly I wanted it . . . not to drive until I was old enough but just to work on and make run. Dad took a look at this piece of rubbish and told me what everyone else had—that clunker will *never* run again. But I had worked hard and saved most of the money and I was determined. So Dad gave in, anted the rest of the price and helped me lug the pieces to our back yard.

Dad was perfectly happy about my interest in cars. He helped me in every way—with money, with advice and with his strength when I needed it to lift something or break loose a rusted stud. What he was against was my becoming hipped on speed, becoming a hot rodder. As a police officer he saw every day what other boys were doing with old cars. No one knew any better than he what they were doing: driving recklessly, illegally, racing on the streets, occasionally killing themselves and, much worse, often taking innocent bystanders with them. He wanted me to develop my mechanical interests in a nice, socially useful way. I know that he sensed and feared the worst, but he never said no.

So I went to work on that Chevvy; poured kerosene on the frozen pistons, and hammered them out. After school, nights and weekends I slaved over it, tore it down to the last nut and bolt and learned how a car is made. I repaired the damage of fifteen years of rotting in a field and began putting it back together. Finally, one evening, Dad and Mom came back from a visit to friends and there was the old Chev, sitting in the driveway, ticking over at a steady, healthy idle. Dad knew that I hadn't driven it anywhere, that I'd just fired it up because it was ready and I was bursting with pride and the thrill of achievement. We all got in, Dad drove it around the block and back into the back yard.

"I wouldn't have believed it, Mickey," he said. "You've done a wonderful, man-sized job and made me proud. But don't let being a good mechanic get your mind off of going to college now. And now that the Chevvy's running what are you going to do with it?"

I got that strictly stock Chev running so good that I was able to sell it for $125. I bought a junked Model A Ford roadster for nine dollars and began the process all over again. But now I was fourteen and there was no longer any challenge to putting a machine together as well as a factory had done. That A-bone was my first hot rod.

3

BACK IN 1959, AFTER I'D GONE FAST IN CHALLENGER AND A NUMBER of other things, people began referring to me in print as America's Number One Hot Rodder. They couldn't have thought of a title I would have worn with any fraction of the pride with which I wear that one. I've always been a hot rodder and always will be. Hot rodding, as I define the term, is a whole way of life and it's *the* way for me.

The term is sadly misunderstood. In the 1940's and early 1950's the country's newspapers milked the term for all the sensational value it had. A fox tail on an antenna or a set of lowering blocks under a car's axle made it a "hot rod." Any young driver who got into trouble at the wheel of a less-than-new car was a "hot rodder." As the press used the term, it meant juvenile delinquents on more or less tired wheels.

Serious, self-respecting hot rodders called these irresponsible idiots *squirrels* and regarded them as their worst enemies since it was they who gave the sport its worst name. Admittedly, without legal drag strips where we could let off steam, we often got too rambunctious on the streets. Still, in order to exist, we did our best to stay within the law and out of trouble. We tried to confine our really fast driving to the dry lakes and our street racing to the most remote, deserted roads we could find.

Back in the 1940's there were countless hot rod clubs between San Diego and San Francisco. Gradually they drew together into large timing associations which also dictated over-all policy to the member clubs. We all knew that in order to enjoy our cars we had to stay out of trouble and the big associations laid down stern rules of conduct. If you behaved like a squirrel or outlaw, you were thrown out of your club and no other decent club would have you. Extremely high standards of safety were laid down and periodic safety inspections were held. Your car had to be much safer than the family barge or, again, you were out of the club until you fixed it. The clubs and associations did all they could to make hot rodding a positive contribution to the community. Rodders were urged to give emergency help to *any* motorist in trouble, to carry flashlights, tools, flares and other equipment for this purpose and to be Good Samaritans on the road. They were impressed with the difference between what we call the sanitary or *clean* hot rod and junk "shot rod" and urged to keep their equipment looking good at all times. They were urged to cooperate and work with local police in all possible ways and to volunteer their services to their community for every purpose. Still the press went on frightening its readers with the "hot rod menace."

In the late 1940's a fine organization, the California Highway Patrol, recognized that hot rodders could be useful citizens and decided to work with the clubs toward that end. Two officers, Ezra Erhart and Chuck Pollard, covered the hot rod beat between San Diego and San Francisco, meeting with clubs, giving talks, discussing problems and doing all they could to encourage the potential good citizenship which the Highway Patrol had recognized in the sport. The example of the highly respected, statewide Patrol was followed by many local police forces and this respect and cooperation between law enforcement bodies and hot rodders helped greatly in keeping hot rodding from becoming the "menace" which helped to sell newspapers.

In 1948 *Hot Rod Magazine* was founded with Wally Parks, long-time official of the Southern California Timing Association, as its editor. Through this publication, which reached speed enthusiasts all over the nation and then throughout the world, Wally drummed home all the positive, constructive messages of hot rodding and attacked its negative, destructive aspects. The magazine was another fine influence on the sport. Then in 1951 Wally organized the National Hot Rod Association with "Dedicated To Safety" as a motto. Through these means he lifted the sport in the course of fighting its enemies on all fronts.

The arrival of legal, organized drag racing and the establishment of hundreds of drag strips across the nation eliminated any excuse whatsoever for street racing—provided there was a drag strip not too far away—and thereby, in one stroke, eliminated any serious threat of a "hot rod menace." People still smoked rubber on the public roads but most of them were just ordinary citizens. Rodders had everything they needed for the safe and legal enjoyment of their sport—a local drag strip for weekly acceleration competition, the dry lakes for really high speeds and Bonneville for an annual showdown at ultimate speed.

Due to all these developments the press gradually relaxed its feverish persecution of hot rodding. Instead it began to find good copy in who did what at the local drag strip last weekend. The press also discovered a juicy advertising dollar where one make of car went faster than all the rest. Aside from an occasional hysterical magazine article aimed at terrifying the parents of teenagers, peace arrived and rodding become accepted as a part of the American way of life and here to stay. At last we were able to relax and feel like reasonably normal citizens of our country—not like outlaws.

But I still haven't defined hot rodding. Actually it would take a whole book to spell out this way of life in all its wonderful, rich, exciting and educational aspects. But that is not the purpose of this story and so I'll just quote some words of one of the strongest spokesmen for the sport. That's Griff, and his writings over the years also have been a force in lifting hot rodding from where it was to where it is, so that now we can take just and open pride in saying, "Me? *I'm* a hot rodder."

Griff says this:

Hot rodding is improvised motoring, with emphasis on performance. It's building your own machine out of available components and making it go better than a mass-produced machine which is powered by similar components. It calls for an unusual degree of mechanical ability and it calls for creativeness . . . the more the better. Among other things it's a sort of machine-age art form.

But it's a great deal more than that. In these days of ever-increasing conformity and standardization, hot rodding provides a dynamic outlet for the expression of individuality, particularly of technical individuality. The conforming masses may be content—even secure—in their peas-in-a-pod clothing fashions, tract homes, cars and beliefs. But nonconformity, independent, original thinking, is the very source of human progress. One of the greatest built-in dangers to a technological culture is the standardization, the conformity which evolves within it in the interest of efficiency. Without various checks and balances this can lead to deadly stagnation and I believe that hot rodding is precisely one of those compensating factors which keeps our American culture vigorously healthy.

It is a purely American phenomenon which is made possible by our unique technology and standard of living. It owes its existence to our technology, but it also helps to nourish that technology by training tens of thousands of young people each year in advanced mechanical skills. This is why the U. S. Air Force for many years has been a steady, heavy advertiser in hot rod publications; the Air Force wants and needs more than just hack, run-of-the-mill technicians.

One of the greatest problems that faces any growing technological culture is finding enough people to create and operate its technical equipment. The hot rod sport is an outstanding producer of such skilled citizens. It is a national asset—one that must or should be envied by many other nations, both friend and foe.

The sport has many creative, constructive aspects. There's the building of machinery for show; the modification of stock machinery for improved performance. There is the social side and its varied club activities; and the community side, where individuals and clubs render a variety of civic services. There's even a religious side—church groups that sponsor dragsters, and drag strips that provide free bus service between the strip and their town's churches. These are some of the less spectacular but important facets of rodding.

And then there's competition. It's a lot more than just going fast against a clock or another car under legal conditions. Whether he likes it or not, the competing rodder is forced to become much more expert in matters of safety than the average motorist. Drag strip and racing association rules insure this. And the unique discipline of competition forces him to sharpen all his reflexes, thought processes and analytical abilities. The man who performs consistently well doesn't do it by brute strength, sheer luck or gobs of money. He does it by thinking and working to closer tolerances than his competition.

The racing side of the hot rod sport—at legal drag strips, dry lakes and Bonneville—is one of the most fantastic chapters in the world's automotive history. What American hot rodders have achieved, year after year, by modifying mass-produced Detroit iron is nothing but magnificent. When, back in 1952, the Hill-Davis streamliner—built at a cost of $2,000 and a million dollars' worth of dedication and ingenuity—broke the FIA international record-

which had been held for fifteen years by a costly machine sub-
sidized by the Nazi government, a new series of achievements
began in which all Americans could and should take at least as
much pride as the Europeans do in the speed record conquests
that they cherish so dearly.

And since the Detroit horsepower race began in the early 1950's,
hot rodding, through legal, controlled, off-the-streets drag racing,
has provided highly safe outlets for the performance of ever more
powerful production machines. These potent vehicles owe their
existence largely to our rich economy and to our superb highway
system but their full potential cannot be used with safety on the
public roads. Nevertheless the temptation is there to use it. Thanks
to the safety valve of legal drag racing its use on public thorough-
fares stays at a minimum.

I couldn't agree more with these observations by Griff on the
sport. When I entered it or just grew into it, most of these positive values of hot rodding barely existed. Still, I could see them
clearly in the future, if only things would work out that way. But
if these things weren't actually present, what were the compelling
attractions that rodding held for me?

Pure love of the automobile was one. Another was the challenge
to my own ingenuity. Another was the thrill and adventure of
pure speed and of controlling and mastering power—and the more
the better.

Finally, there was one of the greatest challenges that rodding
has to offer, one of the greatest disciplines it has to teach. This is
determination, the refusal to quit. To never say die until you're
definitely and finally shot down in flames. For the devout non-
quitter there is no field for activity, for accomplishment, like hot
rodding.

With skill, imagination and unlimited determination a poor
boy can fight the biggest money and win as often as not. I must
have had some of those qualities because money was the most
exotic thing in my life.

4

I LEARNED A GREAT DEAL ABOUT CARS, MOSTLY FROM DAD, WHILE rebuilding the Chev. When I began taking auto shop courses in high school they were a breeze for me. The teacher, Mr. Alexander, and I got along very well. He would excuse me from class so that I could work on my own car's equipment. It was in his class that I did most of the souping of my first Model A.

I couldn't afford a Winfield high-compression cylinder head so I filled the combustion chambers of a stock head with weld and milled the head. I couldn't afford a good high-lift camshaft so I made templates and reground the stock cam by hand on an ordinary bench grinder, just grinding down the heels of the cams to increase their lift. I wanted to use three downdraft carburetors but Stromberg 97's cost two dollars each and I couldn't afford the six bucks. So I ran three updrafts that nobody wanted. I made my own ignition modifications, regeared the rear end, mounted big tires at the rear and was ready for the lakes.

Dry lake beds are a feature of southern California which, along with the dry and temperate climate, are largely responsible for that region being hot rodding's home. The best lake beds are in the high and usually dry Mojave Desert, roughly a hundred miles from Los Angeles. They consist of a mixture of fine dust and alkali which is usually flooded by winter rains so that the surface is restored to a like-new condition every year. The lakes are far from any public roads and are desolate. You can drive fast there and break no laws.

One of the first men to drive fast at the lakes and attract attention to them was Lockhart. At Muroc Dry Lake in 1927 he drove a tiny 91-cubic-inch Miller race car 171 miles an hour. This inspired him to make his attempt on the Land Speed Record.

A few other big names made record runs there, including Eddie Miller and Ab Jenkins in the very early 1930's and, at the same time, wealthy motor sportsmen such Gary Cooper, Zeppo Marx and Tommy Lee began using Muroc to exercise their Duesenbergs, Mercedes and Bugattis.

Also at about that time the poor go-fast boys of the Los Angeles area began trekking to Muroc in Frontys, Rajos and Cragars. The Gilmore Oil Company, later absorbed by Mobil, set up the first really organized meet for hot rods at Muroc in 1931 and in 1937 the Southern California Timing Association was formed to weld together the small clubs scattered from Ventura to San Diego and to promote and conduct dry lakes racing on a high plane of amateur sportsmanship. And then the Russetta Timing Association was formed of which I was one of the original members. These two groups continue to be the big wheels that govern dry lakes hot rodding.

By the time I was old enough to start making the Mojave pilgrimage every weekend throughout the long dry season, World War II was on and Muroc, the biggest and best of the lakes, had become Edwards Air Force Base. So the hot rod fraternity moved over to El Mirage Dry Lake, which had a course almost three miles long. Sometimes we used Rosamond Dry Lake. It was smaller but well into the season the surface of El Mirage could get pretty badly torn up by the cars.

So I was fifteen when my first A-bone was ready to be clocked. My Dad, who had been too young for the first war, had sort of forced his way into the Navy for the second one or I probably never would have been allowed to build the car at all. I told Mom that I was going to take the A to the lakes for timing, letting an older friend drive since I was too young to get a driver's license. She didn't put me on the spot by asking who was going to drive on the lake bed itself. She just went out to the back yard and took a long look at the A. Then she said, "Those tires on the rear can kill somebody. Get some new ones, Mickey. I'll find the money."

Those two Ward Riversides cost thirty-two dollars and were by far the most valuable part of the outfit. I didn't bother to tell Mom that those things on the front were farm implement tires which were guaranteed to be safe up to five miles an hour. We found, in 1952, that they came apart at about 160 MPH.

So my buddy and I drove to El Mirage and I clocked 79 MPH

on my first trip, which was very close to the class record. That was the start of my teenage reputation for having the fastest cars in the school, and the crudest, sloppiest looking. After all, there never was time enough to make them go as good as they could and what little money there was all went into go; there never was a cent left for show.

For the rest of that season I never missed a lakes meet and, although I never was first, I was always in the top three of my class unless I broke something that was hard to repair, like scattering an engine. Since I was doing this well on next to no money and most of the competition was well-heeled, I was encouraged. I went to school all day, maintained a good standing in athletics, worked at jobs after school, worked on my car at night and got by with almost no sleep.

On Friday afternoon I'd rush home from school and work on the A until about three o'clock Sunday morning. Then, off to the lakes to arrive by sunrise and get in a full day of racing. Then, back home by ten or so to mull over the lessons of the day and to plan modifications and strategy for the Sunday coming. I never was tired; never had time to be; never wanted to be. Racing was in my blood, all right, but beyond that I had found something to test myself against—something that would tell me, prove to me, things that I had to find in myself. Like, how capable am I? What is the power of hard work and determination? Can it ever match the power of money? What are my limits? Do I have any chance of getting to the top?

Lockhart had gotten there and had risen from very grim poverty, so I knew it could be done. What I had to find out was could *I* do it?

I threw a V8 engine in the A-bone and again laid in the top three in class, consistently. Then Dad came home, took one look at the roadster and said, "Son, *get rid of that!*" That was one of the few times he ever said no and I heartbrokenly sold the A and bought a square-looking '39 Ford coupe, which I proceeded to turn into a bomb.

It was at about that time that I met Judy. But before that I came too close to death for the second time.

5

I BARELY MADE IT THROUGH CHILDHOOD. THE FIRST CRISIS CAME IN 1937, when I was eight years old.

Dad had worked very hard all his life and was one of the lucky ones who had a steady job all through the Depression. He and Mom had skimped for years to reward themselves and the family with a real vacation and this was the time. Dad bought a brand-new Dodge sedan and we all bundled off for Yellowstone Park.

We cut across Nevada, entered Utah at Wendover. I'll never forget that first sweeping view of the Great Salt Desert as we came over the last ridge. It filled three quarters of the horizon. I had never seen anything so immense. It was gleaming white, without a speck of life that you could see. It was spooky and beautiful.

"Down there, Mickey," Dad said, "is where the fastest cars on earth have been racing lately. You've heard of Campbell, Eyston and Cobb? That's where they run."

You can bet I knew about them. I might miss the funnies but not the sports pages and I devoured every line about racing.

Then Dad drove us right out onto the Salt and I had the thrill of standing on the world's fastest speedway, seeing it close up, walking around on it, feeling it—even tasting it. Those were the days when the Salt was at its best, before it had been spoiled by potash mining operations. It was smooth, moist, cool and flat and hard as a concrete slab for much farther than the eye could see. Knowing that there was such a speed course in the world and knowing that it was only seven hundred miles from my home probably had a more profound effect on my thinking than I'll ever really know. I didn't know that Brigham Young had said *"This* is the place," but I sure thought that for anyone who wants to go really fast, it was. Later, when I began building cars, that vast white expanse was in the back of my mind.

We went on to Yellowstone and had just entered the park

boundary when some drunk came hurtling around a blind curve and crashed into the left side of the Dodge, where I was sitting. Dad boiled out of his new car, more the outraged citizen than police officer, and dealt more than sternly with the man.

Dad, Mom and Colleen were unhurt. But the rear door had been bashed in against me. I looked at my left arm and saw the forearm bent in an unnatural direction. I had a severe compound fracture of that arm, and the shoulder and all the fingers were smashed, also. They got me to a doctor in the nearest town, Ashton, Idaho, sixty miles away. He set the various bones and whittled a splint from a lug-box board. Then we went back to Yellowstone to camp among the beauties of nature, as planned.

I took it very easy, spending most of my days being fussed over by the whole family and playing with chipmunks and squirrels that were tame as house pets. Then I began to feel worse and the arm began to swell. By the time I was booked into the little hospital in Yellowstone Park, the arm had swollen to about three times normal size and looked like a piece of rotten meat. I had gangrene.

Dad found that there was a man with an excellent reputation as a bone specialist over in Montana and had him flown in within hours. He was a rugged, independent Westerner who regarded his own word on anything as final. He had such contempt for women that Mom could not approach him. The first time she asked him about my condition he just snarled, "If you want to know anything, go ask your husband." Under normal conditions Dad would have given him a stiff lesson in manners, but right then we needed him in one piece.

He examined me, looked at the arm with a fluoroscope, and when he made his report to Dad he handed him a paper to sign, authorizing the amputation of my arm. Years later Dad told me what followed.

In his police work Dad had had plenty of exposure to emergency medicine and he knew much more about things medical than the average layman. And Mom was a nurse. They both believed in radical surgery only as a last resort and they knew enough to do some reasoning of their own.

Dad said no to amputation, that there were other things that could be tried.

The doctor said, "If you think you're a doctor what the hell did you send for me for? *I* know what I'm doing."

Sounding very authoritative now, Dad told him, "Doctor, it's my considered opinion that the man in Ashton who reduced that fracture has the artery caught between pieces of bone. I believe that if that condition is relieved circulation can be restored."

The doctor said, "Listen, Mr. Thompson. Just what do you want? To save the arm or save the boy?"

Dad said, "If you put it that bluntly I guess I'm going to have to be pretty blunt too. If I bury the arm I'm going to bury the boy along with it. There will be no amputation at this time."

The doctor gave in. He put my arm back on the fluoroscope, studied it from many angles and then said to Dad, "It's a very long shot but you just might be right. We'll give it a try."

So the doctor held me and Dad pulled the break apart and worked the arm until they both agreed that if the artery had been pinched it wasn't pinched now. It wasn't a pleasant experience for either of us but Dad says I never whimpered. This, of course, was his training.

After that someone massaged the arm for every minute of the day and night. Part of the time it was a nurse. But most of the time it was Mom or Dad. Finally there was evidence that the circulation was coming back. The swelling began to go down and the color improved. Then the doctor put a new cast on me. For some reason best known to him it was put on with my arm folded, hand against the shoulder. He had told my parents that the arm would never grow.

All this took many weeks and finally, back home again, the cast was taken off. I could not move the arm. It had frozen in that vertically folded position. Again Mom and Dad had the answer. They took a toy sand bucket and every morning taped its handle to my hand. I had to carry it all day, every day. Each day they would add another ounce or two of sand. It was painful, but gradually the arm began to straighten. As soon as it was straight enough they put me to work with a bow and arrow.

Finally, I took up boxing as a means to force myself to straighten and strengthen the arm. In the beginning many kids who knew my handicap took advantage of it, but I wouldn't stop until I had enough strength in my arm to come out on top. After about a year I had almost full use of the arm that the specialist wanted to amputate. For a while it did not grow and looked as though it never would. But eventually it caught up with the other arm to the point where only an expert could tell the difference.

The next nearly deadly blow fell when I was fifteen. It was in October and I came down with infectious mononucleosis. Very little was known about the disease at the time. First one doctor tried to diagnose it. He couldn't and called in others until there were five doctors milling around, all trying to cover their own confusion. Meanwhile, my neck was swollen larger than my head; my tongue was so swollen that I couldn't close my mouth; and I was running such a constant, high fever that there were two beds in my room. I was kept in one while the other was drying out. I was *sick*.

This dragged on through November and far into December and finally the doctors told my parents that I wasn't going to make it. So Mom set up a Christmas tree in my room and we had our Christmas on the twenty-second because I wasn't supposed to be around on the twenty-fifth.

But Mom did something else on the twenty-second. She desperately called the pediatrician who had looked after Colleen and me when we were little. We were very fond of each other, he and I, and although his practice was limited to infants, he came rushing when he heard Mom's story.

Three of the other doctors were there. Doctor Hamilton took one careful look at me, turned to them and raged. "What in the name of God is the matter with you people? Don't you know what's the matter with this boy?" He was furious.

He turned to Mom and said, "Take all that medicine and throw it out, pull these shades down and go to pray. There is no medicine that can help. All you can do is give him nourishment, darkness and absolute quiet . . . and just hope that he can pull through."

Instead of looking for a virus the doctors had been looking for a germ, which, of course, they never found. They had been pumping me full of penicillin, which was a waste if it wasn't downright harmful. Dr. Hamilton had a portable laboratory brought in that same afternoon; confirmed his diagnosis, and told the other doctors to get lost.

During the first week of January I began to pull out of it

slowly. I had had a lot of kidney damage and it wasn't until April that I could go back to school. Again, Mom and Dad somehow were with me constantly throughout the whole ordeal. Dad had managed to get the Navy to assign him to duty in Los Angeles and on nights and weekends he lived by my bedside. I wondered if he ever slept. Dr. Hamilton told me later, "Kid, if you'd been in a hospital you never would have made it. The thing that saved you was that unlimited tender loving care."

I don't tell these stories to brag about what I've been through. This is the story of my life and these crises were real high points in it and therefore I think they should be recorded. I'm not sure what they all add up to, but they do help to explain why I didn't graduate from high school until I was eighteen and why I stayed small and frail for a long time. And the people closest to me say that the first real change in my personality followed the mononucleosis attack. But I'm not sure about that. I think that I did begin to take things more intensely and began to drive myself harder. I probably had picked up a pretty good appreciation of how fleeting and precious life is.

I know that I never was worried. I knew that Dad wouldn't let them whack off my arm and I knew that between the three of us —Dad, Mom and me—I'd pull through the mononucleosis. I knew that my time hadn't come. Those people loved their kids with a power that was stronger than anything. It was far bigger than my poor Dad's income and it was bigger than dismemberment and death.

Once I snapped back I snapped back fast—to the world of cars and girls . . . and Judy.

6

I HAD TURNED SIXTEEN THE WINTER I WAS SICK AND ONE REWARD OF getting well was getting my driver's license. I spent most of my spare time working on my '39 coupe and going to the lakes on weekends, where I continued to do well in spite of the everlasting money problem. I belonged to a hot rod club in my part of town called the Rodents. It was made up entirely of kids like me who had hardly a nickel and had to really scratch to buy their club plaques. We knew every junk yard in the city and what was in it. One thing I learned from Dad, although he never had to tell me directly, was never to come home with a part without a bill of sale for it in my pocket, unless it was unmistakably junk. Getting parts from the Midnight Auto Supply—meaning stealing them—sooner or later led to big trouble.

Across town, in West Los Angeles, was a club called the Coupes, made up mostly of kids from wealthy families. What they needed they bought for cash over the parts house counter and they even had access to a dynamometer for tuning their cars. The Coupes were the Rodents' natural prey and they were the guys that I in particular lived to beat. I really loved to prove that there were bigger, more powerful things than money in racing and I usually did prove it except when some junk part let go on me.

One weekend during summer vacation I was invited to spend a couple of days at the beach resort of Balboa. I skipped the lakes for once and was purring down the Pacific Coast Highway at about one in the afternoon when I heard the rap of a big, full-race Merc coming from a sharp '41 Ford sedan in the next lane. I looked at the five girls in it, wondered what they were doing in such a keen hot rod, smiled at the pretty blonde who was driving and gave her the questioning nod that meant, "You want to go?"

She smiled back, punched the throttle and the sound of that big-bore Merc came booming out of a pair of straight-through pipes. Just as I put my own foot down I shot an automatic glance into the rear view mirror and there, about a quarter-mile back, was the familiar black and white 'cycle with a pair of red eyes. The fat wasn't in the fire yet and I hit the panic beat on the horn. The blonde looked around, I waved her to cool it and she got the message. We just loafed along and the officer went on by. Pretty soon the '41 pulled into the parking area of a little beachside apartment house and I pulled up too.

The girls got out and the blonde gave me a friendly smile and said, "You're a real gentleman. Thank you for saving me from bad trouble. Some guys wouldn't have." That's how I met Judy. Street racing. She was staying with an older girl friend at Balboa and the girl's husband was one of the dry lakes boys, away in the Air Force. That's where the hot car came from.

There was an ice machine in the parking area and Judy had to buy ice. I asked if I could carry it upstairs and she accepted. The landlady braced me at the door and said, "All right, young man. Get in with it and get right out." I said to Judy, "There's a dance at Sleepy Hollow tonight and I'd sure like to take you." She said, "That would be nice."

Things didn't go too terribly well. She was two or three inches taller than I was, which only brought out the cockiness that was part of me anyway. I sort of gave the impression, "Okay, honey, I've taken you out for this real big time. Live it up." While we were dancing some big lout planted his elbow in Judy's back and I came close to smashing him on the spot. Judy never had been out before with a boy who got into fights and she didn't like my feistiness. But I got her home not too badly shaken and she let me have her phone number. She told me later that she never expected to hear from such a cocky character again and if she did she didn't plan to do anything about it.

Well, it was about a week later and we were back at our parents' homes, mine in Alhambra and hers in Glendale, about fifteen miles apart. I called her and asked her to go with me to another dance. She told me that she'd like to but had a tentative date. Would I call back in a couple of hours?

Much later she told me that it was no date that made her hesitate. My cockiness was a lot to take but what really got to her was my height. I was much shorter than she was and weighed only 125 pounds. She discussed it with her mother and said that if she was going dancing she was going to wear heels, as a well-dressed young woman should. Her mother said, "That's nonsense. If you go through life letting trifles like that rule you, you'll be a very sad person." So Judy wore flats and we had another date.

For some reason she began to like me. And I liked her immensely. Temperamentally she was just like my mother—warm, happy, cheerful, always helpful and always on the same even keel. Just the opposite of Dad and me with our extreme ups and downs.

And there was a whole lot more to Judy. I needed help with my schoolwork and she wanted to help me. She did. And more, she understood my love for racing as though it was the most worthwhile thing in the world. She shared it and helped me with it. Man, *how* she helped me with it!

Her disposition was pure sunlight and just to have her around was to be made happy, encouraged, fortified and inspired. She was as much a partner as any guy could be, and she was a really attractive girl! She was a match, at least, for most boys in things they could do well. Yet she was wonderfully, purely feminine. She was a real prize and I knew it. She still is and I'll always know it.

After that second dance in the flat slippers we began to understand and really like each other. I had been a precocious kid, strongly interested in girls, and I was loaded with girl friends. But Judy was different and I lost all interest in the others. The same thing seemed to catch her and from that time on we spent every weekend together. But not in any conventional way.

We got together every weekend and often during the week. Usually she drove over to my place in her parents' car. She helped me with homework and with whatever car we were racing. She was a wholesome, constructive influence on my life and my parents knew it. Her parents, too, thought that what was going between us was good and headed in a good direction. So we had everyone's blessing. We went steady and a year later, when we were both seventeen, I gave Judy her engagement ring.

Our whole life was cars . . . maybe not the royal road to romance but it was the right one for us. We would go to a movie rarely but nearly all our dating centered around racing. The midgets were really charging in those days and we never missed a race at Gilmore

Stadium and the Rose Bowl and caught most of the good sickel racing in the L. A. area.

We built our cars together. The Ford flathead V8 was *the* engine for hot rodders and we haunted the alleys behind Ford agencies, rummaging through junk bins and lugging home every sort of part that could be patched up and used. That was the equipment we *raced* with—equipment that was no longer fit for the streets. I welded up junk blocks, heads, rods and pistons and made engines out of them. Judy washed parts, then learned to grind valves, clean and gap plugs, swap carb jets. She became more helpful all the time. She didn't do only the light jobs. She shuffled a thousand cylinder blocks across the garage floor and I could toss her a crankshaft and she'd catch it without batting an eye. Judy was a woman and a lady. She had that wonderful feminine softness without there being weakness. She was strong—a strong human being who never hid behind her sex or asked for privileged treatment because of it. That was the kind of woman for me.

During the lakes season we rarely missed a meet. Judy would drive her folks' car over to my place Saturday morning. We'd work on the race car into the night. Judy would sleep with Colleen and then we'd get up at about four in the morning and head for the lakes. We'd drive up there, arrive in the freezing dawn, yank the gasoline carburetors, install the ones that were set up for alcohol and race until the sun went down or something broke. Then, home again by hook or crook and Judy would head back to her folks' place and we'd start another week.

I guess it was a pretty crazy life. Yet it seemed like the only one possible for us. Like early one morning we were heading out of Alhambra for the lakes when the suicide axle on our car broke off clean and there we were in the wee morning hours with the whole front end lying there by itself in the middle of Main Street. Judy had learned that a rodder never quits until he—or she—is hopelessly wiped out.

"Can we fix it?" she asked.

"Well, we've got all the hand tools we need, but it'll take welding equipment," I told her.

"I'll get it," she said. We flagged down a lakes-bound buddy, who drove Judy back to my place, helped her load the oxygen and acetylene bottles and brought them to the scene. In the meantime,

I began working on the damage. We slaved for two hours in the middle of Main Street, gluing the car back together. Occasionally a policeman in a patrol car would stop and let us see by his headlights for a while. And so we got to El Mirage a bit late. But we broke our class record that day and the accomplishment was sweetened by the extra effort we'd put into it. We have hundreds, maybe thousands of memories like that one.

During the rainy season there was no racing at the lakes and that was when street racing was at its awful height. I was not one of the wild ones who itched to burn rubber any place, any time. I was careful where I ran and with whom. The place had to be as safe as possible from the standpoints of ourselves, the public and the police. I wouldn't run with the irresponsible squirrels and I wouldn't run with too large a group. Both spelled quick, bad trouble.

One of our favorite spots was Fifth Avenue in the settlement of La Puente. In spite of its citified-sounding name it was just a narrow back road way out in remote citrus farming country. It had about a one-mile straightaway and there were only a couple of farmers on that stretch to complain to the police. We'd usually have cleared out of the area before the police arrived.

The procedure usually went like this. We would meet a group of other rodders at a drive-in restaurant and start discussing who could beat who. Guys whose cars were pretty evenly matched would choose each other off and then very quietly—because nobody wanted a crowd—would arrange to meet at the usual spot in Puente that night. If I liked the setup I'd include us in at the rendezvous and we'd park someone's car across the road at each end of the straight and the battle was on.

Usually I'd blow off car after car and time and again some disgruntled loser would start smarting off and I'd say, "Aw, forget it. Not only can *I* beat you. I can put my girl in the car and she can beat you too." And that's just what used to happen. I loved it because it really sank the needle into my competition; really was humiliating. And it proved that it was more than my driving that made me a consistent winner. It proved that my workmanship was all right. And it proved that I had a very, very special girl.

Sometimes the police would be laying for us in the darkness and once our show was under way they'd pull a raid. It was absolute madness. Roadsters and prowl cars rushing in all directions over the rough ground, dodging orange trees and smudge pots. The police kept their headlights on but we didn't. We also had it over them in power, light weight and maneuverability. We usually got away—across country.

But not always. After Judy graduated from high school (at seventeen) she began going to Glendale State College. She belonged to a sorority that met every Wednesday night. I would usually wait for her and after the meeting she and a couple of her sorority sisters would follow me, in Judy's folks' car, to a drive-in.

Well, we were blasting along one night, Judy behind me and playing bumper tag with me. We came tooling around a sharp right, going twice as fast as we had any right to, and there were the red lights and barricades. We had been *had*.

We were all terrified because we had absolutely no excuse or defense and we knew it. The police asked for both our licenses, turned a flashlight on mine and said, "Oh *we* know *you*. We know your Dad, too. We'll take you to him."

I begged them, very close to tears. "*Please* give me a ticket," I wailed. "Take me to Juvenile Hall. Lock me up in jail and throw the key away but *Please* don't take me to my Dad."

They took us both to my Dad.

There he was, sitting on the porch, when the whole convoy rolled up. He could guess pretty closely what had happened. He didn't even look at me. He looked past me, straight at the officers, and said, real icily, "What is it, boys?"

They told him and he said, "Thank you for bringing them here. You can count on me to handle this." They knew that already and they left.

He turned to me and didn't say a word. He just held out his hand. Anybody would have known his meaning. I fished out my driver's license and handed it to him in silence.

"Mickey," he said, "I want you to tell me when three months have passed. Then you can have this back. Until then you may not drive any vehicle. You may not *ride* in any vehicle . . . a friend's car, a bus, anything, unless it's a genuine emergency. And the next time it will be *six* months."

He turned to Judy and said, "When you think this over, try giving a moment's thought to how it affects *me*. You can go home."

I never got in that kind of trouble again. At least not without going awfully far from home to find it.

When you get older you think of all the mad things you did in your youth and wonder why you weren't killed a thousand times. You remember that being killed or even badly hurt was the farthest thing from your mind. Racing was the only thing that counted.

Later, hearing people knocking and fighting legal, organized drag strips would send me into a rage. It's not just that legal drag racing provides a sane outlet for pressures that are built into our American way of life and it's not just that it keeps the participants from maiming themselves in droves. It's the innocent bystanders that I really think of. The little old couple, out for an evening or Sunday drive, that may get in the way of some fearless individual who feels that he must experiment with the power and freedom of the machine that is practically his birthright in our wonderful country. Organized drag racing protects this individual but, much more important, it protects the other ninety-nine per cent of the population that uses the roads but never goes near a drag strip.

Judy and I went through the same crazy, scarcely disciplined school together. When we were given the chance to help organized drag racing, as we were, we gave it all we had and we still do because no one knows better than we do what a healthy and needed thing it is for rodders, for the public at large, and for the country.

7

I CAN'T SAY THAT I WASN'T A VERY WILD KID, ALTHOUGH THEY CAME a lot wilder. But along with all the wildness I had a strong sense of personal responsibility and of justice, fair play and morality. These I learned mainly from my parents, who didn't so much teach as set examples by their own behavior and use gentle, indirect suggestion.

Mom has always been a faithful church-goer. She belonged to the First Christian Church in Alhambra. The pastor, Dr. Ira Ketcham, baptized Colleen and me and, when the time came, it was he who married Judy and me and then, later, Colleen and my buddy Gary Campbell. I was very active in that church until I was fifteen and began running out of time for all the things I felt I had to do.

I never felt guilty about drifting from the church, probably because of Dad. He would say to people, "I don't lean too strongly toward any type of religion but I think it's a good thing for those who want it." But I could see that he lived a more truly and ideally loving Christian life than a lot of people who made a big show of their piety. So I just eased away from church in order to concentrate on athletics, work and cars. But I never stopped looking to God for guidance or trying to serve Him in all my thoughts and actions.

I was popular enough with kids my own age, but usually we did not have a lot in common and I sought out the company of older boys. I never went through the gang phase. When kids of my age had discovered it I had already discovered what fun and good company girls could be. I never ran with a pack.

It's not at all that I was a teenage Don Juan. Nothing like that. Because of all my training and my love and respect for my mother and sister I had an almost fanatical respect for womanhood as such. That may have had something to do with the way girls tended to seek me out. Girls my age would honey up to Colleen, three years younger, trying to get an in with me. If I was cocky with them, as everyone says, I still probably let them know that I didn't think they were one bit inferior to my own sex.

I was pretty clean living. All my life I've tried to keep a clean mouth. I slip occasionally but I'm really sickened by vulgarity for vulgarity's sake, as opposed to the cuss word which is well placed to emphasize a point. Then or now, if anyone should say something filthy in the presence of any woman I even remotely respect, and I'm there, he can be sure of getting my knuckles in his face. It's happened more than once.

All this was part of my parental conditioning; of the values and attitudes that I soaked up. For example, during Prohibition my Dad always had a jug in the kitchen, like millions of other Americans and a large percentage of police officers, who are human too. His buddies would drop in of an evening and be sitting around discussing the day's events over a glass of corn and I, hardly out of knee pants, would say, "Dad, I'd like a shot."

In my memory's eye I can see that big Irishman throw the group a deadpan look, which said, "Don't smile, boys. No reaction at all. Clear?" Then he'd take a glass, turn his back, splash a few drops of whiskey in it, top it off with ninety-nine parts of water and hand it to me with a little friendly smile. Sometimes I'd drink it down; sometimes only taste it. The story was the same with tobacco.

These adult privileges and habits were neither denied nor encouraged by my Dad. He just minimized their importance completely and so I never felt the need to smoke and alcohol for me never has been more than a relaxing nightcap or something to drink socially and moderately. I hate to see alcohol used heavily. It stands so brutally between where a person is and where he could be.

In high school, classes naturally ate up most of my time. I resented them all except the shop, math and physical ed courses. My parents told me that I could do anything I set my mind to and I knew it. But it didn't help. I did miserably in English and the teacher would often say, "Mickey, you can spend this hour working on my car again today."

When Mom discovered that I was doing automotive maintenance when I should have been getting culture she lost no time in cornering the teacher. "Mrs. Thompson," the teacher said, "don't worry about your son. He has what it takes and he'll be making dollars when most of these A students are just working for dimes."

She meant it, and this cheered my mother considerably. She was a wise teacher who knew how not to fight the way the twig is bent. I got her car running like a watch. She and Mom still get together occasionally and talk about my academic failure and what I did in spite of it, because of it, or whatever.

I loved sports with a passion. One of Dad's ambitions was for me to become a top-notch baseball player and for years when he came home each evening we worked out until dusk in a vacant lot with bat, ball and glove. Baseball was good but it was too smooth, too slow, too easy; not rough and demanding enough.

After my big sickness I was a real runt, small and frail compared to all my classmates. I chose track and football to show that these handicaps didn't count. I was no good as a sprinter; I was slow. But I had determination and stamina and those worked for me in long-distance events. In the long dashes and relays I shut off the flashier runners and made a good name. I also did well at putting the shot.

In football I played first string on the C team while I was a freshman and on the B team when I was a sophomore. But I never grew in high school, so I was lucky to make the junior varsity because of my weight. I was the lightest player on the entire team, weighing 135, against the team average of 180 pounds. But I made 80 of the 107 total points for the team that year.

I got broken up a lot—legs, arms, ribs—which kept me out of football during my senior year. But it meant a lot to me that I could at least hold my own in really trying sports in spite of the arm that should have been crippled or gone and in spite of the disease that should have done me in.

I was a "retarded" child in the sense that I was a couple of years behind my age as far as size was concerned. I wanted out of high school in the worst way, but the problem was to make passing grades in the courses that bored me stiff. Here Judy really rallied round. She helped me with my homework and when I had no time or stomach for it she did it, forging my own handwriting. So somehow I scraped through the semesters and one day found myself on the auditorium stage, receiving a diploma. Judy was in the audience and I learned later that the principal got her to one side and said, "Dear, thank you. We know how helpful you've been to Mickey. We love all our students but we're always glad to see them move on into the world." It seems we really hadn't fooled anybody.

Meanwhile, we lived for racing. It was a time when coupes were practically unknown as a form of competition hot rod and my challenge was to beat the roadsters. Eventually I gutted the '39 until it was just a resonating shell and threw a big Merc into it. I pruned the roadsters so successfully and consistently that I attracted a lot of startled attention in the sport and plenty of protests about my engine, which was perfectly within the rules. Then I built a '40 coupe, which was even more successful. We massacred the competition in street drags; and at the lakes we moved from being consistently in the top three in class to often being in first place. And when the first legal drag race took place at Santa Ana, we were there and made a good showing.

At first I financed this budding speed career by mowing lawns and selling papers. As I became better as a mechanic, I began to fix people's cars for profit. Eventually Judy got a secretarial job and that really helped. I would meet her at lunch every Friday, take her paycheck to the bank, cash it, go back, give her her allowance and go on home and back to work. It used to drive her mother wild.

"Was Mickey there today?" she'd ask.

"Just like Old Faithful, Mom."

"Did you put any money in the bank?"

"Well, no."

"His cars are getting more expensive, aren't they?"

"That's right."

"Where is this ever going to stop?"

"Well, Mom, Mickey says that when we need more money for the cars I can get *two* jobs." The question was a silly one, Judy thought, so she gave it a silly answer, which you often have to do.

Today people ask things like, "Say, how did you get started in this Land Speed Record business?" You start to say something and then just gulp for air. They take it for granted that it happened recently, as the result of some abrupt decision. You don't have time to tell them that it began when you were a kid in a back yard full of junk and how you worked your heart out on old clunkers for all those years. How there was a girl who believed in you and slaved to help you on your way, whatever it was. How everything you did was a step to a higher achievement until there was nothing left but to become the world's fastest man on wheels. And you go ahead and give that challenge your all and then start looking for something to do for an encore.

Questions like that get Judy riled. Newsmen like to ask, "Why do you do it, Mr. Thompson?"

"Because it's there to be done, you fool," Judy mutters to herself. She never asked those naive questions. She dug the answers without being told. She went square on me just once.

8

WE WERE NINETEEN. WE HAD BEEN ENGAGED FOR TWO YEARS AND had been leading a wonderful, exciting and rewarding life. Then one day out of the blue Judy said to me, "Mickey, there is no future in the way we're going. All this racing is just for nothing. There are two ways it can go and neither of them are any good. You can squander every cent we ever make or you can get killed. I want a better future for us and for our kids if and when we have them. Either racing goes or I go."

I pulled a deep breath and said, "Judy, I love you with all my heart and there isn't another woman in the world but you. But if you put it that way, we've had it. You *know* perfectly well that racing is my life. If you're with me you're with racing and it can't be any other way. *That is it.* Now tell me goodbye if you don't want me."

Some tears were shed, a couple of days passed, and life returned to normal. That was the first and last time that Judy ever spoke a word against racing; against the compulsion I lived under and still do. Things have been a million times rougher on many, many occasions but she never has murmured one sound of complaint. When she decided to stay in my corner she never wavered again. I often wonder how she does it.

When I first broke the wedding news to Dad, he didn't say a word. He just looked way into me and his blue eyes puddled up and big tears rolled down his cheeks. He took it as a personal affront. It wasn't that I had found a strong love outside the family but he seemed to feel that he and Mom had failed. That if they had made a really happy home I wouldn't be rushing away from it. But this was not the point at all. He never did a thing to try to stop me and when I'd try to talk to him about my wedding plans he'd say, "I'll do anything I can to help but just don't talk to me about it.

I don't want to hear about it." It upset him that much. That's how soft that tough old cop is inside.

Mom was quite different, naturally. Judy had been like another daughter to her and she didn't look on twenty as a too-early age for marriage and she was confident that we'd be under foot all the time anyway. And instead of thinking just of our generation she was thinking of the grandchildren we'd no doubt bring into her life. She was fine.

Although I didn't have a "decent" job and depended for my security on garage work in my back yard, Judy's parents cheerfully resigned themselves to the situation. Both families joined in the preparations. It was a mammoth wedding at the North Glendale Methodist Church and between Judy's friends, my friends and the friends of both our families, there were about five hundred people there, including seven bridesmaids and seven ushers. We could have done without some of *my* friends.

The gutted '39 coupe was utterly unfit for anything like a honeymoon trip. So we had borrowed Judy's folks' Chevvy, which we parked and locked outside the church. I knew my practical-joking buddies well enough to know that there was going to be the devil to pay and tried to take every precaution. One was to borrow a pair of handcuffs from Dad and I shackled Judy to me before we arrived at the church. Once inside I took the cuffs off but as soon as the ceremony was over I snapped them on again. The older folks thought that this was a cute, quaint thing for the son of a policeman to do but the young ones knew better.

So there was a reception at the bride's aunt's home and everything went well. Then the time came for us to head away on our honeymoon. That meant changing into casual clothes and that meant taking the cuffs off. That's what they had been counting on and that's when they grabbed me.

About fifteen of my so-called pals swarmed all over me and began hauling me off to a car. It was a knock-down, drag-out battle and I messed up quite a few faces before they cracked a couple of my ribs and sat on me. Then they took all my money, drove me around for a few hours and finally dumped me five miles away in Glendale. They left me afoot and battered and ragged at a popular hot rod drive-in, where the whole audience could have a good chuckle.

In the meantime another group had broken into the Chevvy, driven it up into the hills and abandoned it. They had broken into Judy's suitcase and decorated the surrounding brush with her intimate clothing. It was four in the morning before I got back to Judy and many hours later that we tracked down the car and got out of town.

Pretty lousy humor, I thought at the time. But I got my revenge every time one of those characters got married and when Gary—who was one of those fiends—and Colleen tied the knot I set a terrible trap that he walked into like a round-eyed baby.

Judy and I were married in January of 1949 and we both had just turned twenty. We rented a little house in Alhambra for $25 a month and I worked constantly on the '39 while Judy continued to plug away at her secretarial job. I made a just-adequate income repairing cars at home and working in a nearby service station when they needed help. We kept right on racing, of course, and I didn't give any thought to really serious breadwinning until Judy became pregnant that summer. Then I decided that if I was going to be a family man, I'd better settle down and get a real job.

One fellow who used to bring me his car to work on spent money on it like a madman. I decided that I ought to work where he worked, which turned out to be the pressroom of the Los Angeles *Times*. I went down there, spoke to the foreman and it so happened that he needed a flunky to push paper, the lowest job in the place. He asked when I could go to work, I said now, and that was it.

That pressroom was a fascinating place to work in, with its roaring main press, almost a city block long. I worked hard. There's a lot of idle time in a big newspaper plant, during which most of the workers just sit around and swap talk. I never enjoyed that, but instead found things to keep me busy. There was a fine machine shop in the building. I got to know the men who ran it and they let me use the tools.

Through hard work and an ability to learn mechanical things quickly I raced through a five-year apprenticeship in seven months. Most of my free time I devoted to designing and building devices to make my job easier, quicker or safer. A lot of those gadgets were really practical and the management noticed them and had them duplicated throughout the plant. All this led to very rapid advancement for me and I was pushed past men with five, ten, even fifteen years of seniority over me. This made me a lot of enemies, which hurt me deeply. I can understand not liking a man and letting him know it if he is a shiftless bum. But not liking a man and letting him know it just because he puts enthusiasm into what he does and gets good results seems like the most unjust thing in the world to me.

There was one job I really had my sights set on—working the color press that the funnies are printed on. It's a relatively small press and would give me top pay along with a high degree of independence in the shop. It was almost like being in business for yourself. Then one day after work I stopped and talked with Dad.

"What's the matter, Mick?" he said. "You look like you'd lost your last friend."

"Well, it's about like that," I told him. "I've got the chance for the advancement that I've really been working for, but I'll be darned if I can take it."

"What do you mean?" Dad said. "Aren't you qualified?"

"Sure I am," I said. "It's not that. But a lot of the guys I have to work with just won't have anything to do with me. I've gone around them and they really resent me. It's rotten to be boxed up with people that you know hate you."

Dad said, "Mickey, never let that sort of thing worry you. Just don't do anything to harm anyone. Any time you're qualified for another advancement, another raise in pay, don't think about the other people. Take everything that your boss sees fit to put in your way.

"Look at me," he said. "There are men in my department who have been there twenty years longer than I have. And they're working for me, just because I dug for it. I prepared for the exams, worked harder than they did and I attempted to show more initiative. Not only am I not ashamed of that, I'm proud of the advancements I've made and you should be proud of yours."

But it was then that I decided that I would never be happy or satisfied with working for someone else, no matter how important the job or how high the pay. I declined the advancement and started marking time until I could be my own boss; have my own business. This was in spite of the fact that working for Norman and Otis Chandler at the Los Angeles *Times* was as ideal as an employment situation could be.

I stayed with the *Times* for seven years and never missed a day's work even when I was falling down sick and could barely drive to work. In fact, I worked double shifts whenever I could and worked triple shifts until the timekeeper would catch up with me. More than a few times I worked seventy-two hours on two jobs straight through.

Until I smashed my back I had stamina that very few people could understand. All my life I've been burning with energy and never have been able to sleep more than about three and a half hours at a stretch. Today I can be dog tired, go to sleep at midnight and at three-thirty or four I'm wide, wide awake. There's no point in fighting it. I keep a notebook beside the bed and while Judy gets her rest, I plan my activities for the coming day, design things and just work with ideas. I do like an occasional catnap and nothing lulls me like being driven someplace in a car. If I'm just being driven around the block the first thing I do is kick off my shoes. If we're going a few miles or more I drop right off to sleep. Fritz Voigt, who was to become one of the top drivers and automotive geniuses in the hot rod field, has driven me millions of miles in a sleeping stupor . . . me in the stupor, not Fritz.

With the '39 coupe we were highly successful and set a number of Russetta records at the lakes. As soon as I began earning an honest living at the *Times*, I became a terribly righteous family man and laid down the law that we've stuck to ever since—income from the main job is for the family. It is sacred and cannot be touched for non-family purposes. If we were going racing at all, and we always were, that had to be financed with income from something other than the basic, bread-and-butter job. Consequently I *always* had at least two jobs going and sometimes three. There was the *Times*, and all the overtime I could wangle, which equalled two jobs much of the time. Then there was all the automotive repair and hop-up work that I could squeeze in. Soon we could afford the better '40 coupe.

Judy began carrying our son Danny in the summer of that year of 1949. But she kept working until she was eight months along, which helped our income a lot. She ran the house on a tight allowance but, on the sly, she skimped for our first Christmas. What she surprised me with—it was for *us*, of course, for the whole family, present and expected—was the most wonderful gift I've ever had. A rebuilt boring bar!

This was terrific. It put me solidly in the garage business at home and was a big help to our income. And it was an equally big help in our own racing activities of course. We could reclaim junk blocks with economy and ease and we could bore each cylinder a different size to fit the odd-size pistons that we'd salvage from junk bins.

The '40 shaped up real fast and the night that Danny was born —it was suffocatingly hot—Judy was barefoot in the garage, seating in the engine's valves. Danny came into the world without a hitch. We were the happiest of families and soon we were racing as a family. During the lakes season of '49 we set more Russetta records at El Mirage. And with legal drag racing at last in full swing we raced almost every weekend the year round.

After Danny came, Judy didn't work for a year . . . on an outside job, that is. But she loved to help me with the car and I loved her help. When we'd get home from the lakes late Sunday night and I'd have to tear off to work in the morning, I'd come home Monday night to find that she had everything stripped from the engine—manifolds, heads, everything. She'd have the motor mounts disconnected, the chain hoist in position and hooked to the block. All I had to do was spin the chain on its sprocket to lift the engine out. She would have done that, too, but she knew that I wouldn't consider it ladylike.

I couldn't stand paying rent—buying property for landlords— even if it was only $25 a month. So we found a little place in San Gabriel with a good garage and back yard work area. We borrowed the $1,000 down payment from my parents and Judy went to work, preferring to take on herself the responsibility for that debt.

She applied for a secretarial job at Aerojet and they asked if she would be steady.

"No," she said, "I want to work until I've made $1,000 and then I'm going to get pregnant again. Four months after that I'm going to quit and go back to raising a family full time."

They must have appreciated her honesty and clear foresight because they hired her. She carried out her plan to the letter, gave us our beautiful daughter, Lyndy, and also managed to buy us a porting grinder out of her earnings.

It was after Judy and I were married that I began to grow again. It was after I was twenty that I began to grow up and out; just why, I'll never know. I do know that all of us Thompsons always had been very light eaters. Judy loved to eat and to cook and she was and is happy and full of good ideas in the kitchen. I began eating much more and within a couple of years I was up to five feet eleven and a hundred and ninety pounds. Life with Judy really agreed with me.

I worked and raced harder than ever and it was with a '36 Ford coupe that we built together that I first raced at Bonneville.

9

IF THERE EVER WAS A PLACE TO INSPIRE THE SAYING, "GIVE ME MEN to match my mountains," it's Bonneville. Bonneville is not a town, it's short for the Bonneville Salt Flats, which are ringed by fine, jagged peaks. It's an amphitheater on an absolutely colossal scale. God could not have created a more majestic arena for the battles of giants.

There are three approaches to the Salt: from east, west and southwest. They are all very spectacular but the eastern one is the least so. Leaving Salt Lake City you drive about 120 miles across the most absolute desolation before reaching the western limit of the Great Salt Desert. There, against a long range of barren, sharply eroded desert mountains, lies the lowest point of an ancient land-locked sea which once filled hundreds of thousands of square miles of the Great Basin.

During each of the Ice Ages glaciers stretched far to the south and made this a humid region of heavy snow and rainfall. The floor of the Great Basin is about 4,200 feet above sea level and the huge inland sea would rise as high as a thousand feet above it. You can still see the old beach lines high up on the mountains.

All this water dissolved billions of tons of salts out of the surrounding earth and rock. When the last Ice Age ended, the sea—

which an early geologist named Lake Bonneville—dried up and
these salts were deposited at the lowest point of the Basin, creating
the Bonneville Salt Flats. Under ideal conditions this slab of pure
white salt covers an area of about two hundred square miles.

From the east the approach to the Salt is by level ground. From
west and southwest the first view of the Salt is from the upper
slopes of high mountain ranges. It's about as breathtaking and
unforgettable as the Grand Canyon. From a distance of fifteen
miles or so you look down on the whole, brilliant white Salt Desert
and it stretches north, east and south as far as the eye can see. It
has a very weird quality—burnished and glistening-clean and lifeless.

It has always been a forbidding place. The Indians who lived on
its borders believed that it was haunted, a place of death, and they
never ventured onto the desert itself. No wonder. It is absolutely
silent. Animals who stray too far die from lack of water. And every
day, as the sun climbs, the whole horizon becomes filled with eerie
mirages. Sometimes impossible things appear in the sky—one time
a complete city, another time a marching army. The old settlers
learned to live with it, to see these strange things and let them pass
without asking any questions.

In 1845 Captain John C. Frémont made history by making a
dash from Skull Valley, ninety miles to the east, to 10,400 foot
Pilot Peak at the western edge of the Salt. That was the distance
between water holes and he did it with light cavalry. The next year
the Donner Party used Frémont's short cut to the West but they
were in heavy, slow wagons and almost died of thirst. That was a
real lesson to travellers and few tried to cross the Salt Desert until,
in 1907, the Western Pacific Railway managed to lay a track across
its wastes.

Seven years later big-time auto racer Teddy Tetzlaff put his
Blitzen Benz on a Western Pacific flat car and rolled it off at
Salduro, the whistle-stop on the Salt where a potash plant had been
built to provide chemicals needed for World War I. Tetzlaff was
clocked at a fantastic 147 MPH way back then but the Salt was too
remote and no one tried to follow his lead.

Official Land Speed Records were being broken constantly but
under conditions that were much more convenient for challengers
and official timers. Brooklands track was in the very lap of wealthy
British sportsmen. Arpajon Road was narrow but straight and less

than an hour from Paris. When speeds got higher the English beach called Pendine Sands came into use but still it was racing in your own back yard. Speeds got still higher and required longer straightaways and even Britons went as far as Florida's Daytona Beach. It was sand, narrow, soft sand, but it seemed perfectly adequate at the time.

Utah claims that Ab Jenkins, great record breaker and one-time mayor of Salt Lake City, was the modern discoverer of the Salt as a high-speed race course. There is another school that holds that California's Art Pillsbury was the real father of all that has happened on the Salt since the early Thirties. But we don't have to settle that argument here. The point is that after Lockhart's death at Daytona in 1928 enthusiasm for that course steadily waned. Jenkins in '32, '33 and '34 set a brilliant series of endurance records on the Salt and these led to Sir Malcolm Campbell bringing his *Bluebird* to Bonneville in 1935 and setting a new LSR at 301.13 MPH. That was on September 3 and was over 24 MPH faster than the same man and machine had been able to go on the Daytona sand a few months before. Because of this and the breaking of the 300 MPH barrier for the first time in history, the perfection of the Bonneville Salt Flats was praised around the world. It finally was recognized as the world's best and safest course for all-out speed.

One of the Salt's greatest virtues is that it restores itself—or at least it used to—each year. During the dry season, roughly from the end of June to the end of October, the sprawling, crystalline slab expands, contracts, cracks and warps. During the winter season rain and snow make it a huge, shallow lake which dissolves surface roughness. The high winds swirl the water around and scour the surface irregularities so that when the water dries it leaves a cement-like slab that extends in all directions as far as the eye can see.

It's a stock joke that it isn't speed that kills, it's the sudden stop. Well, on the Salt there's nothing to stop against suddenly. A line of black oil is painted from south to north and you steer down that line. If you happen to drift off it at high speed there is no need to try to get back on the course. In fact, any attempt to do so is potentially deadly because the vehicle is more than likely to overturn. On the spacious Salt all you need do is lift your throttle foot, give the machine its head, let it slow down to a stop and try again.

There is nothing to run into. No sea, no rocks, no trees, no obstacles of any kind.

Another great blessing of the Salt is the table of brine which normally lies just below its surface. During the sweltering days this cool fluid is drawn to the surface by the sun's heat. It keeps the surface extremely cool and therefore extremely kind to tires, the components which are most likely to fail under the pressures of really high speed.

My good, fine friend Captain George Eyston brought his *Thunderbolt* to Bonneville in 1937 and pushed the LSR to 311.4 MPH. The following year he raised it by an incredible margin to 345.5 MPH. Then, a month later, Sir John Cobb's *Railton Mobil Special* lifted the LSR to 350.2 MPH. Eyston came back in '38 and boosted the LSR by another 7.3 MPH. Cobb hit back in 1939 with 368.9 and in 1947 he pushed the two-way, official LSR to 394.2 MPH. His best one-way speed was 403.1 MPH. All these records were set by what fairly can be called locomotive-size vehicles, powered by immense aircraft engines. And the LSR stayed where Cobb nailed it.

Meanwhile, back on the dry lakes, speeds were increasing and so was the need for a larger, safer course. Back in '39 fewer than thirty out of hundreds of SCTA contenders had broken 100 MPH but by 1948 contenders in SCTA competition were *averaging* 130 MPH. This led Pete Petersen, publisher, and Wally Parks, editor, of the then brand-new *Hot Rod* magazine to make a pilgrimage to Bonneville and to Salt Lake City to attempt to arrange with the responsible authorities for an annual week of speed for hot rods. The result was the SCTA-sponsored Bonneville National Speed Trials, the World's Series of hot rodding, which was launched during the last week of August, 1949.

The first Nationals necessarily was a hastily-organized affair that was announced at the last minute and in which only about fifty of the faithful were able to participate. In a really magnificent performance for the day the Xydias-Batchelor streamliner set the top speeds of that first meet with a flathead Merc engine. They were a one-way 193.54 and a two-way average of 189.745 MPH. Mighty good for a hot rod. Mighty good for a backyard-built bucket of bolts.

I promptly went to my boss at the *Times* and put in for my next year's vacation—the last week in August. Destination—the Salt.

10

AT THE FIRST LEGAL DRAG MEET AT SANTA ANA IN 1949 THE OVERALL winner, Jim Woods, turned a top time of 99 MPH. In the '36 coupe I broke 90 MPH, which was fairly wailing for a machine that was as streamlined as an Iowa barn. As time went by and the new sport sorted itself out, I was among the very first to turn 100 in the quarter-mile, then 110, 120, 130, 140 and 150, right up that scale. When the 150 MPH era came in in 1955, I continued to be a front-line competitor in drag racing but my thoughts turned more strongly to Bonneville.

My first year there for the Nationals was 1950 and I drove up with a buddy only as a spectator. It was a fabulous show with over a hundred entries and a mob of about six hundred hot rodders. When it was all over the officials had clocked 1,307 runs and no one had come close to being injured. The Xydias-Batchelor streamliner clocked a one-way 210.8 MPH and Bill Kenz of Denver with a streamliner powered by two Ford engines, clocked 210.77 one way and his driver, Willie Young, set a wonderful two-way average of 206.50 MPH. I was really burning to be in the midst of the competition.

Something else that thrilled me that first year at Bonneville was the clean amateur spirit, the spirit of cooperation and fellowship that ran through that big, motley crew. It was like the lakes, only everyone was much farther from home, much more dependent on each other, more aware of being a part of genuine speed history and a part of a great adventure. The poor souls who never saw the Salt could never know what pioneering rodders were doing there. The whole show was the dream of a lifetime come true, of pinch-penny kids turned loose on the world's greatest race course.

They conducted themselves so well that we all took new pride in being hot rodders. In the little village of Wendover, about seven miles from the Salt and where we all somehow managed to find food and lodging for a solid week, there was no real unruliness. There had been dire forebodings of a repetition of "the Hollister massacre," when the sickel boys ripped up that town. But the clubs, publications and big associations had gotten the message across that there was no place for kooky show-offs or for any sort of irresponsible character in this sport. Most of the guys didn't need telling in the first place and the week was a festival of hot rodding at its constructive best. It told a lot of us that we hot rodders were becoming big on the national scene, that our big meet someday could rival Indianapolis as the last word in American speed. Few of us dreamed that, within a few years, our little meet would be recording speeds that were absolute, all-time records, the fastest in history.

We continued storming in the drags and as summer rolled around I built two engines to run in the coupe at Bonneville. One was for Class B, 183 to 260 cubic inches and the other was for Class C, 260 to 305 cubes. And we also picked up a beat-out old '39 Ford sedan to use as a tow car. We barely made it.

Between Los Angeles and Bonneville there are several mountain passes to cross that are about 7,000 feet high. And there are many other long, steep grades. We had both machines loaded with tools, spare parts and cans of fuel and on three occasions the sedan just couldn't pull all that weight up the grades. So we'd unload everything from the two vehicles, leave Judy guarding the junk by the side of the road, and I'd haul the race car to the summit. There I'd disconnect the tow bar, leave the race car and go back and pick up Judy and the equipment. Nothing worthwhile comes easy.

That first year we stayed in one of the little shacks behind the Western Services station in Wendover. We were lucky because in those days there was practically no tourist accommodation in that whole part of the country and most of the Salt pilgrims had to camp out. In the cabin next to us there were about a dozen guys bunking, along with a fifty-five gallon drum of nitro fuel. About midnight one night when everybody was snugly tucked away I said to Judy, "Watch this," and lobbed a cherry bomb through our neighbors' window. Their first thought was that the fuel had blown up and they came boiling out of windows and doors in pajamas, shorts, T-shirts and just plain skin as though they'd been shot from guns. It was a fine sight. Of course the humor was pretty infantile but all of us used to play pretty rough. Thank God they never found out who tossed the bomb. Judy and I still break up over that scene.

We started out with the little engine in the pure white coupe and made run after run but for some reason that we still don't understand the car just wouldn't trip Otto Crocker's photo-electric timer. We talked it over with him and he suggested that we try a little color on the car and see if that wouldn't break the light beam. We painted big, hairy, purple flames all over the front end. That cured the trouble but the best time we could get was 122.282 MPH, versus the 126.582 of top man Bud Fox. But this was our first time out on the Salt. We were still learning to tune for the altitude and we felt encouraged.

We got impatient with going slow, snatched the little engine out and dropped in the Class C mill. There were eleven entries in that class and we managed to turn the fastest one-way time of them all—141.065 MPH. Our nearest competition in qualifying was Clark Cagle at 137.614. But I got greedy when I made my record try, tipped the nitro can a little too bravely and dumped the whole bottom end of the engine onto the Salt. Cagle went on to wrap up the two-way record at an average of just 133.688 MPH. We had the satisfaction of being the absolute fastest in the whole class and we drove home in high spirits, hatching big plans for the next year.

I was fond of the coupe classes, if only because of safety. The body structure gives some protection in itself but, beefed up with a husky roll bar, it's a very safe place to be. Too many builders of competition machines are born kamikaze pilots. They happily operate on the assumption that nothing will go wrong and, if it does, there'll be no surviving it anyway. I have always been chilled by that approach.

I have always thought of myself as a real nut on safety. It's true that when it comes to actual racing, to climbing into a car and *going,* I used to get completely carried away. In the heat of competition if someone offered me a ride in his race car it just never entered my mind to take a slow walk around it and see if all the welds look good and the cotter pins are in the spindle nuts. I just got in and went.

But when I'm building something I've always thought, "if this thing were to get upside down at high speed what would it take to come out of it alive?" I've always tried to figure out the answer to that one and then build it that way. Some of the people who have looked at my roll bars and said, "Chicken" would be alive today if they had been a little more "chicken."

So I decided to stick with coupes for a while. I wanted the smallest, most compact body I could find. It came in the form of an old American Bantam. And this time I was determined to come back with the Bonneville record in my class and give the rest of the boys something to remember. I decided to use two engines.

Bill Kenz had done this very successfully, letting one engine drive the front wheels and the other drive the rear. But for the speeds and acceleration that we both were concerned with at that time, I could see no need for the complexity of four-wheel drive. I decided to couple my two engines together at the crankshafts and let them both drive through the rear axle.

There was another reason for taking this route. If you want to be successful, then you have to think of something that hasn't been tried before. It may lay an egg or it may be a real improvement and show the world the rest of the way. But you don't have to be very smart to figure out that by imitating the most successful combination, you can only hope to equal its performance and no more. That's been my philosophy as a builder of racing machinery—and it's one held by a lot of successful men.

I wanted to go fast and to go faster than anyone in my league. Kenz was going very fast with two engines so I would use two engines. But I would use them differently, coupled together. When other rodders heard that I was doing this, they jeered and said it would never work—that I couldn't whip the problems of synchronization and that one mill would fight the other. None of us knew enough automotive history to know that that's just how the first straight-eight engines were made—by coupling a pair of four-bangers in line. But it seemed like a highly promising direction and I took it.

It was in early '52, while I was working on the Bantam, that Rodger Flores came to live with us. Rodger was a poor kid; he was struggling to go to high school and is one of the nicest, wholesomest people that God ever put on this earth. And let me say this at this point. Nobody, but *nobody*, ever accomplishes anything big alone. Behind every successful person there are the patient, hard-working others who have provided lots of the muscle and sweat and drudgery and often a lot of the ideas that have made the success possible.

For all his brilliance, Lockhart, for example, could not have achieved much without the helpers he gathered around him from his early youth on. The same is completely true of me. I've never been able to operate without capable help; never have been able to translate one important idea into reality without that help. And the higher the goal the more important that help becomes. Rodger was one of those vital helpers and I'm happy to say that he's still with me today.

Rodger was a fifteen-year-old Mexican-American, a born gentleman, mannerly and intelligent, born in the States. A lot of fellows used to drop in at my place just to watch the madness in progress. One of them was Ron Ellico, whose father owned the Ford agency in Alhambra. He and Rodger were buddies and one day Ron brought Rodger over to see what I was slamming together. After that Rodger used to come over every day after school, just to help out, and we became inseparable. He knew almost nothing about cars but was eager to learn. For someone like myself, for whom the accepted way of doing things must be no more than the point of departure, this is the best kind of helper there is. You can train him your way, without having to wear yourself out trying to break down "tried and true" thinking.

Rodger was eager to learn and was glad to learn to do things my way. He needed a place to stay and we had an extra room in the little house that Judy had worked to make the down payment on. We gave him board and room and money as he needed it. He went to school, baby-sat for us, and helped on the cars and became one of the best mechanics and welders that I've ever seen. It was a happy arrangement all around and it had a lot to do with me getting into the Mexican Road Race.

11

So WE PUT THE DUAL-ENGINED BANTAM COUPE TOGETHER. IT WAS THE first tandem-engined hot rod and it presented some minor problems which we didn't have much difficulty in overcoming. I managed to induce a lubricant-additive manufacturer, Auto Moly, to sponsor the machine to the tune of $250 and that cash helped with the cost of our '52 Bonneville campaign.

I've always had a certain gift as a promoter. Without it I'm afraid I wouldn't have gotten far. I've always had furious, blind belief in my projects and when I've needed help in the form of parts or money I've usually been able to hustle it somewhere. Without this kind of help you'll never make it in this game, whether your name is Joe Hot Rodder or Donald Campbell. You can give your all, but it's never remotely enough to meet the endless expenses. There are business people who stand to profit by your success if you succeed. They're terribly hard to sell when the project is nothing but a dream but I've always worked hard at it and had better than average luck.

The Bantam's two engines had a combined displacement of 592 cubic inches. In later years we could get close to that from a single Detroit block but back in '52 it meant stroking the two Merc flat-heads to the limit and boring them out to the water. I fitted them with good Harman & Collins magnetos and cams, dropped them in the coupe's rails, hooked the tow bar to an old pickup and headed for the distant Salt.

Judy was seven months pregnant with our daughter, Lyndy. As we'd done the year before we checked Danny with his grandparents. There was room for the three of us—Judy, Rodger and me—on the seat of the pickup but seven hundred miles in a straight-back seat would have been a lot for Judy then. So I rigged a canvas cover over the back of the pickup and spread a tarp over an intake manifold to make a cozy place for her to stretch out. That was the style in which we rode to the Salt in '52. As always, we had scarcely any money and never would have been able to operate without credit cards. Racing's debt to credit cards never will be told. Now it's a little bit different for us. We skim over all those miles to the Salt in a powerful, luxurious, air-conditioned station wagon and recall those good old days that we somehow endured and survived.

On the Salt our bright yellow, long, tiny-bodied monster was greeted with curiosity and ridicule. Granted, it was sort of brutally put together but it was the cleanest looking machine that I'd built to date. The technical committee tried hard to find fault but couldn't. Everybody came around to look at the oddity and I kept overhearing comments like, "Man, will you look at that Rube Goldberg lashup!" and "I wonder how many RPM difference it'll take before those crankshaft flange bolts shear?" and "Just stand way back when that thing comes to the line."

Well, it didn't blow. The existing record was 146 MPH. I shoved my throttle foot deep down on the first northbound run, constantly flicking a glance at the tachometer. It climbed steadily and strongly until it said that I was about 25 MPH over the record and then I eased back and held those revs through the traps. I turned out, returned to the pits and found that Crocker had clocked me at 172 MPH. Not bad for a first run.

Well, I wound up turning 196.72 MPH—a solid 50 MPH over the existing record—and backed that up with a two-way record of 194.34 for Class E Competition Coupe/Sedan. I had built and driven what was decisively the fastest coupe in the world. With open wheels and everything hanging out I had come within an ace of the then-magic 200 MPH mark that only fully streamlined machines had broken.

The hot rod sport is a pretty sociable one. The guys swarm together more or less tightly and love to discuss the things they know best—the tried-and-true combinations again. I never was in that league. I was a sort of lone wolf type, untalkative, and I know I was resented for that. It wasn't secretiveness that made me refuse to discuss machines that I was still experimenting with. I just didn't like to make claims for anything until it was proved. I'm still that way. But once I've proved a design then I'll tell anybody anything they want to know about it. I don't mind giving secrets away because the current machine is always obsolete. Knowing that sooner or later somebody will come along with a faster machine, I'm always planning way ahead, designing the machine to beat the machine that I know perfectly well must beat my machine. I'm eager to give the old ideas away, hoping that they'll be used, that they will be my competition in the future.

The great Chrysler *Fire Power* engine with hemispherical combustion chambers was brand new in '52. Similar Ardun heads for the Ford-Merc flathead had been around for years but had hardly ever been made to run well and so the Chrysler was ignored by the hot rod fraternity. I thought I saw a terrific potential in it and made it my secret weapon for Bonneville in '53. That may have shown a little foresight but I really did some pioneering when I adapted a GM Diesel 4-71 supercharger to that engine. To the best of my knowledge that was the first of the blown Chryslers which eventually took over the whole sport and dominated it for years.

During this period Rodger and I had gotten acquainted with Ray Crawford, heir to a supermarket fortune and a gung-ho racer. He'd been active in the Mexican Road Race and had a car entered in the Indianapolis 500-mile classic, with Bill Holland driving. Rodger and I volunteered to help him with his car at the Speedway and he accepted the offer. That was one of the most enlightening experiences of my life.

If there was one thing that Rodger and I lived for, it was working on race cars and racing them. We knew that you never quit short of absolute exhaustion, blowing up, or until the finish flag fell, because you never ran out of things to do. The more you work on a race car the more intimately you know it and the more things you realize can be done to make it go just a little bit better.

Well, we had seen our share of alleged hot rodders who seemed to go racing for lack of anything else to do. They'd break a two-bit part and then sit on the sidelines, toying with their crash helmets and goggles, while the real racers let nothing stop them. But Indianapolis was a revelation. There were all those entries—nearly a hundred of them—representing millions of dollars invested, and with a hundred-thousand dollar purse at stake. And yet the great, great majority of car owners and crews seemed to have come to Indy just to have a good time. While the guys were puttering around all day, playing hero racing mechanic and applying decals and body wax they'd be talking about the riot they were going to raise in that dull town that night.

Rodger and I liked pleasure, too, but only after the racing is over —because there's no pleasure, no activity like racing. In the garage area at the Speedway we worked far into the night, every night. What we never could get used to was that in that whole, gigantic stable, there were very few other burning lights at night. We just shook our heads and said to each other, "*This* is racing?" And we agreed that out of the ninety-nine entries and thirty-three starters the winner of the race had to be one of about four, because that was the limit of the entries that approached the challenge in a really determined and professional way. "Man," I thought, "if I just had the loot, what I could do back here. They're all copying each other and a really new idea would throw them into panic . . . a new idea that could do some good." I dared to dream that I'd have my own car at the Speedway someday but I didn't dream that it would happen as it did just nine years later. What I did promise myself was that if I ever made it—and I would—it would be with a car the like of which never had been seen before.

At the Speedway that year I had plenty of opportunity to watch Clay Smith at work and to talk with him over the weeks of qualifying and practice. People used all the superlatives in describing Clay. They called him the nation's greatest racing mechanic, a great natural engineer, a wizard and a genius. He was all these, plus being one of the greatest strategists in racing history. Yet he was also one of the most modest, humble and friendly men who ever lived. The people who knew him at all really worshipped Clay and I was one of the many.

Clay was a Long Beach hot rodder who began grinding camshafts for flatheads. He had the touch and they performed outstandingly. Then, because the action of the valve gear is so direct and similar, he began grinding cams for the Offies and they worked far better than those that the Meyer & Drake Offenhauser factory made. Then Clay added race-car preparation to his activities and soon began managing whole seasonal campaigns for car owners and drivers. He continued to get top results and Ford Motor Company used his talent in the Mobilgas Economy Run. It was said that Clay could have won the Run pushing a wheelbarrow, and he of course won it for Ford. Ford gave him greater responsibilities and in 1952 Clay singlehandedly master-minded Lincoln's sweeping and history-making one-two-three victory in the Mexican Road Race, with the very valuable assistance of Bill Stroppe. I used Clay's camshafts a lot and used to haunt his little shop and factory in Long Beach just to watch a real master in action and to catch whatever gems would fall from his lips.

As Clay would be working on some utterly trifling part of an engine he would say, "No matter how small the job may seem to be, the thing you're working on at any given instant is the most important thing in the world." He didn't work fast. In fact, he took much longer for any given job than other mechanics did. But he worked precisely, efficiently, and just didn't make mistakes. That's why *his* lights didn't burn at night, even though he took no part in trying to paint the town red. I'd love to learn a fraction of his patience but my temperament is different and I never will.

At any rate at the Speedway in May of '53 I spent all the time I could at the Agajanian garage, where Clay did his work. The Mexican Road Race was the big topic of discussion and the winning Lincoln drivers, Chuck Stevenson, Johnny Mantz and Walt Falkner were in and out constantly, telling their stories of that high adventure. Clay had been Stevenson's copilot and, according to the winner, Stevenson only held the wheel. It was Clay who dictated every brake, shift and cornering speed. Clay told him how to drive every one of the 1,923 miles.

All this really had me bug-eyed. Indianapolis was Big Time and I wanted to race in the Big Time in the worst way. But Indianapolis is not for poor boys. Mexico also was Big Time. Some of the best drivers and most important factories in the world took part in it. At the same time, anybody with an acceptable car and a little money could get in the act and show what he could do. After we had all returned to southern California I continued to drop in on Clay and pump him for details on the world's longest and wildest road race, just in case I somehow might be able to make it. At least I could dream. And meanwhile we got ready for Bonneville that August.

I could only afford one Chrysler and the Bantam looked weird with an unblown flathead in front and the blown Chrysler coupled behind it. My hopes were very high. The Chrysler, by itself, had pulled four hundred horsepower on Weber's dynamometer and nobody could believe it.

But Bonneville that year was a sort of fiasco for me. I never could get that combination running properly and I couldn't get the Chrysler to stay together.

The first day out the engine blew. We hauled the car back to Wendover, worked all night and got it back in shape. The second day we blew up again and spent the second night the same way. The third day we blew up again but this time the block was ruined.

I wasn't about to quit. We hauled back to Wendover, pulled the engine out of the car and tore it down to the bare block. We tossed the block into the back of the pickup and drove all the way into Salt Lake City. We parked right at the door of a welding shop, slept in the truck and when they opened the doors in the morning we were the first ones in.

We got a couple of liners welded into the block, then ran it to a machine shop and got the new liners bored and honed. Then we dashed back to Wendover and worked for the rest of the day and all night putting the engine back together and getting it into the car. We were ready to go the next morning and you know what? We blew up again and really totalled most of the engine that time. We may not have achieved anything but we learned a lot and knew that we had done our absolute best. And I couldn't be bothered to be too disgruntled because I had this other thing burning in my mind.

I'd said nothing to Rodger all that summer except once to ask casually, "Say, Rodger, how do you speak Spanish?"

"Just barely," he said, and I dropped the subject.

But driving home from Bonneville, in the back of the tow car, I was still smarting from having done nothing on the Salt. I said to my sixteen year-old driver, "Rodger, what do you think of our going racing in Mexico?"

"It would be nice," he said, "if we had a decent car to race."

I said, "How do you think we might be able to promote a new car?"

Rodger thought for a minute and then said, "Gosh, all I can think of is Ron Ellico's dad."

"Let's get home fast," I said. Rodger nodded and bore down on the throttle across the Nevada wasteland. I put my head in Judy's lap and went to sleep and dreamed up a storm.

12

In mexico it was called the carrera panamericana "mexico" but in the States everyone just called it the Mexican Road Race or the Panam. It went on for five years and all the most hardened, most experienced veterans agreed that in all the world there was not another speed contest to compare with it. There was nothing else as long, as gruelling, as diversified and challenging for both sports cars and touring cars and for the drivers of each.

The first Panam was held in May, 1950 as a means of letting the world know that it was now possible to drive the length of Mexico, from the Texas border to the Guatemalan frontier. It was part of the inauguration ceremonies for the brand-new Christopher Columbus Highway and wasn't taken too seriously as a race. Any and every kind of automobile was eligible to run in the one big class, providing it was a "standard" make. There were 123 entries, including 57 from Mexico and 50 from the U. S., including everything from elderly couples on vacation to a heavy turnout of Yankee stock car handlers. The race started at Ciudad Juarez, across the Rio Grande from El Paso, Texas, and ended 2,106 miles later at Ciudad Cuauhtemoc, on the Guatemalan line. It was won by an American, Hershell McGriff, in a 1950 Oldsmobile and at an average speed of 78.4 mph.

The second Panam, like those that followed, was run from south to north. The leg between Ciudad Cuauhtemoc and Tuxtla Gutierrez, capital of the state of Chiapas, was eliminated. It was the only unpaved part of the whole highway and was better ignored. The new total distance was 1,934 miles and again all competitors ran in one big class. Italy's Piero Taruffi won in a Ferrari with an average speed for the distance of 88.09 mph.

Finally the pointlessness of having heavy touring cars competing on an equal basis with light, powerful sports cars dawned upon the organizers and for the Third Panam, held in November of '52, two categories were recognized—standard production cars was one and sports and racing cars was the other. Karl Kling, driving a prototype Mercedes-Benz 300SL, won in the hot-car class with an average of 102.6 MPH and Chuck Stevenson's Lincoln took the other class with an average of 91.0 MPH.

Participation in the Panam by both American and European factories had gone far beyond the expectations of the race's organizers, who decided to sweeten the pot for the Fourth Panam in '53. They created four competition categories—one for big sports cars and one for small ones, and one for big touring or "stock" cars and one for smaller ones. This news was released from race headquarters in Mexico City in time for us to hear it from Clay Smith while we were all together at Indianapolis. It was the small stock category that really made Rodger and me prick up our ears. It was open to the sort of machinery that we knew best and which also was relatively cheap. Also, there was a first-place purse of $4,000. The lucky winner could almost break even.

As soon as we got back from Bonneville in '53 I took a few hours' rest, then cleaned up and made an appointment to see Mr. Jesse Ellico, Ron's father. He had a warm spot in his heart for hot rodders, appreciating the good promotional job they did for Ford products. Ron had told him about some of my exploits so I didn't approach him as a stranger. He gave me a chance to make my speech and when I got through I almost fell over when he said, "Ronnie's already convinced me that you've got a whole lot of ability. Now I see that you've got plenty of drive and guts. Okay. I'll fix you up with a new Ford sedan and I'll pay for the painting because I want to be sure that Ellico Ford is spelled out in big, bright letters all over the car. Can you take care of the rest?"

I must have been just one big, nodding grin. I was too overcome to speak right up and my mind was a whole three months in the future, racing in Mexico. So Mr. Ellico just reached for my hand and said, "All right, Mickey. You can pick the car up tomorrow. And all the good luck in the world to you and Rodger."

Rodger was in school, but I was at the agency when the doors opened the following morning. The paperwork was taken care of and I drove straight home and began tearing the car down, right to the frame. Rodger bolted home from school and for the next three months we lived with just one purpose and that was Mexico.

I got a copy of the race regulations from Clay. They demanded that all cars in the standard or stock categories be absolutely, strictly stock in every respect that could affect performance. So I got a copy of the Automobile Manufacturers Association specifications for the Ford Six and Rodger and I took our car right out to the limit of those specs. We hand-finished the combustion chambers until the volume of each was identical, right to the last cubic centimeter. We used the last permissible thousandth of an inch of bore and stroke, the biggest permissible clearance and the optimum venturi and jets for the carb. We worked furiously because there was so little time but still I don't think we overlooked one shred of advantage that the rules allowed us.

We lifted the body off the frame and where the factory had put two welds we put four. We reinforced every stressed zone and doubled up on shock absorbers. We stripped all the stressed parts of the running gear and had them X-rayed or magnafluxed and replaced anything that showed a hint of possible weakness. We rigged up heater blowers to direct cool air against the brakes and installed a roll bar that was probably three times stronger than what anyone else would think of using. It was also three times heavier but I didn't begrudge that investment in safety. I even built a little hand-grip bar and installed it on the transmission hump where it would be handy if someone had to dive for the cellar. And where the rear seat had been we installed a sixty-five gallon fuel tank to supplement the stock tank. All these modifications were within the limits of the rules, which were wide open in their allowances for safety.

This expedition was going to take plenty of money and lots of spare equipment and so while Rodger slaved over the car I spent a great deal of time scrounging around town, begging, borrowing, mortgaging, promoting. Always promoting. When we finally were ready to leave we still were on an absolutely threadbare budget but nothing could hold us back.

In spite of all the good counsel we'd had from Clay and all the other facts and rumors we'd been able to smoke out, we still had almost no idea of what we were getting into. We'd been cautioned by everyone about food, milk, water and so on in Mexico, particularly in the back-country parts. So Judy, who was staying behind, prepared and packed all the food and drink that we'd need for the whole campaign—dried milk, canned stew, pork and beans and all such wholesome stuff. The plan was that she would meet us in Ciudad Juarez, on the Texas border. That's how green we all were. We actually took it for granted that we were going to finish the race.

Finally we took off, about three weeks before the start. It's about 3,000 miles from Los Angeles to Tuxtla and we just drove on down, practicing as we went and taking our time, checking out the best speeds for the trickier turns, narrow bridges, deep dips and so on. We were not ideally set up for real racing practice. The car was groaning under the load it was carrying—food, spare parts, clothing, lots of tires. Rodger and I were just wedged in among all this debris. Two weeks after we left Los Angeles we had our buddies Mel Noriega and Bill Weber start out for Tuxtla in Mel's old International flatbed, with the major load of spares and food. Mel's truck was to be our service vehicle during the race.

I've done a lot of things that are supposed to be brave. Or maybe they're considered foolhardy. But the point is that when I do admit to being scared occasionally people point the finger of scorn and say, "Hey, dig old Fearless Thompson. His knees are rattling." This is part of what you get for being a public figure. I'll have more to say about fear later on, but right now let it be clear that I make no pretense of being braver than Dick Tracy.

For example, neither Rodger nor I knew much about Mexico and I didn't know the language at all. I had gone to school with plenty of Mexican kids, plenty of whom were plenty tough. I was as tough as they were, and we got along all right. But I kept getting stories about the way it was in the *patria*, as they call it. The *patria*, *donde la vida no vale nada*—where life is worth nothing. You get out of line there, brother, and they whittle you down with a machete and that's it. Nobody blows a whistle for a cop. You mess around with me or a member of my family and you'll get justice right now—from *me* and not from anybody else. I had learned that you walk very politely among Mexican people in the States, and in their own country you had just better not get out of line at all.

So, Rodger and I were booming along, south of Durango, heading out of the desert and into the endless agricultural country to the south, when we ran out of gas. It's a long, long way between filling stations in that part of the world. We tossed a coin to see who would walk for it, and I lost.

There I was, nearly a thousand miles into an alien country, on foot with an empty gas can in my hand. I trudged along the little-travelled road for over an hour. No motorist stopped for me and I didn't see a single field worker. I really felt alone and had no idea if it would take me five minutes or five hours to find a source of gas. Then, over in a field, I saw a little burro grazing. My feet were tired and I thought, "I'll just ride that little critter and bring him back later."

Well, I strolled real casually over to where the burro was, trying not to scare him off. He couldn't have cared less and just kept chomping away. at the weeds. I made friendly noises at him and sidled up and grabbed him around the neck. He skittered and I hung on, gas can flapping around. Then, right out of the earth, rose up about twenty Indians, most of them with machetes in their hands or tucked under their arms.

Well, the sweat really rolled down my hide. I could see the whole thing as it must look to them. Cattle rustler. Stranger trying to make off with their livestock. Quick justice. Chop and crunch. Bury the thief in the field and that would be the end of it. Nobody would ever know. I'm telling you that I had it all figured out and it looked horrible.

So of course I let go of the burro and started trying to explain, in English. I pointed to the gas can and held it upside down to show that it was empty. I pointed to the road and made signs that said "automobile." I made gestures about riding the burro away and then riding him back to that spot again. Finally these witnesses to my crime put it all together, smiled, laughed, held a discussion among themselves and offered me food. They felt friendly toward me instead of feeling anger and I've never mopped my brow with greater relief.

This little scene took place about 300 yards off the highway and I was just finishing the second ear of roasted corn when I saw the Ellico Ford coming my way. I leaped up, waving arms and gas can, and stampeded to the road. Rodger had gotten some gas from a passer-by. All I could say was, "What in blazes took you so long!" He looked at me and laughed and then I laughed, but I was still shaken. We passed out some soft drinks among my new-found friends, shook hands and continued on our way. But I was still scared of those completely strange surroundings and was in for real terror before I got out of Mexico that year.

13

THE ROUTE FOR THE '53 PANAM COVERED 1,908 MILES OF TWO-LANE pavement. For many weeks before the race thousands of laborers worked at patching potholes and put the surface in top-notch condition. At every danger point such as a tight curve, sharp dip or narrow bridge, clear signs were posted. The Mexican government went all-out to make the event safe and successful.

The distance was broken up into five stages or legs, which were to be covered in five days, starting on November 19. The first leg, Tuxtla to Oaxaca, covered 329.4 miles and was by far the most difficult in the entire race. From Mexico City to Ciudad Juarez the highway becomes increasingly level and straight. Between Mexico City and Oaxaca, to the south, there is a pass almost 11,000 feet high and the road twists through mountains and shoots straight across broad, flat valleys. Between Oaxaca and Tehuantepec is one of the most fantastic mountain roads I ever hope to see. The mountain ranges themselves are stacked up like accordion pleats and during our second year we charted over 5,000 curves on that stretch. Then there is a 90-mile straightaway beyond Tehuantepec and after it crosses the Isthmus the road climbs again through wild mountain country to Tuxtla Gutierrez, the quiet little capital of remote and isolated Chiapas, Mexico's southernmost state.

On our way south, in the mountains on both sides of Mexico City, we kept picking up another Ford Six, just like ours. Its driver was practicing with a real vengeance and so were we and with our almost identical machines we fell into staying in sight of each other and racing each other all the way down to Tuxtla. The first time we stopped and had lunch together I found out that this silver-haired,

youngish man was the one named on the side of his car and not just
a flunky breaking it in. He was Piero Taruffi, a great European road
racing driver, a veteran and past winner of the Panam and holder
of many of its leg records. He was the sort of racing driver who
would drive a Ford when he couldn't get a Ferrari and would drive
either car with the same will to win. He also was a collector of
straightaway records in machines that he designed and built himself, and this gave us a big interest in common.

Taruffi speaks English very well and almost the first thing he said
to me was, "Where did you pick up your European driving style?"

"Are you kidding?" I asked him. "I've never raced on anything
but streets and straightaways in my life. The way I'm driving here
is just what seems to me to be the common sense way. I don't know
any better than to do what I'm doing."

"Well," Taruffi said, "you've got real talent. Stay behind me on
this next stretch and maybe I can show you a few tricks."

He did, then and later. When Rodger and I got to Tuxtla we
found Noriega and Weber with the flatbed and had a few days in
which to get the car back in shape and to rest before the race began.
Taruffi's car also was based in the big garage of the Anza Brothers'
Ford agency there and of course I went over to see how he was
making out.

He needed a whole lot of help. He was used to Italian cars, not
American ones, and there were a thousand little details that I could
explain to him and that were really helpful to him. Finally it got to
where we were working side by side on his car late into the night.

"I just can't understand it," he'd say. "Here you are, a competitor in a race that's just hours away, and you're helping me, a
rival in your own class."

"That isn't unusual for Americans," I told him. "There are tens
of thousands of them that have the same attitude toward racing.
At any big hot rod meet if you break a part and a rival has an extra
he's almost certain to let you use it. If he still beats you, it's a
prettier victory for him. I've loaned the wheels and tires off my car
to a rival so that he could make a run, then I've re-mounted them
and run against him. And we never mention sportsmanship. We
just enjoy playing the game that way."

"*Come bello*," Taruffi said. "How nice. It's not that way in
Europe any more, although it was in England many years ago.

Look. Let's go driving together tomorrow and let me show *you* a few more things."

It would still be a few years before Taruffi wrote his famous book on race-driving techniques but in those days, just before the '53 Panam he outlined it all for me, in action as well as in words. It was a lot to absorb—how to slow down without touching the brakes, just by rocking the steering wheel; how to hit a curb at speed with the least damage; how to take savage dips and maintain good control. It was a funny friendship, between an American hot rodder and an Italian aristocrat and engineer. But it was a solid one and it has lasted to this day.

On the way down to Tuxtla we had many opportunities to prove that our Ford was faster than Taruffi's by a couple of miles per hour. Still, that didn't tell us too much about the rest of our competition. But once we were in Tuxtla, where the whole entry list was assembled, we soon got the precise information we wanted. Our car was plenty tired. We had wiped out one side of the front end against a cow and the other side against a cliff. We had thrashed the engine for 3,000 miles and had the simple-minded idea that it was just nicely broken in, while the truth was that it was worn out. Anyway, we got engine and chassis in the best possible tune and continued to practice on the roads around Tuxtla and to look for cars to practice against.

Well, the Anza brothers knew their Ford products and on top of that they knew the local roads as almost no one else did. They had prepared two Ford flathead V8's for the race and two nights before the start we met one of them out practicing on the open road. We took him on and satisfied ourselves that we were a good two to three miles an hour faster than he was. That spoke awfully well for our preparation and chances and gave us a lot of encouragement.

The morning of the race they flagged us off at one-minute intervals—sports cars first, then the big stocks, then the small stocks. There were about a hundred entries and we started sixth in our class, which gave us a lot of waiting to do. Finally our departure time was entered in our route book, we buckled ourselves in, the green flag fell and we headed down the straight next to the Hotel Bonampok like it was a drag strip.

I really had no idea how I would make out in this sort of competition because it still was totally new to me. But I stayed on it hard and Rodger kept encouraging me. "You're doing good," he'd say. "You could have taken that last one five MPH faster. You're driving real steady. Push it a little harder." And so on.

Within twenty minutes we overtook one of the Anza boys, and that was like a shot of adrenalin for both of us. We went switching and charging through those mountains faster than I'd ever driven on the open road before. Rodger was as cool as ice, so I knew I couldn't be doing too badly. There is a series of long, one-lane wooden bridges with two-by-twelve planks for vehicle tires to run on. We took those bridges just as fast as entry and exit would allow and managed not to fall off the planks. We were flying. Then we overtook a Lincoln which had left long before us. He·was still moving pretty good and that was another shot in the arm, proof that we were gaining in the turns what we didn't have on the straightaway.

Finally we came out on the long Isthmus chute, I floorboarded the throttle and just sat back and steered. We had a top speed on the level of about 105 and I used it all. The miles sped by and we picked up more cars—another in the big car class and four more in our own class. We had no stopwatch to tell us just how we were going, but we knew that we had overtaken every small stocker in front of us and that this was only the beginning. My confidence grew with every mile.

We were wailing down the long straight at sea level and it was monotonous and terribly hot. Rodger said, "How about a Pepsi?" and I said, "Sure." He undid his safety harness and had turned around to get the bottles from the rear when I hit the brakes and shouted, "Dive!" Rodger dove and grabbed that little hand-grip that we'd put on the transmission hump and that's the only thing that saved him.

Rodger had gone for the soft drinks just as we were approaching the town of Tehuantepec at the far end of the Isthmus. He knew that from there to Oaxaca it was nothing but those accordion-pleat mountains and that he wouldn't have a better chance to maneuver refreshments for us. That would have been perfectly fine, except for a couple of other factors. We had charted the big curve at the town coming down and had pegged it at 65 MPH. If we had charted it the other way we would have experienced its extreme negative banking and put it down for no more than 30 MPH. Fortunately,

we knew that we were so far in front of our class that we had reduced our speed and went into the turn at about 60.

Even so, I probably could have kept the car well under control
if it weren't for the people. As we came shrieking around that big,
sweeping bend there were about a dozen people all over the road.
Dead ahead of me was a woman with a baby in her arms. A policeman was frantically trying to herd the crowd off the pavement.

There was no place for me to get except into the people or off the
road. I braked and with the car still under good control went as
wide as I could around the crowd. I clipped the policeman with the
left side of the car, knocking him into the air, and then the right
rear wheel hit one of the boulders that lined the road's edge. That
did it and over we went in a long series of about thirteen grinding,
crashing, slow rolls, over the bank and into a ravine which lay
beyond it.

I'll never forget that policeman. He stayed right alongside us
for about a hundred feet. We were doing slow rolls and so was he.
He just kept looking in the window at me and I looked at him, both
of us too stunned to even wonder what was happening. I did
wonder, though, why his cap stayed about an inch off his head and
didn't fly away. He must have been wearing a chin strap although I
couldn't see it. By the grace of God he got up and walked away,
with no more than torn clothes and bruises.

It seemed like forever but we finally came to rest on our wheels
in the ravine. The engine and transmission were torn out of the
frame, every bit of glass was gone and it seemed that most of it was
in our faces and clothing. I looked over at Rodger and said, "Are
you all right?" We were both dazed but he grunted, "I guess so."

"Well let's get out of here fast, then," I said, and we started
scrambling. We were both thinking of that 65 gallons of gas that
was in the cab with us and could explode at any time.

We crawled out and, staggering, chased spectators away in case
of a blowup. Then we tried to make our way up the hill, to get
away from the car. It was steep, we were groggy, and we'd crawl a
few feet up and slide back. It seemed like we'd never make it but we
finally got to the top and started walking. The torn-up policeman,
with a friendly grin, took us in tow and led us over to the Hotel
Tehuantepec, where a first-aid station had been improvised and
a crowd gathered.

The policeman found an interpreter and continued to be wonderfully helpful to us. The first thing he did was post a guard by our wreck, which still was full of our belongings. Soon a bush doctor appeared, gave us tetanus shots and checked us over. Rodger's injuries were only superficial but the steering wheel had cracked a few of my ribs and, what none of us knew until later, I had gotten a moderate brain concussion. It was as we came out of our dazed state that the real adventure began for me.

14

Since rodger was in better shape the policeman urged him to go back to the car and remove our valuables and sent a couple of boys to help him. When he came back it was with the news that we had killed five people, which we hadn't known up to that point. The full story of the accident began to take shape.

Three minutes before it occurred another contestant, Bob Christie, had hurtled into the badly banked turn too fast. Seeing that he was going to lose it anyway he spun out so as to cut his speed and also to crash going backwards, which is the safer way. He landed in the ravine, out of sight from the road, and of course spectators began flocking to stare at the wreckage. When we came along our soon-to-be-airborne policeman was trying to clear them from the road and I chose to crash rather than run the people down, above all that woman with a baby. When we came to rest I remember congratulating myself on only having brushed the policeman. I had no idea that we had landed right on top of five people who were looking at Christie's wreck.

A strange facet of this whole weird experience came out later, when *Life* magazine ran a big spread on the accident under the heading, "Disaster at Tehuantepec," in its December 7, 1953 issue (my birthday, of course). Two newsmen were overhead in a light plane when Christie crashed and they circled to take movies of the wreck. Then they saw us coming and they also could see what we could not—the crowd on the road around the bend. So this photographer, Bill Riley of New York, started shooting movies and came up with the spectacular sequence which told the complete story of our crash and which *Life* ran, with a story pointing out how I had done my utmost to avoid hitting anyone. The strange thing is that the man up in the air, Bill Riley, was Judy's cousin. Of course he didn't have the slightest idea that the man behind the wheel in the disaster he was filming was a relative of his.

Now we come back to the fear that I felt in Mexico. I had grown up being taught that if you do an injury to a Mexican you can count on his kin enforcing the law of an eye for an eye and a tooth for a tooth. When Rodger came back with the word that our car had landed on top of five men, who were now being buried on the spot, all I could think of was all those fathers, brothers, uncles and cousins, who would make it their sacred duty to avenge their family blood. I was in a state of shock, my brains were addled, I was reacting to the tetanus horse serum, I was in a wild part of a very foreign country almost 3,000 miles from home and I was scared as hell. I was an oddity, of course, and every human being in Tehuantepec had to take a good look at me. And every pair of eyes that looked at me seemed to say, "There's the killer. There's the man we have to get."

This may sound like a lot of silly fantasy but, believe me, it was plenty real. I never want to go through it again even though, as it worked out, no one came after my scalp. But I still think that was only because the people who were killed were tribesmen from the distant hills who had no kinsmen on the scene.

There was one other idea that obsessed me and that was that I owed it to Mr. Ellico to bring back his property, his car. I had it hauled to the back of the hotel and, while we waited for our truck to come back from Oaxaca where it had expected to meet us, we went to work on the car. It soon became clear that it was totally beyond salvation and so we just stripped it bare, leaving nothing but the frame, body and the .325-wall chrome-moly roll bar that had moved less than one eighth of an inch. The engine, running gear and everything that possibly could be used again we loaded onto the truck and sent home.

Meanwhile, at home, one of the big wire services had had the decency to call Judy and inform her that her husband had been killed.

"Oh no he isn't," she said with complete confidence.

"You're in a state of shock, Mrs. Thompson," the voice said, fishing for a juicy, hysterical quote. "But you must face the facts."

Judy said, "Listen, mister. I don't care what you tell me but I have my feelings and they tell me that my husband is alright. Thanks for calling and now good-bye." She was badly worried but not *that* worried.

Of course it hadn't occurred to me that such a report had gone out over the Stateside wires and so it was late in the afternoon of the day of the crash that I got around to reporting to Judy. Southern Mexico was in touch with the outside world by means of something called radio telephone, on which a dozen conversations went out over the same "wire." After hours of trying I finally managed to get through to my wife. Between all the other conversations in Spanish she said, "Are you alive?" and I was able to say to her, "Yeah. I think so." I told her that Rodger and I were really okay; were heading home, and not to worry.

I was worried frantic about the vengeance committees that I felt sure were gearing to get me. I decided not to ride back in the truck. It had my name and Ellico's painted all over it and my survival instinct told me to get back as inconspicuously as possible. We talked it over and arrived at a simple, workable plan. Rodger would go back with the truck and the parts. Mel Noriega, whose Spanish was perfect, would stay with me. We arranged with a Tehuantepec cab driver to run us up to Oaxaca where we'd catch a plane for Mexico City and from there fly into Los Angeles. Perfect.

Well, the truck headed northward and we were due to take off for Oaxaca the following morning. But before we got to bed that night someone got to me and lifted my wallet, leaving Mel and me with no more than the change in our pockets. I reported the theft and perhaps if I'd stayed around I might have gotten the money back in a week or two. But I wanted to get out of that locality without delay. Mel explained our problem to the cab driver and told him that we could wire for money from Oaxaca and he would be sure to be paid. He said he was sorry, that he'd made dry runs on that story before. The news was around the little town that we were broke and everyone said that the thing for us to do was to hitch-hike. And, boy, that's what we did.

There is very little traffic in that part of the world and most of it is trucks. We got a ride in the back of a fish truck that got us about half way to Oaxaca . . . smelling. Another lift in the back of a beer truck, among a mess of broken glass, got us the rest of the way. There, in Oaxaca, they refused to have anything to do with collect wires or phone calls outside of the country. If I'd been thinking clearly I could have promoted my way out of that mess with ease— by starting with the Oaxaca Ford agency, for example. But I was completely punchy and was driven by just one obsession—to get back to a place called El Monte, California, where I had a loving wife and kids and a home and a bed and a place where I could heal up in safety and peace. So we grabbed another ride and pushed on.

The next thing I remember is that a truck had let us off in the outskirts on the south side of Mexico City, one of the biggest metropolises in the hemisphere. We had hiked a half-mile or so, trying to grab another ride, when Mel remembered that he'd left his camera in the truck that we had just quit. He headed back to try to catch the truck and I waited for him. I don't know how it happened but we got lost from each other at that point and there I was, sick as a dog, penniless and alone in a strange city in a strange country and unable to speak more than a couple of words of the language.

I was a mess. I hadn't shaved for days and my clothes were filthy. The bush doctor who had taped my ribs had taped them far too tight and I was bleeding under the bandage and the blood was dribbling into my pants. I was too sick and groggy to think of contacting the American Embassy for help. I don't know what I ate or how I somehow found my way across that huge city to the highway on its northern outskirts, but somehow I managed. And there I was, standing there like a half-dead hobo, when a car with Michigan plates ground to a stop and a voice said, "Hey, Thompson! Climb in here before the vultures get you!" That voice probably wasn't far wrong.

It was the voice of Bill Toia, owner of Gratiot Auto Supply in Detroit and a pioneer hod rodder in that area. He and Les Viland had entered a Lincoln in the race, blown something and were heading for home. With relief and exhaustion I collapsed in the back seat of their car and slept for most of the two days it took us to gobble the miles to the American border, except when Bill or Les would wake me up to take nourishment. In El Paso I wired Judy for money and flew home. That was my first taste of racing in Mexico.

15

Instead of my enthusiasm for the panam being dampened, it was far stronger than before. For the short while that I'd stayed in the race I had done much better than I had dared to hope I could and that gave me a sort of confidence that I'd never had before. Also, I had learned a million things about that race that could only be learned as a participant. And, finally, my performance in the fourth Panam was terribly incomplete, if it wasn't a downright fiasco. I was determined to go back and do it right.

As soon as I had rested up a bit Rodger and I drove the truck over to Alhambra and presented Mr. Ellico with the remains of his race car. We expected him to be very disappointed by our performance but he wasn't. That publicity in *Life* wasn't going to do him any harm and he knew that I had crashed for good reason—to save innocent lives. "For a pair of rank beginners you did fine," he said. "Keep in touch."

Well, the rules for the fifth Panam were released in March or April of '54. I had already contacted the Ford Motor Company in an effort to get some help with an entry but they ignored me. As soon as I had a copy of the new rules in my hand I called on Mr. Ellico, showed them to him and we talked about doing it all over again, but more professionally this time, in the light of all that we had learned.

I did a lot of powerful persuading and Mr. Ellico went right along. He agreed to provide not only a race car but also a practice car, a big supply of spare parts and a certain amount of cash money.

I needed a lot more money, however, and beat myself to death trying to raise it. I couldn't. I couldn't even promote a set of spark
plugs or a case of oil that year and wound up selling a lot of my
racing equipment, taking out another mortgage on the house and
borrowing every cent I could, which still wasn't enough for the
sort of campaign I had in mind.

This time Mr. Ellico worked through Dearborn and arranged for
me to go to the Ford assembly plant in Long Beach, pick out the
car I wanted on the assembly line and have it assembled according
to my own instructions. I stood there and told them where to apply
extra welds and where to beef up the body and frame. One day in
late June they handed me the keys and I drove the car to El Monte,
where Rodger and I promptly tore it down to the last nut and bolt.

I had stayed very close to Clay Smith, who was *the* brain of
Ford's racing department. Up to '53 the old flathead V8 still was in
production. But the overhead valve Six was a much newer, more
sophisticated power plant. It was faster, had more pulling power,
better fuel consumption and was more reliable. In production car
racing no one thought of using the old V8 and everyone used the
Six.

Then in late '53 Ford introduced the overhead valve V8 and it
was generally assumed that it would be a hotter engine than the
Six. I learned from Clay Smith that he and Stroppe were setting
up a pair of the new V8-engined cars for the Anza boys to drive in
the coming Panam. I figured that what was good enough for Smith,
the genius, was good enough for me, not realizing that Clay was just
acting under orders from the factory, which was interested in promoting the new model. I should have stuck with the Six.

Again, Rodger and I went through the engine and brought it to
the exact limits of the specifications and the rules. We had an
identical practice car to prepare also and this time I wasn't going
to wear out the race car by flogging it all over the continent before
the race. I invested in an old stake truck to carry the race car to the
starting line and we had to put the truck in good running order,
too.

The practice car was painted and lettered exactly like the race car
and we drove it to Bonneville just to look on at the Nationals and
keep abreast of developments on that front. Then we blasted back
to Los Angeles on the first of September and made the final, always

hectic preparations for the Panam in November. But this time we were going to practice and chart the course like it had never been done before. We were determined to devote a full month to that.

As always, and in spite of our early start, there wasn't enough time. I kept sending parts out to be magnafluxed. I found a few that had flaws and sent out replacements for magnafluxing until I knew that every part of the running gear was perfect. Except one. The day before I was due to take off I got a rejection on a tie-rod end. I fished a brand-new one out of the spares and installed it, telling myself that it ought to be all right, that the odds were all in favor of it being all right.

This is one of my biggest faults, getting carried away in a frenzied rush, and I know it. Everybody who works with me knows it, reminds me of it, complains about it. But I just can't help it. When there's plenty of time for preparation I'm the most thorough workman in the world and my patience is inexhaustible. But when the time comes to race I switch over to an entirely different brain circuit. This one is concerned only with getting from A to B *now*, and before anyone else does. At that moment that tie-rod end looked to me like the most perfect thing on earth. It had to be.

This is how Mexico went in '54. I sent Rodger south in the practice car to do a rough mapping of the 1,912-mile course. He drove from Juarez to Tuxtla and took notes on every mile. Then he drove back to Mexico City and cross-checked his notes. I flew there to join him and we practiced north to Chihuahua, where we met Noriega and Weber with the race car on the truck. We told them we'd meet them in Mexico City, and drove back to Tuxtla, refining our maps and practicing. Then we headed north again for more of the same. We met the race car in Mexico City, gave the boys some work to do on it, and headed on back to Juarez. Then we headed south again, picked up the race car in Oaxaca, and pushed on to Tuxtla. We socked in over 20,000 miles of practice and mapping! No big bank robbery ever was plotted with greater care.

Our greatest problem, next to money, was tires. Ordinary passenger car tires were costly and they began slinging treads after about twelve miles of running at racing speeds. We had no choice but to run on cheap recaps, which cost about eleven dollars each in Mexico, and we went through them at an incredible rate. By the time we landed in Tuxtla, three days before the start of the race, we were wiped out of rubber and had just a few pesos left to rub together.

That was when I made one of the most important and rewarding connections of my whole racing career. Goodyear, who had been big in the racing game in decades past, had decided to get back into the speed business via fast stock cars. Detroit's horsepower race was running wild, cars were much faster than the tires they rolled on, and Goodyear saw that the time had come for a tire company to meet the challenge that the automotive industry had created. The Panam provided an absolutely ideal proving ground and test lab for Goodyear's new high-speed tires for passenger cars and the company's engineers were on the spot to learn how racing can improve the breed.

Ironically, because of all that practice on cheap but good Mexican recaps, I didn't have enough money left to buy the tires that we'd have to wear out racing to Juarez. I knew the course as few others did, I had a perfectly prepared machine, but I was effectively grounded. On a long shot I went to Goodyear's headquarters at the Bonampok and told the big man about my problem.

"Forget it," he said. "We watched you while you lasted last year and you did all right. We'll see you through to Juarez."

Without that help from those terrific people I would have had to throw in the towel. And, interestingly enough, that was the beginning of a relationship that later would result in the fastest, safest, most radical and original tires that the world has ever seen.

With the tire problem solved our race car was ready and we had three days to burn. I looked up Taruffi who was gamely running a Ford Six one more time. We had kept in touch by correspondence and it was good to see this wiry Roman with the boyish face and silver hair again. Again I helped him to get his car in shape and we spent every evening together, mostly in swapping speed secrets. We got in a lot of daytime practice on the open road and it was clear that his Six had more suds than my new-fangled rocker-arm V8.

16

THIS YEAR THERE WERE SIXTY-FIVE ENTRIES IN THE SMALL STOCK class alone. Although I had been the first American entry in that class we all drew lots and Rodger and I started in twenty-sixth place. Everything was as before except this time we had good maps and good watches and had a good idea of what we were doing. Rodger and I had agreed that this year we would speak to each other only in case of emergency and he would raise his head from his navigational equipment only to check our position on the road. We were coolly organized and felt coolly confident.

We tore out of the broad, green valley in which Tuxtla lies and began lacing our way through the mountains down to the coast. By the time we hit the Isthmus straightaway, we had overtaken eight cars, including one of the Anzas' and two in the big stock class. Rodger had his eye on the watches and knew we were doing well but he wouldn't tell me. The car was handling perfectly, helped by radically beefed-up stabilizer bar, springs and shock absorbers, and we didn't seem to be extending ourselves at all. Finally Rodger said, "If you can't make this thing move I'm going to get out and walk." I got on it harder.

Then, just as we entered the long Tehuantepec straightaway, we came up on Francisco Anza in the first of the Smith and Stroppe Ford V8's to get away. I tried to get around him, but his car was a shade faster than ours and I had to be content to tuck in behind him and hang in his draft, which at least kept him from getting away.

We had covered two or three miles on the straight when a tropical storm broke loose, with high wind and driving rain. Anza slowed a bit and I got past him. But Stroppe had taught him the art of drafting too and he whipped into the low-pressure area of our wake. Then, with his slightly higher speed, he got past us again. We laid on his bumper while mud from his tires covered our windshield. We were doing about 100 MPH and the wiper blades just floated uselessly. By getting way down and peering through the steering wheel I found a spot where the air current kept the mud from settling and I did not reduce speed.

Anza slowed again and we passed him again and this ding-dong swapping of positions went on about thirteen times, for the full length of the straightaway. Then, finally, we came to the curve that had been our downfall the year before. Anza took it with slow respect and so did we, on his tail. With that and the next few curves behind us, we both heaved sighs of relief and Rodger said, "Mick, you can go a whole lot harder than this, you know."

That was like a surge of new life to me and I really began to charge. I pulled around Anza, looking forward to losing him now in the more than 5,000 curves we had charted between Tehuantepec and Oaxaca. As we passed him I looked his way to give him a grin. But he was glaring straight ahead. His eyes were bugging out, his neck tendons were standing out in cords and his arms were locked rigidly onto the steering wheel. I broke our silence and said to Rodger, "Boy, that guy is through. He can't last that way. We've still got almost three hours to go."

It was raining like mad and we were heading toward a turn that we had charted for 85 MPH, dry. I said to Rodger, "I'm going to try to make it, man."

"You won't," he said, and reached for the grab bar.

"Well, we're going to find out," I said and downshifted to second and then punched it into overdrive.

My usual way of cornering in a road race is to go through the turns with my left foot on the brake and my right foot on the throttle. I guess that Anza had gotten used to seeing my brake lights flash on and this time, when I chose to use engine compression instead of brakes he must have thought I was still going flat-out in top gear. He must have tried to follow me that way.

We got horribly crossed up but I managed to horse us around and stay on the pavement. I flicked a glance to the rear view mirror and there was Anza's Ford standing on its nose. I backed off instantly as Rodger watched him flip about five times and shouted at me, "Keep going, you fool. Nobody would stop for us. The natives will help him." I finally was persuaded and got back onto it. Anza was hospitalized for almost six months.

That was at Kilometer 450—the kilometer posts mark the distance from Mexico City. Rodger looked up from his charts and watches and said, "We're running three minutes behind the record. You're driving awfully good and you can go a lot faster and not be over your head." Rodger was only seventeen but he was race-wise and conservative. My throttle foot got heavier.

Rodger's confidence in my driving kept growing and so did my own. He began working up our speed without telling me what he was doing. If we had a turn marked for 50 MPH he'd tell me to take it at 65. If we had it marked for 70 he'd tell me 80. I was getting used to the car and used to the road and feeling more contented every minute and soon *I* caught the bug. When Rodger told me to go 80 I'd go 90, when he told me to go 50 I'd go 70. We closed in more and more on the record time.

One of the things that made the Tuxtla-Oaxaca leg the toughest one in the race was the road surface north of Tehuantepec. The asphalt had been mixed with local volcanic sand and gravel. You can get down on your hands and knees with a strong magnifying glass on an ordinary asphalt road and you'll see that the surface particles have a rounded appearance. But this volcanic stuff never had worn smooth and through a glass it looked like millions of little knives and probably still does. It was notorious for abnormal tire wear and *everybody*, every year, scheduled a stop for tire changes on that leg.

This year I had practiced so much that I had developed a sort of sixth sense for everything that the car would do or was likely to do. When the rain began falling and promised to keep falling for a long time I thought to myself, "This changes the tire wear picture completely. We might make it to Oaxaca without a change and that'll gain us a couple of minutes at least." I sensed that the odds were slightly on our side and decided to make the gamble.

We had planned to use the pit that Goodyear had set up out in the jungle for the benefit of its users. The pit crew was standing expectantly in the rain, poised to swarm all over us as we went flying on by. They jumped up and down, waving wildly, thinking that we had missed the pit or overshot it. I laughed and kept charging.

We caught up with Taruffi and finally edged past him. We swapped positions three or four times and then he gave us the lead, deciding that that sort of game could get us all killed.

To give ourselves some idea of how our tires were holding up we had rigged up a timing light and cut a small hole in the floorboard through which Rodger could shine the light on the right front tire. He began by checking it at ten minute intervals and then, as we rushed closer and closer to Oaxaca, he started spending most of his time on the floor, watching the plies wear through and yelling, "For God's sake slow this thing down!"

About fifteen miles out of Oaxaca a little complication set in. The carburetor needle valve stuck, causing the engine to flood. We had a fuel shutoff valve under the cowl, so I had to loosen my harness and drive that last stretch hunched over, with one hand on the wheel and the other working the valve. When we hit that last long, downhill grade that swoops into the Oaxaca Valley we were wide open and indicating 110 MPH. Rodger kept shouting, "It's going to *blow!*" but I wasn't worried about blowouts on the straightaway. It's the ones on curves that can be impossible to control.

So we swept into the city first in class, among wildly cheering crowds. We had knocked almost *eleven solid minutes* from the class record! In addition to having outrun all the other 64 entries in our category (we were four minutes faster than the second place car) we were faster than three finishers in the small sports class, faster than four in the big sports class, faster than ten in the European stock class and faster than twelve in the big American stock class. Since that was the last of the Panam races that record of four hours, eighteen minutes and six seconds still stands.

This year Judy and Mom and Dad had driven to Mexico City and followed the race from there by radio and television. I shot a wire to their hotel saying

ON TO JUAREZ. LOVE.

There was a big banquet for the whole racing crowd and the winners of each class were honored by the governor of the state of Oaxaca. They were Phil Hill, Ray Crawford, Karl Bechem, Gonsalvo Sanesi, and me. We were all treated like conquering heroes.

A telegram from Judy reached me in the banquet hall. It said:

HAPPY BEYOND WORDS. JUAREZ, SI. REMEMBER YOU'VE GOT TO GET THERE TO WIN.

17

ALL CARS STARTED THE SECOND LEG THE FOLLOWING MORNING AC-cording to their standing in general classification. We, for example, were faster than ninety-three and slower than thirty-three of all the cars entered. Now we were mixed in with big sports cars, small ones, big stockers and small European stockers and this added a big new element of interest for us. We could test ourselves against every type of car in the race.

As mountainous as the Tuxtla-Oaxaca leg is, it is relieved by about ninety miles of flat land across the Isthmus. The second leg, Oaxaca-Puebla, has very few straight and level stretches and is 253 miles long. The third leg, Puebla-Mexico, is only seventy-five miles long but it climbs from Puebla's 7,200 feet to the Rio Frio Pass at 10,480 feet and then drops to Mexico City's 7,200 feet. This leg is nothing but the tightest of hairpins and switchbacks and is one that Taruffi, a real mountain master, has broken the record on repeatedly. I've always been in my element with mountain driv-ing and Rodger and I were looking forward to this day.

We dug out across the Oaxaca Valley and into the non-stop passage of the mountains. Thirty seconds behind us came Joaquin Palacios' Pegaso. He roared past us on the straight but we hadn't been out ten minutes before we overtook him in the foothills of the first little mountain range. I was taking the turns 15 to 25 MPH faster than we had them marked, but the car was under perfect control. The Pegaso could not get away from us and we just lay on his tail, pushing him every foot of the way. This went on for miles until we hit another straight stretch in the little valley beyond. As we came out of the last turn Palacios was already just a dot in the distance, his infinitely better power-weight ratio having been given a chance to express itself. What gassed Rodger and me was that we actually had been taking the turns faster than the costly, thorough-bred Pegaso for we had caught up with it and stayed right on top of it. It was at that moment that I made up my mind to build a sports car for the next Panam. If I could corner that good in a family barge I certainly could do a lot better in a more wiry machine.

We overtook and passed a lot of cars that should have been faster, including small but hot sports jobs and a couple of big Buicks and Lincolns and then we started having trouble. We were going up a grade approaching Teotitlan and I had it in overdrive second. We seemed to be bogging down. I kicked it down into conventional second, the engine revved just a bit too high and a pushrod jumped out of its sockets. We stopped and fixed it. It jumped out again. We stopped and refixed it. It was badly bent and jumped out again. Finally we just pulled two spark plugs and finished the leg on six cylinders. All told, we were dead stopped for twenty-nine minutes but still we managed to make up thirteen of them and come in eleventh in class. I extended myself a little to do it.

There was a thirty–minute layover in Puebla during which it was permissible to work on the cars. I was fairly frantic and convinced that we were washed up. Working like mad, we pulled the rocker covers, intake manifold, carb, valve gallery cover and everything else that was in the way, installed a new pushrod and put everything back together again. We rolled to the starting line with exactly twenty seconds to spare. That's how close we came to being disqualified.

We took off again with the car running like a watch. Then more trouble. But this time it was only those two spark plug leads. In all the frenzy we hadn't jammed them on tightly enough and they had shaken off. That stop took less than thirty seconds and we were back, charging.

We made it over Rio Frio, careened down the other side into the Valley of Mexico. Rodger spotted Taruffi storming up behind us and said, "Now watch the difference between the Six and this miserable V8." In no time he was on us and past us on the final straightaway into the capital. But there was more than just the difference in engines.

As we usually did, Piero and I had sat up and talked the night before. We had become awfully cooperative competitors even if we didn't tell each other *all* we knew. He asked me, "Are you carrying Rodger tomorrow?"

"Of course," I said. "We wouldn't think of splitting up."

"I would," Piero said. "From Oaxaca to Mexico you need every trace of advantage you can get, every ounce you can save. I'm sending my copilot on ahead. I'm stripping the car, carrying no spare tire and not a liter more fuel than I calculate it will take to get me there."

So Taruffi came wailing on past us and, on the straight, he could look over, smile and give us an "I told you so" wave. He was hundreds of pounds lighter than we were and that made its difference on that most mountainous leg, as he knew it would. Still, when we reached Mexico City we were back in third place in class.

In Oaxaca I had received a wire from the Ford Motor Co., whose brass were watching their cars perform from Mexico City. They congratulated us on winning the first leg and offered us all the help the Ford racing organization could give, which was plenty. They were there when we rolled into the impound in the capital and I said to them, "Thank you for your offer, gentlemen. I begged your company for help a few months ago and I couldn't get heard. Mr. Ellico put me in this race and his help is all I ask for."

Again we had an overnight stop but only an hour for servicing the car. In that hour we rebuilt everything. New rear end, new transmission, new brakes all around, overhauling the valve gear and a lot more. We had Noriega and Weber and Ronnie Henderson from the truck to help us, but it was still a well-filled sixty minutes.

From Mexico City north there's a long stretch of tortuous mountain country and then it levels off into nearly a thousand miles of flat-out desert. This day we had almost nothing but big sports and stock cars ahead of us. Our car was running well enough but, due to the mostly open country, we overtook no one. According to the watches, however, we kept moving closer and closer to setting another lap record. And then our oil pressure began to fail.

Up to this point we had had no oil consumption problem and we carried only a couple of quarts in reserve. We used them up in twenty miles and the pressure alarm was on again. We were out in the desert now and I spotted a spectator's old jalopy in a handy spot. I mashed the brakes, warped in alongside him and shouted to Rodger to grab a crescent wrench. I didn't have to tell him what for.

He was under that car before I could scuttle up with an old hat to catch the muck we could drain from this unknown crankcase. The owner was torn between racing fever and private outrage, but we had his glue in our engine before he became violent. Maybe it was a mean thing to do, grounding the man like that, but all's fair in certain situations and this certainly was one of them.

We charged on. Eight cars had passed us during this emergency operation, and that was bad. I saw a gas station and screeched in. Rodger shouted, *"Aceite,"* but the attendants just stood there, staring with blank happiness at the real, live race car and crew that had dropped into their little domain. So I jumped out, stormed into the building, grabbed a case of oil at random, threw someone my last hundred peso note, dumped a gallon into the fuming engine and we were on our way again.

We weren't the only ones in trouble, so in spite of these little delays we were high up in contention in the race. The car was singing after the hour's work we had been allowed to do on it in Mexico City and we were in wide open country now, where the driving was easy and very fast. We had passed Johnny Mantz, who had taken over the remaining Anza Ford, and we knew that our buddy Taruffi was somewhere up ahead. We were out to collect him. We were close to Kilometer 255, just out of San Juan del Rio, when it happened.

At the end of a long straight which we had taken flat out was a wide turn that we had charted for 80 MPH and which I planned to take at about 95. I lifted my foot slightly, turned the steering wheel—and nothing happened. Rodger had observed the action. We threw meaningful looks at each other and Rodger began heaving all his paraphernalia into the back of the car. I hit the brakes hard enough to lay about 350 feet of rubber and quietly and calmly said, "Here we go. Hold on."

The curve curved but we kept going the way we were aimed. Paralleling the road was one of those mortarless stone walls that are all over Mexico. This one was about five feet high and we hit it almost head on, doing about 90 MPH. Big stones flew in all direc-tions, the car went plumb through the wall and stopped lying on its right side. As usual we were overboard on safety. How we stood the deceleration I don't know, but we both remained perfectly con-scious. I looked down at Rodger and said, "Here I come. Okay?"

He nodded. I unsnapped my harness buckle, dropped down on him and then we both climbed out through my window.

We were both remarkably cool about the whole thing. About eight people appeared and helped us tip the car back onto its wheels. We had been shooting movies of the race from inside the car, hoping to pick up a few dollars from the footage. Now that it was clear that we weren't going to make a nickel any other way, I grabbed the movie camera, sat on the roof of the car and shot the luckier ones as they sped on by. After the last race car had passed, I hitched a ride in an official car to Leon and flew home from there. Rodger stayed with our car and waited for our truck. We brought the whole wreck back to Mr. Ellico this time.

It was that solitary tie-rod end that I was in too big a hurry to have magnafluxed that had fractured and put us out of the race. I wish I could say that that was the last time something like that ever happened, but I can't. When it's time to go racing I can think of nothing else. That's one reason that I need help, and good help. Rodger was very good but he was still almost a child and not in the habit of telling me what to do. Eventually Fritz came along and gave me a lot of protection against myself—one of his many invaluable contributions.

18

THE INSPIRATION OF THE '54 PANAM SOON GOT ME INTO SPORTS CARS. But in the meanwhile, during all this Bonneville and Mexico activity, I stayed deeply involved in drag racing and managed to keep in the front line of competition year after year.

It was in late '54 that I decided to build a radically new type of dragster. For years everyone in the sport had been making noises about traction, weight transfer and about getting as much of the weight of the vehicle as possible concentrated on its rear, driving tires. As the whole sport learned to get more and more horsepower from its engines, the need for greater traction became even greater. Still, nothing much happened.

During my usual wakeful nights I used to ponder this and what could be done about it. Gradually the ideas took shape. The big obstacle was keeping the driver between the engine and the rear axle. This required a drive shaft of a certain length, which pushed the engine forward by that amount. Now if you would place the driver *behind* the rear axle you could couple the engine-transmission assembly directly to it and you would really have the main weight of the vehicle focussed on the driving wheels.

There was another problem to traction and that was the amount of rubber on the ground. If you could double the area of rubber on the pavement, you could probably transmit almost double the horsepower to the road before the wheels would spin. That's when I went to dual rear wheels and everybody laughed at my "truck." But I got the results I'd hoped for. Then I went to the A-1 Tire Company and talked them into building molds for the first recap wide-tread slicks, which I seem to have invented. This paid off some more.

One of the biggest factors limiting dragster performance in those days was directional stability—the things were just desperately hard to keep going in a straight line. I felt that this could be helped by approaching as closely as possible to a three-wheel configuration with the front wheels very wide apart and the rear wheels just as close together as the width of the driver's body would allow. So I built a dragster that way. I also thought, and I still do, that a dragster should be as streamlined as possible and I enclosed everything but the front wheels. I couldn't afford to have a body built of aluminum so Rodger and I made a framework and stretched fabric over it. That was the *first* enclosed dragster.

As it gradually took shape, the result of all these ideas made me the butt of jokes all over southern California. They called my car "The Monster" and "The Tractor" and other needling names. But the funny thing was that it *ran* and one day at Santa Ana hot rodder Leroy Neumeyer said to me, "You know what that beast reminds me of, Mick? A slingshot. You know, the way the driver sits back there like a rock in a slingshot." That was the name that stuck and the configuration proved to be so successful, so unbeatable, that within a couple of years it became the standard of the sport, which it continues to be. My old original slingshot, incidentally, is still running and it *still* meets the latest safety requirements.

When that car was still new, top dragsters were running in the high 140's. I started out with a Ranger four-banger aircraft engine in the slingshot and it never clocked higher than 119 MPH. But I don't think we ever got beat, whether Rodger drove or I did. We'd usually go into the first clock about half a car length ahead of the competition and come out of the last clock maybe two lengths behind them. But our ET—elapsed time—was lower, and it's ET that counts. Another fifty or sixty feet without regearing and we would have been wiped out. But I had a knack for choosing ratios and for calling ET's to within a tenth of a second. These predictions were strictly for the crew. To make them publicly would be to jinx our luck and to ask to be made of fool of.

I've also always had a remarkable knack for sensing speed, like the time at San Fernando on the historic occasion when I officially broke the 150 MPH barrier for the first time.

I had every kind of engine in that poor little car—Ranger, flathead V8, De Soto, Chev—we'd try anything that happened to be available. We'd torch up some new mounts, drop the mill in and *Oops!* the frame or something wouldn't fit. Out with torch and shears and hammer and we'd chop and weld and pound until it did fit. The car got to looking worse and worse. But it ran better and better up to the time we wanted to go even faster and started begging Ray Brown to lend us his very hot Chrysler engine.

We must have made fifteen trips to Ray's shop in Hollywood before he broke down and agreed. We installed the big Chrysler in the little rail, regeared the quick-change and headed for San Fernando. Rodger was with me, along with a new racing buddy, Dr. Milton Schwartz, a general practitioner and police surgeon in El Monte. He had that typical racer's disease of everlasting needling.

We were running unblown, on fuel, and after a few warm-up runs I made my first real try. Ray was with Rodger and Doc and when the time of 151.4 plus and 10.08 ET rang out over the announcing system, Ray almost jumped out of the pickup. History had just been made, and with his engine, which also had powered the FIA record-holding Shadoff Special.

Of course I was out of hearing when they called the time. As the crew drove down to pick me up Doc said, "Now let me handle this. None of you guys say *anything* to Mickey. Just look kind of sour."

They arrived and I was sitting there wearing an ear-to-ear grin and I shouted to them, "I *did* it!"

"You did *what?*" Doc asked, dead-pan.

"I *did it*. I broke 150," I said.

Doc knew that the only instrument in the car was a water temperature gauge and he said, "Yeah? What the hell makes you think so?"

I said, "Why didn't you wait until they called the time? I *know* I turned 151 something. I can tell by the wind and the sound of the car."

So I was three-tenths of a second off. My next run, when I lost second gear, was 152.7 and I called that just as close. It's just a sense that I have and it stays accurate no matter how fast I drive. The people who know me can vouch for it.

This was a thrilling and terribly active period for me in drag racing. It went into another very important phase in late '57 when I sold the old slingshot and got busy with a new, dual-engined, four–wheel drive machine. But I'd been getting into a lot of other trouble in the meantime.

The '54 Panam experience had convinced me that sports cars were the way to go. Early in '55 I went to work on a chassis and had Sorrell build a body for it. I was just getting ready to set the world on fire when the Panam was cancelled, for that year and the foreseeable future. But by this time I was hooked on sports cars and road racing. I had to find out what they held for me.

There was plenty of road racing activity in southern California at that time, but I quickly learned that it was a far cry from what I had tasted in Mexico. There, there was a man-sized purse that *real* racing people competed for. They made no pretense of being anything other than men doing a demanding and dangerous job and doing it, they hoped, for material gain. If you were a racing man you were treated as an equal. If you were an amateur you were treated with friendly respect ... and with caution, because you might get somebody into trouble. And, just as in hot rodding, if you were a phony no one had any time for you.

The sporty-car yo-yo's at that time were a totally different breed.

That whole field held a few very rich playboys and lots of ribbon clerks who liked to believe that a down payment on an MG made them aristocrats. They were a sick crew in the mental health department. It was a rare one who could change a spark plug or would want to. Phonies found a happy home in their ranks. They prided themselves on racing for pewter mugs.

Another group was made up of the men who drove for the importers of these cars and for their dealers and, occasionally, for the rich playboys. They were about as "amateur" as Yogi Berra but they still looked down on anyone who could possibly be ranked as a peasant. Around 1960 this sickening situation began to clean itself up and men like Dan Gurney, Phil Hill, Ritchie Ginther, Carroll Shelby and many others—*real* racing men—could stand openly for what they were. Until then, mixing with the phonies of the amateur sports car set was enough to make any self-respecting racing man sick. It did it to me and I was just one of a great, great many. Still, I took it for about three years.

I was well along with my own sports car—I was campaigning the slingshot—when I got a lead on a very special Kurtis, the last Indianapolis roadster-type sports car that Frank Kurtis built. The price was so right that I decided to give it a try and arranged for the owner to trailer it to Palm Springs, where I could try it out in one of the major events of the '55 season. I brought Rodger along and asked a couple of new-found buddies to help out in my pit. They were Doc Schwartz and Fritz Voigt and this was the first time we ever went racing together. We were all totally green at this kind of racing.

We arrived on Saturday morning and took the Kurtis over. Its tires were thoroughly unfit for racing, but that was okay. I cut some practice laps and went out to qualify. The car handled badly. It had a very short wheelbase and had flipped with two top AAA drivers. But I went storming around and did well enough in the qualifying heat until something broke on the last lap. I coasted until I was about a half-mile—no closer—from the finish line, then got out and started pushing in the desert heat.

I had the impression that I had to cross the finish line without outside help in order to qualify and I was determined to run in the main event. Part of the way was slightly uphill and I pushed my lungs out and my tongue was down to my knees when I got across the line and collapsed. That's when Fritz said to me. "Hey, you dizzy dramatist, you didn't have to do that. But you sure put on a nice show for the customers." Fritz is still with me and he's never stopped being lippy with me or anybody else.

So we were qualified for the next day's big race. But the car was a mess. The rocker arms of the Cad engine were starving for oil. The shock absorbers were over the hill. And we had to find new tires and mount them.

We worked all night. I did a lot of welding and picked up several painful flash burns. By the skin of our teeth we arrived on the starting grid just twelve minutes before race time. I was a wreck but that was par for the course. I buckled on my helmet, Doc whacked it on the top and said, "Sic 'em, Mick."

I was in the twelfth row when the flag went down but I was the first one through the first turn. I lifted my foot and found that someone had forgotten to hook up the throttle return spring. I made it through the next two turns with my shoe hooked under the throttle and then on the backstretch, while going full bore, I managed to undo my shoelace and loop it around the pedal. Don't ask me how, because I'll never know. I ran sixteen laps that way, most of the time running third to Phil Hill and Carroll Shelby, until I had to come in on a flat tire. We only had a small, flimsy passenger-car jack in our pit and the Kurtis fell off it. By the time we could borrow a decent jack from Ken Miles, there was no point in going on. Doc sat there and cried like a baby and if I hadn't been so mad I would have done the same. Fritz's comments were philosophical but unprintable, which is a pretty good three-word portrait of Voigt, my favorite mechanical genius.

So I bought the Kurtis and stretched its frame and went racing at all the Southern California circuits. I was always in contention, but never on top and never really happy with the dingalings who infested the sport. Finally, in practice at Riverside in '57 I crashed and shattered a kneecap and spent the day of the big Grand Prix watching from a wheelchair. That was another one of those situations where the doctors had one idea and somebody named Thompson would have none of it.

"We're going to have to remove that kneecap," the doctor said.

"Why?" I asked.

"Why, if we don't you're going to have a stiff leg for the rest of your life."

"And if you do, how good will the leg be?" I asked.

"Well, it'll still be a very stiff leg," he admitted.

"So leave the kneecap alone," I said. "Later on we'll see just how necessary it is to chop pieces off me."

So we compromised on putting the leg in a cast, where the doctor said it would have to stay for six to eight months. A month went by. I had to go racing and I couldn't do it with a cast on my leg. I sawed it off and the leg was stiff as a plank, the knee joint just welded together. I sat on a chair and put another chair under the thigh of the bad leg. Using the other leg like a sledge hammer I banged down on the bad one, trying to break the knee loose. There was no result the first few times except the feeling that I was going to die. But I knew that something had to give—either the leg or the knee, and the knee was the weaker of the two. I had nothing to lose because the kneecap was already broken. Finally the knee bent and I moved around on crutches until it almost was as limber as it should be. Now it locks up in cold weather but if that kneecap had been taken out, I would have been crippled for life.

19

I HAD A BUSY LIFE IN THAT PERIOD AFTER THE FINAL PANAM. I WORKED out the slingshot, went gung-ho for sports car racing and became a drag-racing impresario. At the same time I was making a living and not a bad one. It's no small wonder that I wasn't seen around Bonneville for three years.

From the very beginning of legal drag racing, I had had the feeling that I could run a drag strip better than anyone else and I had a burning urge to give it a try. I talked about it a lot and many people knew how I felt. Then one day in April of '55 a buddy called up and said, "Say, why weren't you at that interview tonight."

"What are you talking about?" I asked.

"Why the one to pick the manager of this big, brand-new drag strip that the Lions Club is going to build at Long Beach. Too bad you didn't know about it. But it's too late now."

"Listen, *pal*," I said. "Next time don't call me after it's too late. Now what's the name of this man that I should have been interviewed by and how do I get to him?"

Two minutes later I had him on the line. "Is it too late?" I asked.

"It sure is. Sorry," he said.

I asked, "Could I just come over and talk to you for a few minutes?"

"Don't bother," he said. "We've *made* our decision and we're very content with it."

"That's fine," I said. "I'm on my way. I'll be there in twenty minutes."

In less than two hours his signature and mine were on a contract to manage the Lions' Drag Strip.

Only the preliminary grading had been done, so there was a lot of time for me to get my plans organized. I liked the arrangement with the Lions. They paid me a small salary and a very small percentage of whatever profits the strip might make, meaning that the harder I worked and the better the results I got, the more I would benefit. And I liked the Lions' approach. They didn't build the strip just to make money, which is the motive behind so many strips. They built it because they believed that drag racing is a good thing for the community, particularly for its young people, and I believed that too—with a vengeance. The strip was just a reclaimed truck farm out in the desolate tules, but I knew that I could get the people to come.

We took the slingshot to the NHRA National Championship meet at Great Bend that year and got back just in time to prepare for the opening of the strip on October 6. That first day was total madness. We had ten thousand spectators and a thousand entries, it seemed, and we scarcely knew what we were doing or why. I had raced at strips all over the country and thought I had strip operation completely figured out. But there were a million problems that you can't anticipate until you're on the organizing end. For instance, someone was supposed to keep track of the times. But he didn't show up.

Judy was there, of course, just to share the experience and watch the show. I braced her and said, "Honey, we're in a terrible bind. We've got to have somebody to fill in tonight. Take this pencil and pad and go up there in the tower and the announcer will tell you what to do." Judy went up the tower that day and many other days when someone was needed to fill in. And she did a whole lot more, like handling press relations. She could even run the whole show when I would have to be away on business.

We learned fast and quickly and if the routine we developed was followed, everything would run smoothly. I was very fierce about safety regulations and set up my own, which were often more severe than those elsewhere in the sport. Anyone who didn't like them could find another place to run, but my job had as much to do with the safety of participants *and* spectators as it had to do with competition. That first responsibility was sacred to me.

Both spectators and drag racers seemed to like the way I ran the strip, and I ran it with an iron hand. It soon became one of the top strips in the country and quite a few authorities call it the best of them all. A natural sense of showmanship helped here. I managed never to run out of ideas to give the crowds a better show almost every weekend than there was anywhere else in the area, if not in the nation. I saw that money was spent on the very finest of timing equipment, and the most fair and foolproof. There never has been any question of phony times, favoritism or dishonesty at Lions. That helped to attract the very cream of competition and the crowds naturally followed. It's said that Lions has made more money than any other drag strip in a single year. I didn't make that money but I helped to make it. And I love to keep on with this work because if it weren't for our drag strips the mayhem on public roads today would be a national emergency.

Lions helped my income, which made it possible for me to pursue an ever more active racing career. I held down my job at the *Times*; devoted about fifty hours a week to the strip, and set up a commercial garage in El Monte. I called it Mick's Service Center and it's still going strong under the management of my original partner, Farrell Backer. My combined, total income ran between $350 and $400 per sleepless week of endless work. It wasn't a bad income but there was a big lag between it and the outgo that my plans called for.

Lions did something else for me that I couldn't have bought with money from anyone, anywhere. That was teaching me how to get along with my fellow man. To put it more bluntly, it taught me not to fight like a wild animal every time I was crossed in the smallest way. Lions taught me to learn tolerance, patience, understanding and to turn the other cheek. All these were things I'd known little and cared less about. But during the first six months that the strip was open, every time someone would get mad at me and mouth off, I'd settle the difference on the spot, with fists. I never came off second best. I became so snowed under by law suits based on broken jaws and noses and lost teeth that it became a question of getting civilized or going bankrupt. If I didn't get civilized, I at least got some sense and it was learning to handle that unruly mob of youngsters that beat sense into me.

It really pained me when, on March 23, 1963, I resigned as manager of the Lions' strip. My kids and my business both were growing and both deserved much more of my time.

20

I GREW UP IN A TOUGH NEIGHBORHOOD. I HAD A FATHER WHO WAS harder than nails and he taught me to take no guff from anyone. All that would have been fine if I hadn't been handicapped and made a runt by accident and illness. In high school the combination of feistiness and frailness produced a belligerence in me that I didn't lose when I got my late, second growth. I still have to fight my brawling tendencies. But at least now it's just myself that I have to fight.

I still manage to get into a good battle occasionally but the problem used to be infinitely worse. I made firm rules at the strip and backed them up. I'd come up to a bunch of punks who were drinking or being disorderly in some way and say, "I'm sorry. You're going to have to stop that."

"Oh, yeah?" would be the answer. "And who's going to make us?"

Now that's an approach that I never could stand. It's like a red rag in front of a bull. It's a challenge that I *had* to take up without an instant's hesitation. Those are the guys that I used to knock over the fence like clothing store dummies. They're the ones who taught me a little tact, diplomacy and self-control when the lawsuits began piling up.

I always have loved to see a bully get whipped. I can sit back and watch and think that it's a good thing. I never have been able to stand seeing a little guy get whipped by a bully or by several other guys. What's fair is fair. That isn't. I never could stay out of a fight like that and still keep my self-respect. I've been in an awful lot of fights where I knew I was going to get whipped, but I didn't care what the odds were, just as long as I could take a few of the others with me.

I learned when I was puny that you have a real big advantage if you *think* you have it. A couple of my mental advantages were bulldog determination and contempt for pain. I learned to whale the tar out of awfully big guys just through perseverance. I used to get whipped badly and often but it never slowed me down a bit. Eventually the word got around that there was no point in messing with me because I didn't care how badly I got beaten as long as I got in some telling blows, which I usually did. Fighting was like any other effort for me—you *do not* quit until you've won or been smashed. My Dad drummed that into me and I've drummed it into my son. If you ever quit on anything, if you give up once, then it becomes easier and easier to give up in the future. I've *never* given up on anything in my life.

If this book is important, then the fighting thing is important, because it helps to explain the way I tick. Like one night a bunch of us who worked at the strip went down to Huntington Beach for a picnic by moonlight and firelight. A ruckus began nearby and I saw about twenty guys, in their late teens and all drunk, slugging a man until he fell. A kid about thirteen—the man's son—came rushing our way with these drunken punks after him. They caught up with the boy and began pounding him.

I was blind with rage, leaped up and shouted, "What the hell are you rotten characters trying to do to that kid?" It didn't matter that there were twenty of them. It could have been two hundred and I would have had to do the same.

I knew that I had six of my own guys around me and, usually, if a small group will stand back-to-back a larger group of bullies will melt away fast. I looked around for my guys and they were the ones who had melted. And there was that little kid, shaking in terror and looking at me like I was his last hope in life. Then someone took a swing at me and the ball began.

It was one of those fights where every time I threw a punch somebody got in the way. They really knew nothing about fighting and fell like tenpins. I stood my ground until only one guy was still facing me, but he was different. I couldn't understand him. I could knock him flat and he'd bounce back like a toy. I must have knocked him down ten times before I finally jumped on top of him to finish him off. Then of course the others closed in and began hammering on me from all sides.

I was so exhausted by this time that I could hardly move my hands, but I managed to break away and run into the water. It refreshed me and I made it a point to keep lined up with our bonfire so I could see the silhouette of anyone who came after me. Four of them came. I could see them far better than they could see me and I drove them off. By this time the little kid had long been gone. Fritz, who had gone for supplies, had just come back to the fire and was bellowing for me. If he had been there before I would have had some *real* help. But I was battered to a pulp and, utterly through, staggered to Fritz and rasped, "Let's get out of here *now*."

Fleeta—who worked at the strip and has been my executive secretary since I started Mickey Thompson Enterprises—and Judy actually were the only ones who stood their ground and got in some licks against these maniacs. We read in the papers the next day that they had gone on terrorizing the whole beach, beating people up and finally shooting at them, until word got to the police and they came. It was one of the big, bad, local news stories of the year.

The impulse to fight is a lot like the impulse that I have to race. Nothing else counts other than accounting for myself in the very best way that luck, God and my own abilities will permit.

There was a time, for example, when Doc Schwartz and I were in my pickup, going to get a part welded. We were stopped at an intersection, waiting for the traffic to pass, when a car with five characters in it went by and one of them leaned out and shouted a mess of profanity at me. I was just sitting there minding my own business and had never seen any of these guys before. Well, I saw blinding red.

I peeled out after that car and chased it about ten blocks until I forced it into the driveway of a used car lot. I don't know what Doc was doing all that time; probably yelling at me. They all came out swinging and I took on the lot. I had decked two of them and was ready to massacre the rest when I saw them back off. The next thing I knew, Doc's arm was around my neck and he was choking me down the way police medics subdue maniacs, painlessly and harmlessly. I blanked out for an instant and when I came to Doc still had his hold and said, "We're getting out of here, Mickey. Right?"

I admired and trusted Doc and got the message of reason in his voice. Two guys were still sleeping it off on the pavement and the others weren't asking for any more. We got out.

"Mickey," Doc said, "you were completely out of your skull. You would have taken on an army and gotten yourself dead. You've got to learn to roll with life a whole lot more."

I tried, but had little success until it became a question of taking it easy or losing the strip, which was a whole world to me. Now, instead of getting into two or three fights a week, it's just one every three or four months. I save these for people who really try to treat me badly and will track them down if it takes years. I'm slavishly loyal towards friends but with enemies I know of just one way to be and that's ruthless.

Many times when I've been in a fight or have been racing someone and *know* that I can win, yet he keeps fighting back doggedly, I give in. I admire and respect a person who is that way and it makes me feel good all the way through to see that spirit. But if I'm fighting or racing someone who has superior equipment or advantages, the harder he presses me the harder I'll battle back. If he has any trace of the quitter in him I do everything I can to bring it out.

It's surprising how often it's there; how often it can be counted on for winning a contest. Determination so often is as strong as brain or muscle or money and very often it's stronger.

21

ANOTHER BIG THING THE LIONS' STRIP DID FOR ME WAS TO BRING me together with Fritz Voigt. Fritz was one of the top hot dogs of the sport when we opened and he was the first Top Eliminator that we had. He came back almost every weekend and wound up TE many times. It was actually the friendship that developed between Judy and Fritz's wife, Dorothy, that led to our friendship. We talked about the lakes, where he was active and I wasn't. I made a few trips with him to the lakes and watched him become the SCTA's top-point man in 1956.

Fritz was and is very smart and a very wild man in a conservative way. He was right at the top in drag racing when he decided to give it up and did. He saw all the writing on the wall. Up to that point you could save your engine and still be a top man. You could race for a whole year on just one engine. Then the pace began to quicken. Everybody began winding mills tighter and tighter and the first thing you knew almost everybody had a new engine every time out. Fritz decided all that expense wasn't for him and that with things getting so lickety-split, it was getting too easy to get yourself killed. He decided to retire a champion and that's exactly what he did. The height of his ambition was just to run his small but profitable little commercial garage in Maywood, make a modest, steady, square living, raise a family and have nothing to do with that racing nonsense ever again. But he got tangled up with me.

It's not that Fritz is a man that anybody can push around. Just never try. He's a big, husky brute who has worked very hard all his life. He can take care of himself and quite a few others in almost any situation, including the ones where brains and wit pull the weight.

But there was something special going between Fritz and me. You can't tell an old locomotive engineer to forget about railroading. Fritz was so deep into racing and knew so much about making machinery perform that he could never hope to kick the habit, which we had in common. We were good, good friends. I wouldn't say so to his face and his words about me I'd rather not have to hear. Still, I'd lay down my life for Fritz if he needed it and I know perfectly well he'd do the same for me. Perhaps Judy knows better than I how deep and good Fritz's friendship is because she has witnessed it under the most telling conditions, when I have only been a vanishing dot on the horizon. We all know how we feel about each other but in our day-to-day behavior we get along like a pack of ornery cats and dogs. As a matter of fact, our goofy hound is named Fritz.

Fritz is four years older than I am. He is a phenomenal hot rodder, meaning that he's a real genius of a mechanic. What's already built he can make run better. What he's lacking he can design and make out of thin air and junk. Machinery comes apart or goes together under his hands as though it led a life of its own and all the while Fritz rattles on, delivering profound statements on psychology, then some profanity, then some profound engineering statement, then a smattering of obscenity, then a burst of philosophy, then some more that's unprintable, then some deadpan humor that cracks everybody up.

Fritz uses "dirty" words like the air he breathes but he doesn't think in a dirty way and the words never sound dirty, coming from him. He just happens to spice his speech. The effect is at least witty when it isn't brilliant. And I say that, being a violent hater of dirty-mouthedness. Fritz is a hot-rod Mort Sahl, Lenny Bruce, Lord Buckley and all the hip comics you can think of, rolled up into one muscular mass that's balding and going slightly blubbery.

Fritz also is a genius at human relations. His own personal, emotional life would be the despair of any head-shrinker but he tosses out the solutions to other people's problems as readily as he retailors a spark-advance curve. People flock around him just to bask in his happy and practical view of the world.

He can work as untiringly as I can without ever getting edgy, as I do. At Bonneville with *Challenger* I used to have to work the crew almost to death. After days and days almost without sleep all our tempers would be strained to hair-triggers. Fritz would be working harder than any of us but he could feel the trouble crackling in the air and say something wisely ridiculous that would make everyone bust out in uncontrollable laughter. The crisis would be gone.

I could fill a book with stories about Fritz, his virtues and wonderful straight-faced antics. But one of the greatest things that Fritz did for me was never to yes me; never to treat me as anything but an absolute equal; never to treat me as a big shot or employer; never to stop thinking entirely for himself while, at the same time, I knew that he was looking out for my interests and welfare with everything he had. His honesty and judgment were as dependable as sunrise. Just so the friendship wouldn't get soggy we always gave each other plenty of trouble.

For example, in that brawl at Huntington Beach I had shattered one of my fists and, sort of typically, had it in a cast. I had just recently finished the twin-engine FWD dragster with a lot of help from Fritz and was racing it at Lions. According to my strict safety rules I never would have allowed a contestant to drive with his hand in a cast but I didn't make the rules to apply to myself. I drove the car all day and nobody said a word, knowing darned well that they might get that cast in their mouth. Finally I was due to run for Top Eliminator.

Fritz had quit racing, had been away from it for a long time. I came up to him and said, "Man, you're going to have to drive this thing. My hand is hurting so bad I can't shift very fast any more."

"Oh, _keen_," Fritz said. "It's the TE run and he lets me drive it and I've never even sat in the weird, miserable thing before!"

Fritz was burned but he also liked the confidence that I had in him—plus he owned one of the car's engines. The run was against Ted Cyr, who hadn't been beaten in six or eight months. Fritz got in that strange bear and smoked off the line and shut Cyr off so badly that he broke his reign. Cyr began losing often after that and Fritz went back to happy oblivion as far as hero-driving was concerned.

I've said before that no one does anything important alone. I've been blessed in having some tremendous help. Judy has been a tower of strength. Rodger was indispensable in Mexico and in drag racing in the mid-1950's. Then Fritz hove onto the scene and added another tower. As a professional doer of big things I insist upon top billing. But I love to give credit to those strong hands that have held the ladder I've been climbing. Judy comes first and, after her, that crazy, great, swinging, non-stop loyal character, Fritz.

22

THE WHOLE THING WAS A GRADUAL DEVELOPMENT, AN EVOLUTION toward a goal that was completely inevitable. If I achieved one minor goal I naturally went on to a higher one that logic put in my way. At the same time, I knew exactly what the big, inevitable goal that I was heading toward was.

Rodger remembers that it was in 1952 that I showed him sketches I made for a streamliner that was to be the fastest car ever built in America. It might even be capable of making an attack on the Land Speed Record.

"That's a brute I'll never drive," I told him then. "But I'll build it for sure and if you want to drive it, you can. You're a good handler, you're smart and you don't have any family responsibilities. Of course, if you weren't around, I guess I'd *have* to drive it." The prospect definitely didn't appeal to me. I just wanted to build the machine to do the job.

I had worked out the drawings that I showed to Rodger in '52 the year before. I first thought in terms of a three-wheeler because I felt it would have the best handling qualities, the best directional stability and the best shape for streamlining. Then I checked out the rules of the *Fédération Internationale de l'Automobile* in Paris, which governs automobile racing internationally. They stated that in order to be considered an automobile, a vehicle has to have four wheels and has to be driven through at least two of them and also steered through at least two. So I drew up a compromise design with the rear wheels placed as closely together as possible. At that time I thought in terms of two Chrysler engines driving the four wheels. I did a lot of talking about that chassis layout and over–all

design and in 1953 Spade Carrillo showed up on the Salt with just
such a machine, except that it was powered by a single Chrysler and
driven through two wheels. Something caused him to flip and
crash at about 250 MPH, which put an end to a great pioneering
experiment. But recently Spade has been working on the twin-
engine, four-wheel-drive version of that design. MG of England
may have been influenced by his '53 car because the MG streamliner EX 181 resembled its unprecedented polliwog shape. That car
was remarkably efficient and Stirling Moss and Phil Hill set a slew
of new FIA records with it at Bonneville. But other influences kept
me from building a polliwog of my own.

It was in '58 that I built the new twin-engine dragster that I put
Fritz in to shut off Ted Cyr. It came into being like this. A wealthy
dairy farmer with an appetite for drag racing, Manuel Coello, had
built a four-wheel drive rail that was powered by a pair of flathead
engines which drove through Jeep running gear. He put the car
up for sale. I saw some parts there that I could use and the price
was right, so I bought it and went to work building a completely
new car, using whatever pieces of the old car that I could.

Of course I was a believer in multiple engines. But in Coello's
layout the driver sat centrally in the car, between the front and
rear engines. I never had liked a forward seat position in a high
speed vehicle because by the time you notice that something has
happened from such a position, it's all over with. The farther forward you sit in a vehicle the less warning there is of any change it
makes in its course. This is one of the great virtues of the slingshot
layout. It gives the driver a sense of detachment. He sits back there
watching everything happening in front of him. In a front–seating
car you can be fishtailing wildly and hardly know it. But the instant
a rear–seating car gets just a bit wiggly the driver knows and can
work to control it. So the first thing I did was get rid of the old
frame and build a new one, slingshot style.

The flathead engines were obsolete and I unloaded them. I still
had the Chrysler out of the old Bantam but needed another one
and had other things to do with my money than go out and buy
one. Fritz had retired from drag racing but still had an old Chrysler
engine and a mass of spare parts in his garage. I hate owing anybody anything or using anything that isn't mine. But Fritz was

different; we were already close friends. So I talked him into going partners in a four-wheel-drive dragster project.

I hauled my old engine over to Fritz's garage and he went to work rebuilding it and his own engine. In the meanwhile a good friend, Kenny Droesbeke, and I built up the new chassis and I drew up a streamlined, full envelope body which Sorrell shaped from aluminum. I paid good money—about $1,000—for that body and Sorrell, a real artist in sheet metal, had great ideas for making it a thing of beauty. I had others. All I wanted was to get the chassis out of the wind and to give it a nose that would penetrate the air smoothly. And I wanted the absolute minimum of frontal area. I just drew up a skin-tight box for the chassis, provided some bumps for wheel clearance and a streamlined nose for the box. It was probably the most ungraceful streamliner ever built and again everybody scoffed.

Also, as far as I know it was the first *fully* streamlined dragster ever built; and it ran well. As I recall, its best performance in the quarter-mile was 159 MPH in 9.72 seconds, on gas, which was plenty good for those days.

We got the new car finished in time to haul it to the NHRA Nationals, which were held in Oklahoma City that year during the last three days of the Bonneville Nationals. Fritz and I talked it over and agreed that we might as well stop over on the Salt for a couple of days and see what sort of top time we could turn. We felt that on a long course we should have no trouble in cracking 270 MPH and that would top Bill Kenz's record . . . the fastest ever by an American.

Bill Kenz and his partner Jim Leslie operate the leading Ford garage in Denver and are devoted, pioneer hot rodders. Kenz showed up for the very first Bonneville meet in '49 with a real weirdo—a pickup truck powered by a pair of flathead V8's. That oddity, which Kenz had built for charging up and down the Rocky Mountains, drew a lot of attention but scarcely got out of its own way with a best speed of 140.95 MPH. But Kenz studied everything on the Salt, above all the 189 MPH Xydias-Batchelor streamliner, which was powered by a single Merc engine.

Kenz was back the next year, this time with his twin-engined truck wrapped in a smooth, streamlined shell. He clocked 206.5

MPH but Xydias-Batchelor (that's Dean Batchelor, now editor of *Road & Track*) still topped him by a quarter of a mile an hour.

In '51 Xydias-Batchelor were out of contention, having crashed during a demonstration run at Daytona Beach. Kenz really got cranking on the Salt that August with a one-way 227.9 and an all-time two-way record for an American-built car of 221.5 MPH. The next year Kenz's car, driven by Willie Young and powered by three flatheads, pushed the one-way record to 252 and turned a two-way average of 244.7 MPH. By 1957 Kenz had maintained his leadership and had boosted the record to 266.2 MPH. He had been America's Number One hot rodder for almost eight years when Fritz and Judy and I clanked onto the Salt with our ugly black-primered brute.

Another thing about Bill Kenz is that he was and is one of the nicest, friendliest, most courteous and helpful men that the sport ever will have. If he and I didn't have some of these qualities in common we certainly had some common interests. Frank Lockhart was Bill's hero too and both Bill and I thought in terms of being faster than anybody and doing it with all-American equipment. The only thing that Fritz and I didn't like, that actually made us feel very badly in '58, was the way we massacred Bill's record. But of course that's what we were there for.

Bill came over when we unloaded the beast and he asked us all about it. It was full of a bunch of outlandish ideas and I was flattered by this very important man's interest and proud to answer his questions about the machine. For example, for running on the Salt I had the front engine set up to operate in high gear only. I planned to get a push start up to about 70 MPH, engage the rear engine, accelerate up to about 160, then engage the front engine. After that, I'd shift the rear engine from second into top gear and get hauling.

Kenz, along with the whole Bonneville technical committee, had grave doubts about the car having no suspension whatsoever. I explained to him that the faster you go the less need there is for suspension and we were going to go awfully fast.

Kenz had seen a lot of eager beavers before and he said to Fritz and me, "Fellows, I was here for several years before I got my car straightened out, you know. You've got a promising thing here but remember that it takes time to go fast and that each tiny increase in speed has to be slaved for. If you don't go over 200 just remember that there's always next year."

Bill was very sincere. He wasn't trying to discourage us. He was trying to keep us from getting discouraged if we didn't cut a fat one right away. I just said, "Thanks a lot for the good advice, Bill." But Fritz blurted at him, "Listen, ole buddy, we don't have time for all that pussy-footing around. We've got to get your record and still make the drags in Okie City at the end of the week!" Bill just shook his head and walked away.

But he was there on the line when I fired the car up on that first day. There was something about the way Fritz had set up those engines—cams, shape and length of exhaust headers and I don't know what else—that gave that car the most savage sound I've ever heard. Those two engines sounded absolutely terrifying. They literally shook the Salt. *Challenger's* four engines never approached that sound.

On the line Kenz still tried to be helpful. "Take it easy now, Mick," he said. "Just ease her through at about 150 the first time." I grinned and nodded but thought to myself, "Man, I've already done more than that on quarter-mile drag strips in this thing. I've got to find out in a hurry how fast it will go."

That first run was on straight pump gasoline, just to feel the car out. I turned a loafing 241. The next run was ten miles an hour faster and the car went straight as an arrow and almost steered itself. And then we decided we'd better drop the pans for a little inspection. We found bearing metal everywhere.

We had known that both engines were on the tired side and that the crank throws in Fritz's engine were far out of round. What we hadn't anticipated was the punishment of popping a clutch in direct drive with a 1.87 gear and of having stock main-bearing caps without steel bars to help them take the load. All we could do was clean up the mess and replace the bearing inserts. But we saw the writing on the wall and we made an agreement. I was to keep on charging and no matter whether Fritz's engine or mine let go first, we'd both share the cost of replacing it.

I made another all-gas run but one of our fuel pumps quit and we burned a whole set of pistons. That meant rushing back to Wendover, phoning Los Angeles, having a new set of pistons flown to Salt Lake City, driving the 120 miles each way to pick them up and working all night to get them in the engine so we could be on the course the first thing in the morning. Just one of those typical hot-rod hassles; one of those little things that you don't quit over.

We were first in line as the day's meet was about to start. Then Chet Herbert's crew moseyed up with their car as though they were going to try to ace us out of our position. It was a crusty trick but it wouldn't have psyched me so bad if Herbert's streamliner with its three Chevrolet engines hadn't been the worst threat we had on the Salt. In the meantime, Fritz had spotted a fuel tank leak and broke the news to me that we had to go back to the pit area and weld it up.

"And let those bums get away with copping our place?" I shouted. "Not on your life. It's me that's going to make the first run of the day."

"You're out of your mind," Fritz shouted back. "There's a steady drip of fuel falling right on one of the exhaust pipes. You'll be fried in your own fat!"

"The hell I will," I yelled. "Give me the fire extinguisher!"

I grabbed it myself and climbed in. And the only reason I didn't make that run was that the cockpit was so tight that there wasn't room for me and the extinguisher, too . . . as though I could have hoped to operate it while trying to control the car at speed. So Fritz won, we went back to the pits and welded the tank and I was still alive, which I probably wouldn't have been if I'd had my way at that carried-away moment. But that's the way I get when I race.

That day, running methanol in the rear engine (because it was the stronger one) and gas in the front engine, I got in a qualifying run at 266 MPH. We hauled back to Wendover, dropped the pans and worked most of the night again, cleaning bearing metal out of the crankcases and installing new inserts. And early the next morning I turned a two-way average of 266.866 MPH. In four days I had wiped out what Kenz had built up over all those years and I was almost ashamed to look at him. But he came to me full of warm congratulations and praise. A gentleman and a wonderful guy, like I said.

We had been so involved in breaking this record and in doing it without nitrated fuel in order to spare our engines that the four days had rushed by. Here it was Thursday morning and if we wanted to make the thousand miles or so to Okie City and make any showing at all we had to leave instantly. We had a pow-wow. We hadn't even begun to put hot fuel to the engines and already had the fastest hot rod, the fastest American car, in history.

Why don't we just stay here and go until we blow?" I asked Fritz.

"Those are the sweetest words I ever heard," he said. "You just keep on doing the driving and I'll try to keep the engines glued together."

I had had the feeling that with better than 800 horsepower available on mere gas, we might go very fast on the Salt that year. So I had contacted Firestone, the only source in America of tires for extreme high speeeds. I told them that I wanted rubber good for 300 MPH and they told me that the new tires they had developed for Bonneville would handle that speed. Unlike the previous Bonneville Firestones, which had a cross-section like a billiard ball, these new ones had square shoulders to provide greater contact area and longer service life. They did a fine job for the other contestants, but *they* weren't going as fast as I was. Even on that 251 MPH run I had begun throwing treads and I didn't like that at all.

Inflation pressures got the blame and we spent a lot of time fooling around with them. On the 251 run we were carrying 75 pounds to the square inch. We kicked it up to 100 pounds and on the 266 runs I only lost about four inches of tread. That still threw the wheels so far out of balance that the car was bouncing and thumping all over the course and it took all my guts not to lift my throttle foot higher than I did.

I got into a terrible battle with the Firestone technicians. They told me that the fault was that the tires were rubbing on the inside of the body. I told them that that was ridiculous. You could just look at the inside of the wheel bumps and see that there had been no trace of friction. They were adamant and I got furious. I grabbed a big axe out of my trunk and hacked the wheel bumps right out of the body that I'd paid so dearly for. The result was an unsightly mess but it made it possible for me to say, "All right. I'm going to make a run. And if I shed treads this time it won't be because the body is rubbing."

I made the run, the treads peeled off, the car bounded all over the course. I came back to the Firestone tent and stood there silently, with my evidence.

"Well, yeah," they said. "Let's try some of last year's tires without the shoulders and run them at 125 pounds."

All this playing around with fuel and tires had consumed most of the week. During that time Chet Herbert, working from the wheelchair that polio had put him in, had been ironing the bugs out of his three-engine streamliner. Late Saturday afternoon—the next to last day of the meet—he qualified at 272. This gave us the old *kamikaze* go-or-blow fever and we put a 30 per cent shot of nitro into the rear engine but left the front one with its egg-shaped main journals on gas. On that run I roared through the traps at what was then a fantastic 286 MPH. Now all we had to do was back that up two ways.

We tore down that night as usual and this time found whole chunks of bearing insert lying in the pan of the front engine. We replaced the mains, put thirty per cent nitro to both engines and started praying.

Sunday morning Fritz pushed me off and when we were doing about 70 he beeped the horn to signal me and I engaged the rear engine's clutch, watched the oil pressure gauges climb, turned on the fuel and then switched on the magneto. The streamliner leaped, went howling down the white vastness and at about 160 I went through the same procedure with the front engine. Both were on a stiff charge of fuel and you could tell the difference in smell, acceleration and noise. The needles of the two tachometers climbed in perfect unison and faster than they ever had before, letting me know that we were making a little history.

Then things began to happen. Before I even got into the quarter-mile timing trap the canopy popped open and began banging up and down. That was very bad. It could come adrift and take my head with it. There was scarcely room in the cramped cockpit to get one arm up behind my head to where I could grab the canopy and hold it steady. I just got my hand through the opening when the lid banged down and laid four fingers open to the bone.

I was too busy to give that any thought and just held on, steering with one hand. The tachs were indicating around 275 MPH when the tire treads began peeling again. I made up my mind to ride it out, and the seconds that followed were like hours. With each bit of tread that would let go the wheels would get farther out of balance and the car would vibrate more violently. With the wheel bumps chopped away I had a perfect view of the tops of all four tires. I just sat there watching more and more of their casings show and wondering which would blow first. The car shuddered so violently that I saw double and then triple. But I made out the red blur that had to be the sign marking the end of the third-mile trap. I lifted my foot and cut the engines and began sweating out the return run.

It had to be made within an hour, leaving no time for attention to the engine bearings that we knew were bad. I was a bloody mess and my hand was beginning to throb hard as we threw on a new set of those tires that scared me to death. As we did this and changed the engines' coolant, Fritz and I worked out strategy for the back-up run.

If there was one thing in the world we could count on it was the terrible state of that front engine, laboring now under a crushing load of nitro. We decided to take advantage of the extra space at the north end of the Salt, go back to where we could get an extra two miles of approach and use only the rear engine for acceleration. The only trouble was that there was no black line to steer by out there and the course had not been scraped.

Well, I was lucky and guessed right. I entered the course proper at just under 200 and only about ten feet off the black line. I climbed up to about 225 and then cut in the front engine. The tach needles swept steadily around and it began to look as though this was it: I was going to be the first American to break 300 MPH. I was indicating about 290 and still had a mile to go before entering the traps. The machine was still accelerating strongly. And then it happened. The front engine scattered before I could even jam in the clutch and there I was, trying to see enough through the smoke and fumes to hold on course.

I was awfully disappointed to have missed the 300 mark. If I'd made it, it would have made it so much easier for me to get help with the machine that I now had to build.

Here are a few points for the record.

On its own initiative Firestone had spent a lot of money on building a better tire for the hot rod sport. They had no real reason to expect the tremendous jump in speed that I came up with. Their tires were completely adequate to my speed except that the tread was a tiny fraction of an inch too thick. Or perhaps it was the torque reaction between my front-driven and rear-driven wheels that really caused the trouble. But those tires took the tremendous centrifugal loading and held their air. Had one blown out I don't see how I could have lived through the consequences.

From the start of that twin-engine car project until I turned the 294 and developed other interests, I spent about $8,000 on it, which of course I could not afford.

The body was ugly but its shape couldn't have been too bad since we had less horsepower than Herbert but went 22 MPH faster in a speed range where each extra mile an hour costs huge amounts of horsepower.

While the big record at Bonneville had been raised by roughly five miles an hour each year I had boosted it by almost 30 MPH. I had topped my own Bonneville record by a cool 100 MPH. I think that I went about 100 MPH faster through the quarter-mile trap than had ever been done; I clocked 272 MPH with an approach of only one and seven-eighths miles. And I made it into the 200 MPH Club by the biggest jump anyone ever had, for what that may mean.

These accomplishments did attract a great deal of public attention and gave me, overnight, considerable stature in the world of speed. Without it the next step would have been much more difficult and, perhaps, impossible.

23

BY TEN IN THE MORNING OF THAT AUGUST 31 WE HAD THE STREAM-liner back on its trailer, all our gear in the truck and were headed back to Los Angeles. Judy and Fritz and I were feeling pretty satisfied.

"Fritz," I said, "I'm going to need your help with the New Car."

"What new car?" he asked.

"You know, man," I said. "The one to go 400. To go after the Big Record."

"Oh of course," Fritz said. "Very dull of me. Well now that you mention it I think that I'll kick this millionaire's habit, forget about striking it rich in racing and just stay in my garage, where the money comes in if you work for it. Count me out, Mick. I mean it."

That was the way it happened; that simply. I just began talking about the New Car that day and that was it. We had come within a tidy 100 MPH of the World Land Speed Record which had been set by Britain's Sir John Cobb back in '47. Cobb had turned his 394 with two huge aircraft engines in a machine almost as big as a boxcar. But with a couple of little automotive engines belting out maybe 1,000 horsepower Fritz and I had come three-quarters of that way. If we doubled our horsepower with a couple more engines we should be able to move past that last quarter of Cobb's record. I had the four-wheel-drive chassis problems under control and my blunt approach to aerodynamics had worked out fine. It was all very simple: it was the obvious, inevitable next step.

Judy certainly thought so. She never batted an eye. We had been together so long that we thought on the same wave-length automatically.

I was pretty quiet on that trip back and pretended to do a lot of sleeping, while Fritz drove his old Cadillac. But I was thinking hard about the New Car—just how I'd put everything together, what old parts I could use and where I might be able to find a little help, because this one was going to take some real money.

As soon as we got home, checked with our parents, reported all the great news to them and picked up our kids and loved them, I said to Judy, "Come on out to the garage."

There I grabbed a handful of chalk and as Danny and Lyndy looked on, I began drawing the New Car's chassis on the cement floor, explaining each step to Judy, who understood it as I went along.

It would be another slingshot streamliner, since the old one had worked so well. It would have four engines and of course it would have to drive through all four wheels in order to have the traction to overcome the terrific wind resistance in the speed range that we were aiming at. But how would I get the power from the engines to the wheels and how would I get the gear ratios to translate the engines' RPM into all those MPH? Not with conventional axles. That was for sure. So I soon arrived at a solution that is so simple most people think it's the last word in complexity.

Naturally, the front engines should drive the front wheels and the rear engines the rear. Each engine would feed its power into a rugged Cadillac transmission. Each transmission would then feed into an overdrive unit—which I'd have to design and build—which would feed into a ring-and-pinion final drive assembly. The front axle would have two final drives, one for each engine, and the rear axle would be the same. So: four engines, four transmissions, four overdrives and four final drive units. Right! Judy listened to all this solemnly, with round-eyed faith in every word I spoke. I said it would go 400 and she therefore knew that it would go 400. But when I began telling other people about it, they knew I had popped my last brain cell.

I had to get back to work at the *Times* but within a couple of weeks I had four wrecking-yard engines on the garage floor and a large pile of junk steel tubing. There were no blueprints, only the chalk marks on the floor, and I began cutting and welding a frame to take the engines.

I had chosen Pontiacs for a very good reason. As wonderful as the Chrysler top end was its bottom end never had been designed with racing loads in mind, so its rod and main bearings often failed under hard racing use. But Pontiac recently had produced a new V8 with one of the most rugged lower ends the industry had ever seen. I didn't want an engine locking up at 300 MPH plus, and the Pontiac promised the greatest reliability by far. I didn't expect power output to be much of a problem, and it wasn't.

Next came tires. Tires are the foundation of any car and above all of any high speed car. Without them you can't move. If Lockhart, for example, had had proper tires he would not have crashed and lost his life. I had had enough trouble with tires at high speed to not dream of taking chances on ones that weren't perfect for the job.

So I went to Firestone and told them that I needed rubber to go 400 MPH. They scarcely bothered to humor me. "You might get going that fast a few years from now," the big man told me, "but not that fast right away. We'll talk to you later."

I begged the man, in desperation, because there was no other firm in the country with the know-how to build such tires, and I would *not* go to overseas sources. But I got the firm, cold, final brushoff.

It was then that I remembered the Goodyear people that I had met and been befriended by in Mexico four years before. I knew that they were interested in stock car racing. This was a far cry from the Land Speed Record but it was a slim possibility, a hope.

I contacted Goodyear in Akron and told them my story. By the wildest of long shots my plans happened to dovetail into a huge development program which they had under way involving tires for high-speed aircraft as well as for almost all forms of racing. The home office asked for all the details I could provide and I sent them, along with photos of the chassis that was just beginning to take shape. I don't know what other checking they did but eventually they decided that I stood a chance to do what I planned to do. So development engineer Gene McMannis got on a plane and flew out from Akron to talk with me. That probably was the greatest single bit of encouragement that I've had in my life.

Up to this time record seekers always had been completely subject to the tire companies. They would say, "I want to go so many miles an hour and my vehicle will weigh roughly so much."

The tire people then might say, "All right. We can give you a tire of such and such dimensions that will do the job." Then you designed the car around the tires and if it had to be boxcar-sized to fit them that was *your* problem.

McMannis spent many hours talking with me about the project. I knew quite a bit about racing rubber after all those years of rodding and Gene recognized this. Finally I said to him, "You know, not only would I like for you to build me tires, I'd like for you to build them to *my* specifications."

"Keep talking," he said.

"Well," I said, "all the LSR tires for decades have been huge, towering things that have destroyed any vehicle's chance at small frontal area. I want the tiniest tires that I can possibly get that will stay together at the speeds we're talking about."

McMannis said, "Okay, Mickey. I came out here with the authority to kill your project or give it my blessing. I'm going to bless it and I can design a tire for you like the world has never seen, and it will be *safe*. How small do you want it to be?"

I measured the chassis. The ideal size would be about 21 inches inside diameter, 29 inches outside, and about five and a half inches across. McMannis said, "All right, you'll *get* just that."

Now I could stop just dreaming. The one insurmountable obstacle had been removed and I could fly ahead with the design and construction of my machine knowing that the tires would be available—and their dimensions. We reached this agreement in January of '59 and there was not a lot of time left for what had to be done. The task ahead for both of us was enormous.

I had scarcely begun to bail out of the cost of the twin-engine car project and here I was in one that demanded more money than I'd ever dreamed of having. I slugged away at the *Times*. I slugged away at the Lions' strip. I slaved away at Mick's Service Center. I borrowed and I mortgaged and still there was barely a fraction of the cash that I needed. I went everywhere trying to hustle support from all kinds of manufacturers. I drew blanks almost everywhere I went.

What would you do if some utter punk came to you and asked for money, saying that he wanted it to break the Land Speed Record? You'd probably humor him, pat him on the head and get rid of him. Well, I got so that I could see that reaction shaping up in the minds of the people I interviewed long before they knew what they were going to say to me. It made me sick and furious; yet I couldn't blame them. I would have done the same thing in their position . . . probably.

There were a few, rare exceptions. I went downtown and made my pitch to Frank Meunier, the Mobiloil executive who had given Cobb backing many years before. This man was a hardened expert in such matters. He cross-examined me to the point of my exhaustion and finally said, "All right, kid. Relax. I'm sold. I like your idea and wish it all the luck there is. We'll help you with some cash."

There were a few others, but very few. From the very beginning Cliff Collins, owner of Harman & Collins and, now chief engineer for Schiefer Manufacturing Co., had faith in my whole approach and urged me on. Champion Spark Plugs eventually lined up with me in a modest way, thanks to their brilliant racing representative, Dick Jones. Ed Iskenderian gave me some very important help. Others who chipped in were Grant Piston Rings, Joe Hunt Magnetos, Stu Hilborn on fuel injection, California Metal Shaping Co. on the basic body panels and Moon Equipment Co. on many accessories.

I absolutely could not do the job alone. I had to work to make money. I had to hustle and promote. I had to build the chassis, designing it as I went along. I had to farm work out to machine shops and keep hammering at them when they consistently missed delivery dates. I had to figure out a body to wrap around the chassis; had to get a mockup built for it and then get the sheetmetal work done. And I had to give some attention to press relations and the problems of insurance and of booking time on the Salt and of arranging for official timing. Those were some of the major chores. You tell *me* how I got it all done, because I'll never know. There also was the important detail of getting engines built.

Fritz was the perfect man for this job in every way—in terms of skill, thoroughness, caution and a temperament that I could get along with under any conditions. I could trust him implicitly. Like me, he would not let another man get into a car that he would not drive. And he was no fool. But he definitely had had his fill of racing just for the love of it and going deeply into hock for the pleasure. I pleaded and cajoled and did everything but threaten him with violence. I told him about the great things that I knew I would accomplish, how I owed him a lot and wanted him to share in my success. But his hard, practical answer was always the same: "I'd like to be in on this with you but I just can't close down my shop and do it at a complete loss. I have to think about my wives, too."

God knows I didn't want charity from Fritz, but I needed him desperately. I knew what was proved later—that he was the one really indispensable man on the project. Finally I got $1,200 from Ed Iskenderian for engine work. I had scrounged six more engines and went to Fritz's garage and said to him, "Here's what I've been able to beg for engine building. Will you set these ten mills up for twelve hundred bucks?"

Fritz heaved a deep sigh, heaved down the wrench he was holding and said, "Well, at least my brood won't starve. You knew I was going to do it anyway, you con artist."

"Sure," I said, "because you *had* to do it. I couldn't do it without you. Now that we're working together again, if we break 400 I promise you a big cash bonus. And if we have any decent luck out of all this, I'll really treat you right."

"I never had any doubts about that," Fritz said. "Let's cut out all this small talk and start hauling the engines over here."

He hasn't stopped working like a galley slave since. But he tells people that I *have* treated him very well indeed. Still, he keeps his old garage business going in the background just to retire to some day. I know that I'm not easy to work for and that if I ever give Fritz a really bad time he'll walk out the door . . . after finishing to perfection whatever job he was working on. I hope that never happens and after what he's endured I don't think it will.

I had pathetically little help. Rodger had gotten married and he instantly carried out an old vow: that the day he got married he would get out of racing in any form. I missed him badly, but couldn't blame him for preferring to feed his family. Now that I'm a respectable manufacturer he's come back to work for me.

There wasn't much that Judy could do on the building end. There was a kid or two who would hang around and try to make himself helpful, sawing, filing and grinding. Every little bit helped and I welcomed it. And then there was my Dad.

Now, for all his passion against my getting "too involved" in fast cars, he resigned himself to fate amazingly well. He disapproved of my racing, yet he never let me down in a pinch. There must have been a dozen times over the threadbare years that I got into expensive mechanical troubles far from home and would wire him, asking him for money. It was rarely less than $1,000 that I asked for and once it went to $10,000. I knew that if he didn't have it he would get it somewhere. And he knew that those debts were sacred to me and that he'd get the money back soon, which he always did.

Dad had retired from the police force, had time on his hands and was handy with them. He saw the terrible bind I was in and was around the shop constantly, helping out in every way he could. It was he, for example, who carved out most of the wooden mockup for the body.

Doc Schwartz rallied around wonderfully and neglected his practice to bird-dog equipment for me, getting it free or at the lowest possible price. And that was about the extent of the help that I had with the staggering challenge of building the fastest car in history. There were a couple of men who helped out whom I deliberately

have not named. One repaid my friendship with arrogance and
wild demands. Another tried to turn my project, *my* total effort,
into a vehicle for his own glorification. I'm sorry. Anybody who
knows me and bothers to take a good look at me knows that I'm as
generous and loyal as any man that ever lived. He also knows that
I will tolerate *no* liberties taken with that loyalty and friendship.
The person who does that one time is through. I'm incapable of
forgiveness when that happens, just as my Dad was when guys in
trouble would lie to him. If all the guys who lent me a hand when
I needed help most had been loyal I would be taking good care
of them today. Since some of them weren't, I don't even remember
their names.

24

MY EQUIPMENT WAS ALWAYS ORIGINAL; THEREFORE WEIRD, OUT-
landish, unproved and ready-made fodder for people who like to
knock other people's effort at any stage—before or after success or
failure. I was used to being knocked but not as I was for *Challenger.* I don't think this was inspired by jealousy to any important
extent at that stage. A lot of it was just lack of belief in the design
and contempt for any little person who would attempt such a big
thing. The general attitude was, "Oh? *You're* going to make an
attempt on the LSR? How quaint. Try not to make too much of
a mess on the Salt."

Hardly anyone took the design of my car seriously. Four engines?
That means 32 fuel injectors and their throttle plates. How could
you ever synchronize them all to a single pedal? Ridiculous.

Two engines running in forward rotation and two in reverse
rotation? No! Ridiculous.

Four three-speed transmissions that all have to be shifted simultaneously? You don't have enough arms. Ridiculous.

Slab-sided body and square tail? About as aerodynamically clean as a truck. The drag will be tremendous and the first good cross-wind will send you rolling. Ridiculous.

Parachute brake? Chutes have barely been tried on dragsters. At the speeds you're talking about any effective chute will yank the frame apart. Look, Ma. Umpteen hundred miles an hour and no rear axle! Ridiculous.

That's how it went: *everybody* knocking and laughing behind my back; being politely, hypocritically patronizing to my face. I expected this from people with backgrounds in formal engineering, but when it fed back to me from my own partners in crime, from the hot-rod fraternity, that hurt. What tore everyone up the most was the idea of solid suspension—no suspension at all. They were unanimous on that point—that it couldn't work. Maybe on a glass-smooth surface but not on the Salt, which is anything but smooth. Rodders with a little knowledge of physics and calculus showed each other jottings which "proved" that hitting a one-inch bump at 300 MPH would impart enough vertical acceleration to the car to put it and its driver into lethal orbit. All of which makes Gene McMannis' faith in the project so fantastic. It was his tires that were going to have to provide all the suspension. In my book he is the world's greatest tire engineer.

This was one of those cases of untried, purely experimental design that I would not talk about until it had proved itself. The whole machine was such a mass of untried features that what I said about it was limited almost entirely to *what*, with no attempts at justifying *why*. And my efforts at selling were confined to possible sponsors.

I enjoyed all the raging argument and speculation, even if it was so negative. I knew that it would accomplish nothing if I told all the doubters that, as far as I could find out, the fastest that a shock absorber can work on a two-inch bound and rebound is a very fat fraction of a second. I was perfectly willing to spring the chassis but I thought, "If I'm going several hundred feet per second, what earthly difference does it make what the springs and shocks did a thousand feet back? They're just starting to react to a condition that existed long ago and far away. What's the good of suspension if it doesn't know what hit it until it's maybe a quarter-mile down the course?" So I just kept on building the car my way, while people shook their heads and guffawed about "Thompson's self-propelled slag heap" and cheerfully waited for me to wipe myself out in a blaze of mechanical stupidity.

Most of those who bothered to drop in on the project from time to time thought they had further grounds for zero confidence. They looked and decided that I couldn't possibly get all that cast iron lashed together by the deadline that I had to meet. I had allowed nine months from the start of construction to *Challenger's* first official run. They were almost right but that's almost always the story in racing, where racing against time is just one set of odds. But it did get to be quite a cliff-hanger.

I wasn't the only one working desperately against time. For the radical new tires I had to have new and very special wheels. I approached Halibrand Engineering to build me a 21 inch magnesium wheel with a 5.5 inch bead-section in January. Ted Halibrand was totally cooperative but he also was totally committed to his horde of Indianapolis customers, and he was generally notoriously slow in meeting his promised delivery dates. So it wasn't until late in May that real work began on the wheels.

Then, to make the whole project really precarious, Goodyear had its problems. Part of the huge development program that I had walked into was the construction of an ultra-modern, million-dollar machine for testing tires up to speeds of about 500 MPH. This was the device that would tell whether McMannis' tires would be able to stand up under the speeds and loads that I hoped to subject them to. But the machine was still in the process of being built and it wasn't completed until mid-June after every kind of crash priority. Only then could the first really serious testing of the tires begin.

That left less than two months to find out if the tires would work and, if they wouldn't, to try to make them work. Akron was in a state of perpetual frenzy and so was I because what I was killing myself to build would be a useless, total loss without tires to run on.

Meanwhile, back at El Monte, conditions were equally frenzied. My timetable called for the first official showing of the car at the Beverly Hilton on July 27! And for the first demonstration at speed at Edwards Air Force Base on August 9! And for me to make the first Bonneville runs on August 14! Of *course* no one believed we could make it. Naturally, no one believed we could make it, but

Fritz and I just kept slaving, knowing that we had to make it and would. Goodyear never lagged for a moment and Mobil let me know that their faith in the project was solid. It was this backing that made it possible for me to keep going, to hold to the schedule and to believe that the whole project wasn't just a mad and idle dream.

Everything was a photo finish, naturally. The last four days before the Beverly Hilton showing were beyond words. There still were no engines in the frame—they were all getting the finishing touches at Fritz's. Don Borth of El Monte, a master craftsman with sheet aluminum, was still ironing out the body panels at his shop. Halibrand had finished the wheels but had shipped them to Akron so that they and the tires could be tested. But somehow everybody sort of met his deadline and in that last four days we got the car together so that it at least looked complete, even though we had no time to paint the body.

Fritz and I had been working for over fifty hours straight through when we loaded *Challenger* on her trailer—a little something else I had to build in my spare time—the morning of July 27 and headed for Beverly Hills on the other side of the city. Then, just as we turned left across traffic on Wilshire Boulevard and into the hotel's entrance, fire broke out in the engine compartment of the pickup that we were towing the trailer with.

It was a wild scene. Hundreds of cars jammed up all around this weird-looking silver missile, smoke boiling out from under the pickup's hood and Fritz and I, gussied up in our best suits and neckties, roaring around like maniacs. The only thing that saved that situation from becoming disastrous was the fire extinguisher in the streamliner. I threw up the canopy, yanked it out, doused the blaze and we pulled up to the entrance of one of the world's swankiest hotels haggard and shaking.

This was Goodyear's party and Cecil B. de Mille couldn't have made it more of a colossal production. Goodyear had hired the Beverly Hilton's huge, gold-draped main ballroom. *Challenger*, in her gleaming aluminum shell, looked like a jewel in that setting and I could hardly believe that this was happening to me and that I somehow had caused it to happen.

Then the people began arriving. It seemed that every newspaper on the West Coast had at least one man there. The TV people were on hand, the wire services were represented and so was every automotive publication in the country, plus many from overseas. It was a huge crowd that gathered first for cocktails and then for a lavish luncheon. Clyde Schetter, Goodyear's top public relations man on the coast, spoke a few confident words about the LSR campaign and then he introduced Gene McMannis, who told the group something about our tires and all that had been gone through to bring them from the idea stage to tested perfection in about six short months. Then Clyde nudged me and asked me to say something. I gave him a nod that meant okay and he rose and introduced me to the members of my first press conference, and one of the biggest that I ever expect to face.

That was one of the great turning points in my life and I realized it as it was happening to me. It was like that crash at Tehuantepec, when my whole life played itself back on a mental screen as we went hurtling out of control, flipping and banging and waiting for death. This time, again, I looked at myself as though I was examining a stranger for the first time and from a great distance.

Here I was, the central figure in this fantastic scene. For all my life and up to that very moment I had been something very different. Just a backyard reef-and-bash artist whose biggest concern was trying to avoid being stomped on by society. Just one of a million or so hot rodders that society lives with uneasily at best, as it lives with various minor plagues. I saw all those years of starvation and seas of sweat, all aimed at a goal that I hardly had the guts to admit to myself. The grimy levis, the junk-bin parts, the race-track romancing, the credit-card racing campaigns, the thousand and one nights and more of working without sleep, food or money just to be on the starting line the next day. Then I heard Schetter's voice say, as though from miles away, "Gentlemen, I now have the pleasure of introducing Mickey Thompson, the man whose vision is responsible for this entire, great undertaking."

It probably couldn't have happened in a better way. My exhaustion was so total that I was incapable of feeling any panic or even any real self-consciousness before this huge group, there to judge me and pass its judgment on to the world at large. I simply got to my feet and let myself start talking. I don't know just what I said but I spoke from my heart and told the people present in honest, straightforward language, all about the project: how it had developed, what we had been through and what we hoped to achieve. I closed by saying something like, "I don't promise to break the Land Speed Record. No one can make such a promise. But I think I can promise you that I will go far faster than any American ever has, which merely means breaking my own record. And I'll do it with equipment that is American down to the last cotter pin."

That was the day when I felt for the first time—and Judy with me—that destiny and I had some fairly important dates from here on out. Up to this point I had just followed a course that was dictated by the drift of my life. At this point that drift crystallized into a sharply defined career that I felt that I could see clearly, almost to its hazy end. Nearly everything I've done since then I could foresee clearly at that moment.

It was precisely at that moment that I looked back on my life-long cockiness and pushiness—some people call it egomania—and knew that they were luxuries that I'd have to start learning to do without. It hit me that suddenly I had become a public figure—my own man, but also a symbol for anyone who might want or need it. Now I could no longer be ruled by the unbridled passions and prejudices of Mickey Thompson, flat-out hot rodder. Now, if I was going to do my job well and reap a reasonable harvest from all this effort, I had to shape up and assume all the responsibilities that any successful public figure assumes. I had to tame myself, learn tact and diplomacy, learn to dress well, speak well, act well and present an image worthy of public attention. I had to start thinking about those hordes of people who endorse and make a public figure, a "star," a culture hero. I shudder to use these terms, which sound so boastful but which happen to be consequences of, part and parcel of, the career that lay open before me. I owed these things also to my few loyal and all-important sponsors. And even to myself and above all to my family, if I wanted to move forward. That moment was one of rebirth for me.

After the speeches we gathered around *Challenger* for pictures and a gigantic question and answer session. While this went on I overheard the snide comments of some writers who said I was out of my mind and that my "bucket of bolts" would come to any one of various miserable ends. Instead of unhinging their jaws, I came up to them with bland patter and didn't let myself get ruffled.

It was a few of the "experts" of hot rod journalism who gave me the worst time and hurt me the most. All my efforts were centered around enhancing the stature of our sport but they preferred to tear me down behind my back while lapping up Goodyear's abundant hospitality. The hack flacks from the big dailies would print anything they were handed and the sharp auto editors would write good, straight stories, but these authorities, who were most qualified to grasp the essence of what I was trying to do, enjoyed themselves by damning it with faint praise. Unfortunately, every sport has its politics, and the hot rod sport is among them. But the big dailies, plus radio and TV, treated me well. Their appetite is for news and I was feeding it.

As we drove back to El Monte towing the shining missile, Fritz fell into one of his sporadic serious moods.

"Mickey," he said, "I believe that everyone has some purpose in life. Today I got a glimpse of yours, whatever it is. One thing I know is that you're tackling what always has been a rich man's field for achievement. I think that you're going to show the world that a working-class man can function in it successfully. If you pull that off it's going to be very inspiring to an awful lot of people and I think that's good.

"I think that I have a purpose in life, too. Fame and fortune don't show me a thing, but I must live for a worthwhile purpose, too. Dig this, Mick. You can count on me to drudge for you as long as I feel that I'm a part of the good thing."

25

THE NEXT DEADLINE WAS AUGUST 9—THE SHOWDOWN AT WHICH I WAS supposed to show the world that the car would run and run fast. This one was rougher than the first. This time the car had to function all the way; not just as an exhibition piece. The two weeks between the Beverly Hilton and the blast-off at Edwards Air Force Base were among the most hectic in a perpetually hectic life.

Long before this I had had to take an indefinite leave of absence

from the *Times,* whose management granted it with cheerful understanding, blessings for success and a command to go out and make
news. Fritz and I and all the hands we could muster labored over
Challenger day and night and by the grace of God had the machine
fully assembled and ready to fire up on the evening of August 6.
Naturally I had to find out if it would work before I made a big
public showing. Would all those engines live together in reasonable
harmony? Would the transmissions shift, would the drive system
work, would the car just go, steer and stop? I should have had much
more time for finding the full answers to these questions. But of
course I didn't.

So on the morning of August 7 Fritz and I hauled the car out to
the Lions' strip where we could feel it out just a little bit, legally and
in privacy. I'm a very hard driver, very hard on equipment. The car
was almost as much dragster as it was LSR machine and I drove
it like a dragster. We got all four engines barking, buckled me in,
and I blasted off hard. It was a shade too hard because I tore up all
four of the ring and pinion sets and split all four of the quick-
change final-drive units wide open. That was a costly lesson—about
$2,000 worth. But the money was the least of the calamity. Two
days later I was due to demonstrate the car before representatives
of most of the world's press at Edwards AFB. All the invitations
were out and there was no turning back.

So once again Fritz and I dragged back to El Monte, told Judy
to keep the coffee and food flowing, and proceeded to do the impossible in the scant, sleepless time that we had left. Fritz made
new final drives out of whatever old rear ends we had lying in
corners and we fitted various quick-change gears to make them all
come out even. Just to make things interesting, Goodyear had a
movie outfit living on our backs and all we did in those final, hectic
hours we did stepping over them as they ground away and said
things like, "Hold it there for a second. Point to that part. Now
make like you're real mad." And so on.

It was two A.M. on August 9 when we put *Challenger* on her
trailer and headed for Edwards—which used to be Muroc—where
we were due to run for a large, important audience early in the
morning. We no sooner got on the freeway than a cop pulled me
over and wrote me a ticket. My nerves were shot, I told Fritz to
drive, kicked off my shoes and went to sleep. Like the streamliner,

its trailer also had no suspension and by the time we got there, Fritz was even more of an exhausted wreck from fighting the 6,000 pound load weaving behind him for all those miles.

We arrived in the cold dawn and unloaded. The press mob was there. We got the engines lighted and tried a real easy shakedown run and the shifting forks broke in low gear. That meant that both low and high gears were useless. I was panic-stricken for a moment until the significance hit me of what it meant to still have the use of second gear. In second I should be able to get up to about 300 MPH and this was merely a demonstration run. I was determined to show those people that *Challenger* would run and run fast, but that should be fast enough. Among those people were Judy, Mom and Dad. They had had more faith in me than anyone and they were the ones that I could let down least of all.

I took some bailing wire and lashed the shift lever in second position. Fritz pushed me off and when the pickup ran out of acceleration at about 85 MPH he beeped the horn. I flipped on the mags and the engines caught but burbled sickly, lugging hard. They coughed and chugged and then got high enough on their torque curves to where they could begin pulling, and then I began accelerating like a shot. "Yeah," I said to myself. "This is sort of what I had in mind."

We were supposed to use the long, wide X15 runway but it was found to have some bad soft spots from recent rains. We were moved to another, narrower one, in better shape, called the Navajo Trail. I was flying down this strip of road-oil sprayed on the lakebed, wandered a tiny bit off the strip and hit a three-inch bump at the intersection with another strip. The car took to the air like a diver off a springboard. The marks later showed that I was airborne for sixty-six feet and according to eye witnesses I was about three feet off the ground most of the time. It seemed like thirty feet to me. I touched down at a slight angle to my forward trajectory, which was enough to send me into a great looping spin. Ollie Riley caught me going through his Chrondek clocks at 201 MPH *backwards!*

I've *always* been able to keep my composure in a racing emergency and thank God I didn't lose it this time. When *Challenger* started spinning I flung the canopy open so I could see where I was going. The tires were screeching but instead of panicking and hitting the brakes or even just getting off the throttle, I kept my foot in it. I had had enough experience with spin-outs at El Mirage to know that when you get sideways on that soft surface the greatest danger is the way the tires build up a wall of dust ahead of them, which the vehicle then trips over. But if you keep your wheels spinning fast they fling the dust away and clear a path for themselves. I kept them spinning and fought the car into a semi-straight line. Then I popped the parachute brake which, like a storm anchor, helped to finish the rescue. I switched off the mags and fuel and rolled to a stop.

Fire trucks, officials' cars and press cars came racing up to the scene as I climbed out, covered with alkali dust and bruised from head to foot. They found out that I was all right and began shouting about what a masterful thing I had done, how nobody else had the skill to have saved that situation from deadly disaster. It was a miracle, everyone kept saying.

Well, my experience had a tiny bit to do with it, but that's all, and I am the one guy who knows anything about it. I had no business coming out of that ordeal alive. None. I got the car back under control by sheer accident. I knew then and I'll never forget that it wasn't *me* who got it straight. Somebody else was helping me steer that car and that's the only reason I lived through it.

Ever since then I've never been a bit shy about getting down on my knees and praying before a run. I do it in whatever privacy is available, like strolling over behind the push truck. But I do it unashamedly and if anyone wants to think that I'm weak or soft or superstitious he's entitled to his opinion and I couldn't care less.

We all learned a lot that day. I learned that *Challenger* could accelerate to over 200 MPH in less than a mile, because that was what happened even though I had the use of second gear only. Any doubts I might have had about *Challenger's* potential were erased.

We learned that Goodyear's tires and Halibrand's wheels could take fantastic side loading and not fail. For a long way the marks made during the spin and slide were made by just two wheels because the other two were in the air. The radical tires were tubeless and a loss of pressure, a blowout or any failure of a wheel would have put an end to the whole project and probably to me.

And the press had a story. Those guys had seen a show in a million, one that they would never forget. It's a pity that all the cameras, TV and otherwise, were far down the course and out of sight of the unscheduled action.

In spite of the incident—or because of it—everyone went home with something that he had come for. I knew that the car was going to be fast and that the tires and wheels were all that I could ask for. I had confirmation that divine help exists. But I knew that God helps those who help themselves and the first thing I did when we got back home was triple the strength of *Challenger's* roll cage. I knew that people would say that Thompson was getting chicken. That didn't worry me either because I had had a taste of what I was up against. They hadn't.

26

Two of the roughest deadlines had been met. They both were irritating because they were essentially press functions that stole time from a racing schedule that was almost impossible anyway. Still, I realized fully how essential such things are. To everyone's surprise and to mine most of all I found myself equipped with a sudden sense of showmanship and of public relations. Perhaps this happens to everyone who becomes a public figure. For the first time I became very conscious of my appearance and of the appearance of my equipment. Everything had to be shipshape, sanitary, professional.

I seized every opportunity to defend and promote the cause of hot rodding while doing my best to fight the negative folklore which intolerant society had created for it. I never had been tactful or diplomatic in my life but I became so overnight. Not altogether, of course, but to an extent that I never would have dreamed possible a few months before. They say that when a country bumpkin inherits a million dollars he automatically becomes smart about handling money. All this responsibility had fallen on me and it made a big change in my life.

Every country that's active in automobile racing has official colors for its cars. America's are blue and white. After that experience with the white coupe that wouldn't trip the timing lights I chose blue for *Challenger*—pale blue—and she looked beautiful.

I assembled a crew—Mel Noriega again, Cecil Schremp, Bill Burns, Jerry and Danny Callahan were among them. I arranged to cover their expenses and they agreed to work for coolie wages, just to help the effort and be part of it. I had uniforms made up for all of them and told them to keep clean, that I'd pay the laundry bills.

We worked like demons until the instant when, on August 22, we all hit the road for Wendover. We had two cars, a pickup hauling *Challenger* and a big stake truck loaded with all our gear, including eight extra, fully prepared engines. We thought we had a big outfit until we saw Donald Campbell's the following year.

We spent August 23 going through technical inspection and getting ourselves organized in space I had rented in the Western Services Garage, so that Fritz and the crew could get to work on finishing the car. The Nationals' tech committee went over *Challenger* with a fine comb and even had some complimentary words to say about her. But they still were worried about the solid suspension. My orbiting at Edwards AFB was food for their fears. But they told me I could run, wished me lots of luck and begged me to be careful.

The following day we were on the Salt bright and early and made a trial run. I only used the short course, turning out after the first trap, the quarter-mile. The plan was to test the parachute brake and the general operation of the machine at what could be called moderate high speed. I clocked 266.27 MPH, just stroking along in second. But I could feel the tremendous latent acceleration. Everything was working perfectly and we all were elated. We pushed *Challenger* onto her trailer and rolled back to Wendover to tear her down completely and make sure that there were no signs of trouble.

You've probably never seen a twenty- by thirty-foot garage with a weird chassis in it, surrounded by four engines, transmissions, final drive assemblies, fuel systems and a jillion other parts, all in a torn-down state and with eight or ten mechanics jostling each other as each works on some complicated task. We could have made a mint just charging admission to the spectators who crowded around the doors, and I wish I'd thought of it.

Fritz and I had agreed that he was the Crew Chief and that I would stay out of his hair as much as possible, letting him keep the mechanical side of the operation under control and leaving me free just to worry about the driving and administrative problems, such as studying the Salt and reporting to Akron on tire performance. This was a good move because two cooks in that kitchen would have created impossible confusion. And, besides, I was so keyed up and nervous much of the time that I would have given everyone the screaming jitters. So, even when I went into the garage, I did it mainly as a visitor and conferred only with Fritz, quietly.

Among hot rodders, among all men who work with machinery, Fritz is a giant and a genius. He rode herd over that crowd of mechanics and that infinity of moving parts with a calm that seemed to say, "This? Oh, I do this all day, every day. Doesn't everybody?"

He delegated a man to each job and worked harder than anyone himself. Still, he knew just what was happening to every part of the car at all times and seemed to be able to *smell* a goof-up when it was made. This is partly why Fritz was indispensable to the LSR effort and quite a few others. I knew to my soul that he would never let me get in a machine that he wouldn't drive himself and that his judgment of what constitutes a properly prepared machine is at least as good as my own. He made it possible for me to relax completely as far as mechanical preparation was concerned.

I didn't just cool my heels in a motel room while all this was going on. I did some sleeping during the day, checked constantly with Fritz and did lots of work at night, mostly studying the course. The moon was near its full phase and I would go out on the Salt and walk it with Judy following in our station wagon. One night I walked twelve miles north and twelve south, in a period of five hours, studying the surface that I had to run on. I had done that in '58 and I did it over and over again in '59, '60, '61 and '62. It's hard and often impossible to detect slight but important surface changes in the snow-blinding light of day. But at night, in angular moonlight or by the light of headlights, areas that are slick, tacky, wet, dry, smooth, pimply, choppy or irregular in any way are thrown into sharp, shadow-defined focus.

I gave equal care to studying the extremities of the Salt, to establishing the current firmness of wide areas of the surrounding mudflats. I never made a run without knowing, precisely, the available escape routes that I could use if my brakes failed. After all, the south end of the Salt is bounded by a high dike on which the highway and railroad are laid. It could be easy to run into, and disastrous. This careful preparation, this meticulous and constant study of the ever-changing course, gave me one of my greatest advantages over other competitors and saved my life many times.

"What is the Salt like?" Donald Campbell's engineers asked Britons who had been there.

"Why, it's just like a bloody billiard table," they said. Of course they were out of their minds, having been dazzled by the incredible white vastness. Their advice was very damaging to the tremendous project that Campbell was putting together on the other side of the Atlantic.

The Salt is not flat. If you drive over it in your grandmother's sedan you know in the first hundred feet that it is anything but flat. Where it has not been scraped and re-scraped by heavy equipment it's almost as rough as a plowed field. The cracks in the Salt make it that way. Brine oozes up through them, evaporates, deposits hard salt which forms ridges and causes slabs and shingles, creating a surface that's almost as rough as driving over railroad tracks.

If you fly over the Salt after a rain you get another picture of its non-flatness. Here, there, everywhere, are ponds and lakes—low spots that trap the water and tell that the Salt is undulating, not flat. There may be other reasons for this but one is the scouring action of the wind as it works on the Salt during the rainy season, when some or all of the vast sea-bottom is underwater. The wind scrubs certain areas and passes over others. The scrubbed ones become basins—shallow to the eye, but deep enough to be critical at a few hundred miles an hour.

Then there are the edges of the Salt, the extreme ends of the useful course. The slab of crystalline Salt feathers out until it becomes lost in the mudflat that is the bottom of the ancient sea. But if you're concerned with ultimate speed you need every inch of useful terrain. As you leave the crystalline slab you can bog down to your axles in blue-gray mud. Or, if you choose your route carefully, you can stay on reasonably solid ground. John Cobb had a 14-mile straightaway at his disposal plus a long, curving approach from solid ground at the sides.

I had different conditions under which to challenge Cobb's record. I had an 8.5 mile course, shrunken by drought and by potash mining operations that drained the brine which had restored the Salt's surface annually for thousands of years. Without the techniques of drag racing I never could have considered an attempt on the LSR on such a limited runway. What made it possible were the facts that *Challenger* was, in essence, a super-dragster and that I was a highly experienced drag racer. The big difference was that I would be accelerating violently for about four miles before I reached the clocks, instead of only a quarter of a mile. Think about that. It's quite a ride.

So Fritz and the crew tore down every part of the car, found everything to be sound, rebuilt the car and the following morning, August 25, hauled it out to the Salt for a more ambitious run. I had no intention of letting everything hang out yet, however.

We pushed to the starting line, Fritz buckled me in, pushed the oxygen mask over my face, checked my helmet fastening and thumped me on the head to let me know that we were ready to go. The push truck fired up behind me and Fritz loped over to our station wagon and got behind the wheel, Judy alongside. Starter Bob Higbee flashed me a grin and gave me his famous "Thataway" arm signal.

The truck's bumper clanked against the push bar. With its solid suspension *Challenger* sounds like a bucket of bolts at low speeds. With its solid suspension and rock-hard tires—about 125 pounds to the inch pressure—the whole car moved over the Salt jolting on each surface irregularity while the body panels acted as a huge resonating box. But with each increase in miles per hour, things became smoother and quieter until I heard the beep of the horn that told me I was on my own.

Engage the clutches. Oil pressure OK. Fuel on. Fuel pressure OK. Magnetos on. The whining scream of all those quick-change spur gears was wiped out by the thunder of the 32 cylinders barking through fat, short, straight-through pipes and spitting bright blue flame. First gear, and I revved to a shift point at around 210 MPH then, *slash*, one movement and the four gearboxes were in second cog. I had barely lifted my foot, jammed it down again, and streaked forward in second. Through the keyhole in the canopy that was all I had to peek through, I saw the Salt and the black line rushing under me. Miles away Floating Island, a distant mountain that rises out of the flat desert and serves as a target on northbound runs, stayed on my mental cross-hairs and grew imperceptibly closer. But the big signs that marked the miles on the course zoomed past and at around 315 I threw the final shift into top gear. It was smooth and perfect and as the four clutches bit and my foot went down again there came that smashing of the back and the still-massive acceleration that might just get me where I wanted to go.

The faster she went, the better *Challenger* ran and handled. I left the final, three-mile trap taching a speed that was just what I wanted for that run, breathed a prayer of thanks, cut the switches and popped the parachute brake.

Came the immediate, hard deceleration and all was well for about a quarter-mile. Then it began to happen. I was still doing over 300 when I felt a force tug the tail of the car to the right. I barely breathed on the steering, got it straightened out and then there was a stronger whip to the left. I thought, "Oh please God, let me get out of this, just for Judy and the kids." Then came a harder whip and a harder one and I grabbed the wheel tight to anchor my arms to protect them when the inevitable flip and crash came. Then the chute got itself caught in a different area of the air stream and yanked me far to one side. That sent me into a tire-shrieking sideways skid for over 700 feet. Again, as in Mexico and at Edwards, I stayed perfectly cool. By a miracle the car did not flip and it slowed to the point where I could steer it again. I brought it back on course in a great arc and rolled and rumbled to the far end where I knew the press was waiting for me.

The big slide had occurred out of sight of all but a couple of isolated course observers and no one else knew what had just taken place. I stood there and grinned for photographers, answered a few questions and then got away with Fritz and told him the story. It had been a really terrifying experience, much worse than the one at Edwards. That one had happened so suddenly that there was no time to get worried. But this one seemed to go on forever, like being on the end of a bull whip, and there was nothing to do but sit there helplessly and let it happen. I was thoroughly dejected and told Fritz that if this was the best we could do, we could go home right now. And for once Fritz had no light-hearted crack to make to brighten our mood.

Meanwhile, back at the starting line, nine miles away, a huge crowd had gathered to watch me take off and see what I could do. I'm told that after I cut my engines they stood there, maybe 300 people, in absolute silence. They all knew it had been a fast run and were waiting for the announcing system to tell them how fast. Soon the word rang out, "Sorry all. Crocker's charts only go to 300 miles an hour. Mickey's times are going to have to be calculated."

That at least told them that for the first time in history a hot rodder had broken 300, and a great roar went up. Then, finally, the times were computed and broadcast. I had turned 274.39 in the quarter-mile, 286.16 in the first mile, 313.64 in the second mile and 332.80 in the third. This was incomparably faster than any American ever had driven. In fact, only one living man ever had gone faster—Captain Eyston. That night I got a wire from Frank Meunier that said:

CONGRATULATIONS. YOU HAVE DONE IN TWO DAYS WHAT JOHN COBB TOOK TWO MONTHS TO ACCOMPLISH.

By that time my spirits were up again. I had walked over the area of the big slide. Fat black tire marks showed where I had gone and I realized the side loading and the scraping that those tires had again withstood without blowing out. And the punishment that Halibrand's wheels had absorbed for the second time. I contemplated the skid marks and thought, "Thank God for that solid suspension. A sprung chassis, rocking on its springs against that side load surely would have rolled." The only problem was the chute and I began pondering what could have gone wrong.

I got together with the chute engineer and said, "You almost killed me. How come?"

"Well," he said, "our scientific tests have shown that the best results are obtained with a tow line equal to five times the chute diameter, and that's what we're using. But apparently the shape of your car is an exception. We'll shorten the tow line by about 15 feet. That should cure the whipping."

"Are you *sure?*" I asked him.

Sure he was sure. I tried the new setup on a 250 MPH run and found myself yanked off the course again.

"You're still sure this is the route?" I asked him.

"Sure," he said.

"All right," I said, "*you* get in the damned car and drive it. Before *I'll* drive it again I'm going to have *two* chutes behind that thing and I want them at the end of a hundred foot tow line. Maybe that will get them out of some of the turbulence."

I won that round and got my way. On the next 250 MPH test run there was no wobbling and I went on to crank on an easy 362.31 MPH and still there was no wobbling. *Challenger* started, went, and stopped straight as an arrow. I had the right combination, it seemed, and I called off further runs. There was no point to wearing the car out during the Nationals since Crocker's clocks, perfect as they were, happened not to have FIA approval. But in September USAC would be on the Salt with their timing equipment that was FIA-approved. I would come back then, in a few weeks, for the big try.

On August 29 the directors of the Nationals came to me and said, "Mickey, we've given you all the help we could. Now we'd like for you to do something for us. We'd like a nice, fat, new, all-time record for the Nationals."

"How fast do you want it?" I asked.

"Any two-way over 300 would make us very happy," they told me.

So we trundled the little blue bomb out on the Salt once more. I decided to give them a good, high one-way figure and cut a 362.31. Only one man in history had ever driven faster, and that was John Cobb. Then I just loafed back, for a two-way average of 330.51 MPH.

Everyone was more than satisfied, me above all. I had been running on an 8.5 mile course and had a 12.5 mile course to look forward to. I had turned the 362 on little more than half throttle and hadn't begun to pour hot fuels to the engines. We hauled back to Los Angeles in high, confident spirits. Except for the chute problem it all had been easy and had gone exactly according to plan.

But big achievements never are that easy. I was less than 40 MPH away from the absolute World Record and what's 40 MPH? Trying for it and achieving it turned out to be the toughest challenge I've tackled in my life.

27

BRITISH MOTORS CORPORATION, WHICH OWNS MG, HAD TIME RE-served on the Salt, had arranged for USAC's presence and had consented to share the Salt with me. I of course would have to make my own financial arrangements with USAC. Captain Eyston was there to supervise the MG EX 181 streamliner effort and his sportsmanship and graciousness toward me had the blessing of MG's managing director, John Thornley, and of chief engineer Syd Enever. All three are hot rodders to the core. Drivers Stirling Moss and Phil Hill, who both dig the hot rod spirit, were content with the arrangement. Our two teams and two cars would not get in each other's way and we enjoyed and valued each other's company

Back in Los Angeles, Fritz had torn *Challenger* down to the smallest of its parts for inspection and made a few improvements that were indicated by our runs in the Nationals. We were due back on the Salt on September 21, but the usually calm season turned out to be a stormy one and as the deadline drew near I seemed to live on the phone, checking with the weather bureau and with big Earl Heath in Wendover. Earl manages the Western Services Garage, knows the Salt as only an intelligent native can and is a helpful friend to the whole speed fraternity.

We were fully loaded up and prepared to leave on September 20 when Earl called me to let me know that a violent windstorm —and they really have them on that immense, flat desert—had come up and had torn USAC's timing and communication wires to shreds. This meant a delay of at least twenty-four hours while forty miles of new wire was procured from civilization and strung. So we waited for that. We didn't know that this small frustration with its accompanying nervous strain was just a mild beginning.

BMC, USAC and my outfit were not the only ones who were under this strain. Goodyear, Mobil, Champion, newsmen, magazine writers, still and movie photographers and many others with an interest in what we were attempting got used to sitting on their hands, just killing time. Just as the new wire was strung, colossal rains fell. Then high winds which almost dried up the water on the Salt. Then more rain.

After ten days of off-and-on-again suspense there came a Crick forecast on September 30 that the Salt was drying fast and that the weather would be dry and clear through October 6. After that, winter was expected to set in, along with steady rain and snow. This definitely was the last chance for an attempt on the LSR in 1959. And, since Donald Campbell's big turbocar was nearing completion and Doc Ostich's jet was under way, it very likely was history's last chance for any piston-engined machine to set the biggest speed records of all. Fritz summoned the crew and we hit the road for Bonneville, at last and once more.

On October 1 we rolled into Wendover and again got set up in Earl's garage. The Salt still was largely under water. We puttered with *Challenger*, getting her in ideal tune. The following morning we unpacked the fresh tires that Goodyear had shipped, already mounted on wheels and inflated. When the first one came out of its crate I took a long look at it and ground my teeth. It didn't look right at all. I rolled it alongside one of the wheels on the car and, sure enough, it was a full inch smaller in diameter than the tires which we had been running and which we were geared for. That inch would cost me 15 MPH in top speed. More frustration and tension.

It was a hard blow but you have to roll with them. I had a big box full of assorted Halibrand quick-change gear sets. I sent a frantic wire to Akron, notifying them of the tire-size discovery, and then spent a couple of hours recalculating gear ratios relative to speed and the new tire diameter. I was ready to change all the final drives and start experimenting again when Gene McMannis roared up to the garage in a station wagon covered with Midwest mud and jammed full of more LSR tires.

"You changed the tires on me!" was the only greeting I bellowed at him.

"Relax," Gene said. "I expected to be here and explain to you before that shipment arrived. It's an improvement over what we made for you before. At speed, those skins will grow to exactly the same outside diameter as the ones you've been using."

That was a tremendous relief and it was an equal relief to have Gene there. Still, it had been an edgy few hours.

This trip to the Salt was different from the one of just a few weeks back. Then I was out to prove nothing other than that the car would run and run faster than any American car ever had. But now the moment of truth was closing in. If it had come on schedule there would have been less strain but all the waiting had done none of us any good. The guys in the crew had to stay away from their homes and families and work much longer than any of us had expected. There was just a whisper of demoralization among them and my conscience was giving me a little trouble because I knew what their loyalty was costing them. That nobody griped at all didn't help. I treated them as well as I could in the barren desert and promised them a big fishing trip on the Pacific Ocean when we got home.

This trip was also different in that, aside from the crew and a couple of savvy writers, there were no real hot rodders on the scene. Instead, Wendover never had seen so much big corporation brass and it was all there to see me perform, to judge me, and it was up to me to deliver what no human being ever had delivered before. They were all easy and cordial and there was no outward pressure, but I knew that they and their big public relations and movie crews were getting edgier by the day. And that gave an extra twist to the stomach muscles and nerves.

Then there was the condition of the course. As dry as it might get, it still would be on the slushy side and who wants to go drag racing toward 400 MPH on slush? And there was the condition of the machine itself. It was far from de-bugged, really. There were weight transfer problems that were far from resolved. At some speeds the front wheels would spin and at others the rear wheels would. At the same time I knew that my clutches also were giving some slippage. What parts of the total slippage were due to tire loading, weight transfer and clutch slippage I still had to find out.

Finally, there was the fact that I was heading into unknown territory. I had gone 362 and that was pretty exciting stuff. Now I was heading up through 370, 380, 390 to 400. At those speeds the air becomes compressed against the vehicle like the thickest molasses, maybe thicker. Anything might happen: body panels tear loose, tires spin and burst. Or what if one engine should lock up or an axle shaft break before I could disengage the clutches? I'd be spinning out there for an hour.

The situation crackled with tension. The delay due to weather had taken more money than I had. I had bought all the life insurance that I could from Lloyd's but it wasn't enough to take care of my family and I couldn't afford more. The whole caper was shaping up for what it really meant and neither Judy nor I had given much thought to what that was until the chips were all the way down. During the runs at the Nationals Judy had shown no particular nervousness. She knew that I wasn't going to put my neck way out. Now we both knew that I had to get it out all the way. Judy never said a word about it but I could feel her tension and I knew that she could feel mine. From the time we arrived in Wendover, Judy—cool and chipper as could be on the outside—lost her ability to swallow. She hardly ate or drank the whole time we were there. As soon as we got back to Los Angeles in one piece her problem disappeared.

The wind continued to blow and the Salt to dry out. Before dawn on the morning of October 3 I was out on it and found it still slushy but drying fast. By mid-afternoon it was dry enough for Phil Hill to smash the FIA Class E records with a best time of 254.53 MPH for the flying mile. But *Challenger* needed a lot more room in which to unwind. Everyone was edgy and wanted to see me do something. Pillsbury told us that he would okay an easy shakedown run and I agreed with him that that was all the course was good for. I loafed north at an easy 337 and the general morale picked up a bit.

While I was waiting to run, waiting for the driest possible Salt that afternoon, a man I'd never seen before came up to me and introduced himself. He asked if I was a Catholic. I told him I wasn't and he said, "Well, please take this with you anyway. It's brought me awfully good luck for a lot of years. Right now I think you need it more than I do."

He handed me a silver St. Christopher medal. I knew what it stood for—safety for travellers—and thanked him sincerely. Then I called one of the crewmen that I knew was a Catholic and told him to install the medal in *Challenger*.

"You want *two?*" he said. "We taped one of those to your roll bar before you went to Edwards."

We all laughed, and I told him to go ahead and tape this medal to the other branch of the roll bar. When we got home I bought a St. Christopher medal I could wear around my neck. I still wear it.

We went back to Wendover for more waiting. The 337 run was the very fastest that the Salt would permit and it continued to dry so slowly that we didn't even haul *Challenger* out there the next day. There was more nerve-wracking waiting during which we couldn't do a thing. Everyone in Wendover seemed to look at me accusingly, as though it were *my* fault that the Salt was wet and the impossible wasn't taking place. We all knew that time was running out; that only hours were left.

Johnny Allen of Fort Worth, Texas had come to the Salt with Stormy Mangham's two-wheeled streamliner, powered by a 40 cubic-inch Triumph engine. He was out to break the World Record for motorcycles which he had set at 214 MPH in 1956. He made his try on this morning and was doing over 200 MPH when his parachute somehow got tangled in the rear wheel, locked it up and sent the tiny vehicle bouncing and skidding over the Salt for a tremendous distance. Of course we all feared the worst, but the first people who got to the wreck found Johnny already out of it and drawling disgustedly, "Aw, shucks. Let's go fishin'." This didn't depress me. Instead, it was another proof of the great safety of the Salt, given a well-built machine and a cool handler.

Around midnight that night the Salt had become tolerably dry and we saw that, given decent weather the following morning, we'd have a course about 10.5 miles long to run on. This wasn't ideal but the weather forecast hadn't changed and now only hours were left for what we had come there to do. So at about 2:30 A.M. on October 5 Fritz and the crew hauled *Challenger* back out to the Salt and unloaded. We waited for the sun to brighten the eastern sky and then Fritz fired up the engines, got the chill out of them, pulled the 32 hot spark plugs and replaced them with cold racing ones. Conditions were perfect. The icy air was without a breath of wind. The USAC panel truck made a run down the ten miles of timing lights. They all tripped the big printing timer as they should and USAC's wise and ever-cheerful Reeves Dutton got the go-ahead over his field phone. "Anytime you're ready, Mickey," he said. "The course is checked and clear."

This was going to be *it*, the first time I ever had let *Challenger* out all the way. We all knew it and driving out to the Salt Judy and I didn't say a word. What is there to say at such a time? Once we got to the south pit where the car was, there was the bustle around it and Fritz's constant kidding and needling to ease the tension. At 6:29 we got the word and Judy helped buckle on my helmet. I kissed her for a long time, squeezed her arm hard and walked over to the car. My feelings were very strong because, after all, I was about to blast off into the dark, absolute unknown. Fritz was beside me and I shoved out a hand and said, "So long, ole buddy."

"So long, *hell!*" he shouted at me. "I'll see you at the other end in ten minutes. Can the melodrama."

Fritz had the right words and the right feeling of gruffness, friendship and devil-may-care humor again and I laughed and climbed into the cockpit. The instant I was sprawled there, lying on my back and looking through my knees at the long road I had to go, all qualms and jitters left me. I became a driving machine again. Fritz buckled my harness, checked the helmet fastening, put the oxygen mask over my face, turned on the oxygen, gave the cockpit a final searching look, thumped me on the head and banged down the canopy. I felt the clang of the pickup's bumper against the push bar and at 6:31 we began jouncing over the far-from-smooth surface, picking up speed. Racing ahead of me and far to one side of the course was our station wagon. If all went well I would be at the far end of the course in just over a minute. It would be another nine minutes before I could see Judy's face, and those minutes had a quality of eternity.

Judy told me later about her state of absolute panic the morning of that first all-out run. As Fritz charged north in the station wagon *Challenger's* engines fired, I went hurtling past and within seconds had disappeared below the horizon. Judy was sitting there, staring at the vacant distance and biting half way through her lower lip when Fritz, who was driving, reached over, gave her a brotherly pat and said, "Everything's going to be okay, Judy. I'm *sure* of it." She looked over at him and saw that two big streams of tears were pouring out from under his sun glasses. That *did* it, and she just sat there and bawled.

The course was short, meaning that I had to accelerate as hard as I could. This was not determined so much by horsepower or torque as it was by the amount of pressure I thought I could put to the drive line without breaking something. If I should, for example, snap the axle shaft to one wheel I might be thrown into a deadly spin before I could lift my foot. So I guessed at the amount of throttle I thought I could get away with and went drag racing down that slush-filled, rut-strewn course.

I had started as far back as surface wetness would permit and was doing about 220 as I approached the beginning of the black line. Due to all the bouncing and correcting that I'd been doing I approached the line about 20 feet to one side and with *Challenger's* nose clipped one of the light wooden laths which I had planted in the Salt to mark the entrance of the course proper. It was a fragile little splinter with a ribbon tied at the top. But at that speed it bashed in the aluminum shell as though it had been a railroad tie. It made an explosive, crashing sound, but I couldn't believe that a mere lath could do any serious damage—I didn't want to believe that it could—and kept my foot on the throttle, still accelerating for all I was worth.

There were smooth stretches and rough ones and I had them all charted. Some of the rough ones I could avoid by gingerly guiding the missile around them but others just had to be taken head on. I was doing about 340 MPH when I hit one of these and a deafening, rasping sound began and it didn't stop.

With all the experience I'd had with tires disintegrating at high speed I thought that I recognized that sound. I wasn't game for a blowout at that velocity, lifted my foot, cut the engines and coasted, grinding and finally clanking the remaining seven or so miles to the north pit.

What actually had happened was that the Dzus fasteners that held the rear of the belly pan had jolted loose, allowing the rear of that big panel to drag on the Salt. It was a good thing that the front fasteners hadn't come loose. As it was, it was potentially just as dangerous as a blown tire, which it could have caused if it had come adrift all the way. Those two incidents—and on a single run— were full of terrible possibilities and I had nothing to do but contemplate them during that long, quiet, free-fall glide to the north end. When I got out I felt a hundred years old and more discouraged than I ever had in my life.

"You fool," I told myself. "You total fool. If you had a grain of sense you'd never climb back in that thing. If you had a grain of sense you never would have gotten into it in the first place."

I felt awful and did little to conceal it when we hauled back to Wendover and Fritz went to work repairing the damage. I was still fighting wheelspin that alternated between the front and rear ends, and the crew worked most of the night, re-gearing the whole machine. Clutch slippage was bad, and they rebuilt the clutches. They were discouraged, too, and terribly tired, but Fritz managed to keep everyone's spirits up. Up to his elbows in parts he said to a newsman, "We don't wear the car out running it, you know. We wear it out taking it apart and putting it together again."

That day the clear skies that we had been having clouded up and became murky. The predicted storm front was moving in and I still hadn't gone any faster than I had weeks before during the Bonneville Nationals. I could imagine what the scoffers were saying at this point, but consoled myself with what I had said publicly a thousand times: "I may not break the LSR but I'll have the fastest car in American history and it'll be powered by American production-car engines. That's all I'm really out to prove."

Still, I wanted and needed more than that and so did my sponsors and so, even, did my exhausted crew. They rallied as they never had before. I had always beaten them to the Salt in the wee morning hours and then ribbed them about it. But the morning of Tuesday, October 6 *they* arrived on the Salt at 2:00. When I got there an hour later Fritz said, "There she is, warmed up and waiting. By the way, what hung *you* up?" All that, just to needle me and to let me know that they, too, would keep slugging until they went down.

Gradually the leaden eastern sky brightened. I made a run down the course in the station wagon and found it hard and dry. The air was perfectly still and when Dutton gave me the go-ahead at 6:40 I thanked God for conditions that were so close to being ideal. I took off in *Challenger* once more, accelerating harder than I'd ever dared to and, at about 200 MPH, threw the shift to second . . . or tried to. Nothing happened. The gears would not engage. Three times I blipped the engines, trying to find a combination of engine and driveshaft RPM's that would help the gears to mesh. It was impossible. Another tremendous effort by all of us, another desperate drag race down the Salt, getting my neck out all the way another time, and all for nothing. Again I coasted to the north pit.

The crew had forgotten what a night's sleep was and could only remember the luxury of naps. But they all pitched in around Fritz, tore the body off the car, then the elaborate fuel system, then the front axle, and then the right front transmission, which was the balky one. Fritz tore it down, there in the middle of nowhere. He was stopped at one point because we didn't have the necessary snap-ring pliers, but this slowed him for only a moment. With our welding equipment he quickly, deftly built a pair on the spot out of odds and ends. He found the burred gears, filed them smooth, put the trans back together and then the gang fell to reassembling the machine. This madness took about five hours, during which the clouds dakened and thickened overhead.

Griff was helping Dick Jones change *Challenger's* spark plugs when Art Pillsbury came over to him and said, "Let me talk to you alone for a minute. You know Mickey and he'll listen to you. If I try to tell him this he may think I'm trying to dictate to him. He's trying to wipe out all the records in just two runs. It's too hard on him and the machine. If he just goes after the World Records from the five kilometer to the ten mile he should get them in a breeze. With those secured he will have accomplished something big and permanent, everybody will feel better and then he can just concentrate on the kilo and the mile."

Captain Eyston had gotten in on this conversation and he and Griff agreed with Pillsbury. Griff came and put the proposition to me and I felt as if the weight of the world had been lifted off my back. Sure this was the answer for right now and I said to him, "Just do this for me. Sell it to the sponsors. They're a lot hotter for the LSR than I am."

Griff blasted off in the wagon and braced them one by one. Some agreed reluctantly, really hungering for the Big Record and thinking of the big advertising campaigns they already had planned. But most reacted like Roger Mahey of Mobil who unhesitatingly said, "Of course. That will give us plenty of birds in the hand and it will take a huge load off of Mick. Then he can chip away at the others for as long as the weather holds."

I was elated by this development because I knew that I could knock over these four records of Cobb's without really trying, without really extending either *Challenger* or my luck. I told Mobil's Bill Taylor to brew me some 10 per cent nitromethane fuel and to fill the tanks.

At 11:55 A.M. I took off from the north end and made a sweet smooth, clean run without incident and far from using full throttle. We checked plugs, changed coolant, refuelled and turned around well within the allowed hour and the return run was just as smooth. This is what I did to the following absolute World records:

Distance	Existing Record	South Run	North Run	Two-Way Avg.	Increase MPH
5 km	326.7	351.95	338.95	345.33	18.63
5 mi	303.2	342.54	338.89	340.70	38.50
10 km	283.0	325.65	329.56	327.59	44.59
10 mi	270.4	282.72	289.68	286.16	15.76

There was a lot of rejoicing and a lot of photography but we got that out of the way as quickly as possible and got on with making the most of what was left of the decent weather. Anyone could see that it wouldn't last out the day so I called to Bill Taylor for a 40 per cent nitro charge and prepared to let everything hang out.

It was at 3:30 P.M. that I took off again from the north pit, the engines barking with more power than they'd ever had before. They caught me going into the traps at 355 MPH when I moved an arm and it happened.

To gain time for the next return run Fritz had gone ahead to the south pit and this was the first and last time that he did not button me into the cockpit. The crew member who did looped the hose to my breathing mask in such a way that just a slight arm movement would be enough to pull the tube from the oxygen bottle, and that is what happened. The normal fumes were bad enough but nitro fumes are highly toxic. On top of that, the front drive units had begun leaking oil. It blew all over the exhaust manifolds of the front engines and those fumes also were pumping into the cockpit. But realizing that I had only about a mile to go under power I hung on, not wanting to ruin a run after all this trouble.

I probably made a mistake by holding my breath as long as pos-

sible and then emptying and filling my lungs. If I'd tried to keep
going on what was in them, plus nibbles at what was in the cockpit, I might have stayed conscious longer. But I felt myself black-
ing out and had sense enough to cut the mags and pop the chutes.
I didn't worry about steering because there's so much caster in
Challenger's front end that she steers herself if left alone. I was
worrying about that telephone pole that stands smack on the
course, about a mile from its south end, when I lost consciousness.
I missed it by a few feet.

I came to rest not far from our south pit. As Fritz tells it, he
looked over, expecting to see me flip up the canopy. It didn't happen and then he saw smoke oozing out around its edges. He yelled
to the crew and came running. He flung open the canopy, saw me
lying there with mucus running all over my face, grabbed the
mask, attached the tube to the bottle, began pouring oxygen into
me and slapped my face.

I came to soon enough and began struggling to get out. Fritz
shoved me back and told me to get back my strength first. But I
didn't want anyone to know that I was in trouble, forced my way
out of the car, flopped down on the tail gate of our truck as though
I were just taking it easy and told Fritz to get *Challenger* ready for
another run.

But USAC's Joe Petrali knew what had happened and demanded
that I get in the ambulance and take more oxygen. To get away
from the onlookers we drove about a mile from the pit . . . *and ran
out of gas!*

At least, that's what the fuel gauge on Ted Gillette's ambulance
was indicating when I looked at it. I could have crashed, and with
the nearest hospital 90 miles away.

"Have you ever been strangled to death, Ted?" I asked the driver,
menacingly.

"Are you worrying about that no-good fuel gauge?" he asked.
"You've got to be pretty healthy to notice that. It never has worked.
But the gas tank is plumb full, if you want to check it. And after
you've done that, check those Thermos jugs. They're full of gas
too."

Still, this fluke made me think. I made up my mind not to run
Challenger again without an airplane and, if possible, a doctor
standing by. I was still railing at Gillette when a gale of wind came

I had my first taste of the Salt in 1937 when Dad took us all off to Yellowstone in his brand new Dodge.

This is pretty much the story of my high school days.

In 1952, I was racing this dual-engine Bantam with two flathead Ford V8's.

With my co-pilot, Rodger Flores, in the 1953 Mexican Road Race. Note the mashed car body.

Scott Fenn

I took a lot of needling about the looks of that first "slingshot" dragster, until the day (above) we pushed through the 150 MPH barrier.

In 1958, I came within an ace of breaking 300 MPH with a pair of Chrysler engines in the dragster.

Griffith Borgeson

I laid out *Challenger*'s frame to fit its engines as snugly as possible. The steel tubing was from a junkyard, all I could afford. I did my best to hide the rusted areas.

My Dad did most of the work on the wooden mockup for the body. California Metal Shaping rough-formed the panels and Don Borth turned them into the finished body.

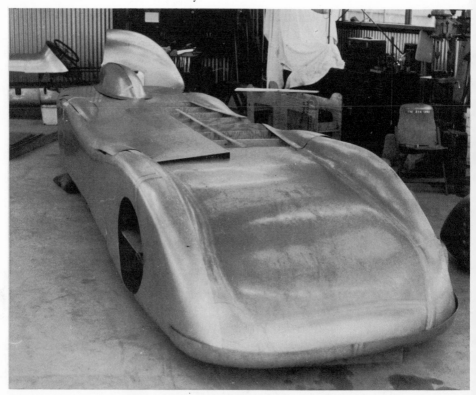

We somehow made the Beverly Hilton deadline, but there was no time for painting the car.

A couple of weeks before *Challenger*'s unveiling at the Beverly Hilton Hotel there seemed to be months of work left to do.

This is how the radical Goodyear tire for the Land Speed Record attempt compared with Firestone's existing high speed tire in 1959.

We finally solved the *Challenger*'s stopping problems with two small ribbon parachutes at the end of 100 feet of nylon tow line. This is the pack ready to be installed in the tail of the car.

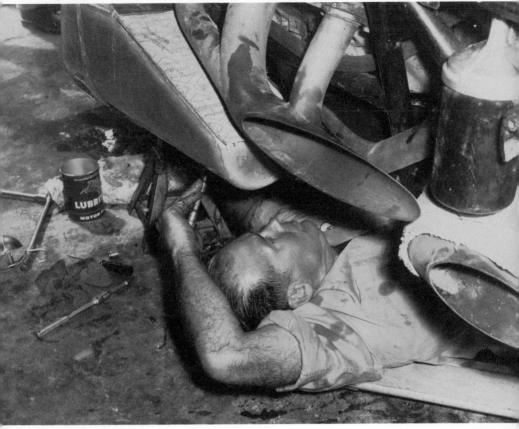

Here is Fritz Voight in a truly characteristic pose.

Challenger's first run on the Salt was made during the Bonneville National Speed Trials in late August of 1959. Here we are ready to go at dawn when the desert air is most still.

The parachutes provided smooth and perfect high-speed braking.

Here, long before sunrise, Judy helps me tape my leathers . . . a little extra protection against fire.

Challenger is amazingly small considering the amount of horsepower it contains. Beside her, Donald Campbell's *Bluebird* looked like a locomotive.

This was the frantic morning in '59 when Fritz rebuilt a transmission on the Salt.

USAC's Art Pillsbury (left) spent his last season on the Salt in 1959, after which Joe Petrali (center) took over his responsibilities.

hurtling in from the south, pushing brine across the Salt. Minutes later the storm broke, putting an end to the season and to our efforts. But there was still a job to do, and a big one. I had a year in which to prepare for it.

28

PEOPLE ALWAYS ASK WHAT IT'S LIKE TO DRIVE *Challenger*. THAT'S A good question because I don't rightly know. There's nothing in the world like her and there's always been so much happening and so much to keep in mind that I've never had a chance to just sit back and think about the ride. Maybe, if I'd ever had a long, long course such as Cobb had, I might have been able to do it. But I don't think so. All five or six of my senses would still have been totally absorbed in analyzing the car's behavior during every split second.

After I'd made many, many runs in *Challenger* I said to Fritz, "Hey, drive this thing. Take it for a little run. It's interesting." He's the only other person who's driven her and he doesn't have much to say about the experience either. What he says is this:

"The noise is incredible, but that's nothing. What's terrible about it is how hard you have to think, with everything happening in fours. Just sitting still and keeping it running—fast enough so that it doesn't load up and konk and slow enough not to overheat immediately—makes a screaming nervous wreck out of you. You can feel your chest swelling, from tension and half-panic. At a time like that if someone were to shout, 'What's your name?' you'd have to think real hard to give him an answer. If a doctor were to put a blood pressure gauge on you, he'd take one look and say you were dead.

"When you take off, the acceleration is like a real hot dragster but you're not on any nice, smooth asphalt pavement. It wants to get ahold of the ground so bad, it wants to accelerate so hard, that it always goes off sideways. I'd always follow Mick as fast as I could and many times I've seen the whole side of that brute as it went clawing down the course.

"You can't even accelerate a passenger car on a washboard road and that was what Mick was running on much of the way. Once *Challenger* starts dribbling like a basketball it's very hard to accelerate. It's real bad to drive until you're over about 200, then it starts smoothing out. Mick's never gotten anything he didn't get the hard way, through struggle and sweat, and when he went fast in *Challenger*, it was no hayride."

People often ask how I can shift all four of those transmissions at once, and how the linkage is made that makes it possible. When I laid the car out I didn't attack all four gearboxes at once. I took on one, told myself that it had to work and made it work. Then the next one had to work, so I made brackets and linkage that made it work too. And I kept going that way until all four were linked up and worked together. I have a knack for sensing optimum leverage points.

I have one lever for low and high gears. You pull it back for low and push it forward for neutral. When you've done that another lever falls right into your hand. You push it forward, in the same plane, and you're in second. Then you pull it back, grab the first lever again, pull it back and slightly to the side and you're in top gear. It's not too much different from shifting a passenger car and it works just about as smoothly, as anyone who has heard *Challenger* run can tell.

At fairly low speeds it's a very rough ride and any good racing driver first trying it would probably be scared to death up to about 200 MPH.. Beyond that, the faster you go the smoother it gets, up to about 350, when it starts skating. It's easy to lose it when that starts happening. I've lost it many more times than I care to remember, but always have managed to drive my way back to a state of control. Unlike the other big LSR contenders, who had courses as wide as 300 feet to run on, I was doing this skating on a 40-foot wide course. When you get off into the rough stuff at those speeds you don't see what keeps your teeth in your head.

I gave *Challenger* just a tiny peep hole to see out of and this has caused much criticism of the car's "limited visibility." After I installed the superchargers and covered them with big air scoops there was even less vision out of the car. But what more do you really need at nearly 600 feet per second? If I could turn around and watch the scenery go by I wouldn't do it anyway. All I'm concerned with are the course markers and the black line and keeping them in front of me. But I realize that most people would get claustraphobia after being shoe-horned into that cockpit and having their helmet pressed into the skin-tight roll cage and having the canopy locked down like a hat that's too tight over their head. It doesn't bother me a bit.

Probably the most difficult thing about driving at such high speeds is all the things that *must* be kept in mind. For me, part of this began with walking the course at night and studying it either by moonlight or by the lights of a car. I tried to memorize every important bump, tilt and other surface change. Of course there are no reference points other than the black line and the course-marking signs, which are mostly at mile intervals. This means that you have to learn to calculate distances in terms of elapsed time.

A couple of hours before making a run I would begin reviewing everything that had to be kept in mind and rehearsing what had to be done each bit of the way. And then all that might be changed at the last minute by a report over the field phone that an eight-mile-an-hour crosswind was blowing at the three-mile post. A lot of what passed for nervousness in me at those times probably was nothing more than the most intense concentration. After all, you're betting your life that you're right and if you're not right, you're through.

The drill would go like this. Two seconds past the one-mile post I've got to start moving ten feet to the left. Farther on there's another rough spot but by that time I'm really moving and what was two seconds' worth of distance now will be three-quarters of a second. I make that correction and now the three-mile is coming up. Move over about seven feet to compensate for the crosswind drift. There's another correction to be made near the four-mile. By this time I'm doing around 600 feet a second—the length of two football fields laid end to end—and it takes about a full second to get body and machine to react, so start *now*. And so it goes, while you also note, calculate and integrate everything the machine is doing.

Challenger has a bare minimum of instruments to be kept track of. Oil pressure must be watched constantly because an instant without it can lock an engine and cause a spin. I had four oil pressure gauges to watch. And the tachometers for the front and rear pairs of engines had to be watched. If the tach needles didn't follow each other almost identically that meant that front wheels, rear wheels or clutches were slipping.

I also had to watch the tachs to gauge my speed in each of the timing traps. If I was accelerating and wanted to average a certain speed through a given trap I had to enter at one RPM level and leave at another. So, I was concentrating, thinking, driving and steering every inch of the way and not just grabbing the wheel and standing on the loud pedal with heroic stupidity.

The widespread belief that that's all there is to driving fast in a straight line undoubtedly is responsible for most of the accidents that occur on the Salt. Athol Graham and Donald Campbell were both of the stand-on-it-and-steer school.

But before you ever get the chance to make just *one* Big Time record run there are the thousands of preparations that must be made in advance. Building the machine and getting it there, along with the parts, tools, fuel and men to make it run. Then there's the approved timing, without which your efforts are officially meaningless. USAC charges $2,500 just to come to the Salt and set up. After that it's only $750 a day, whether they work or not, rain or shine. You have to find that money and you're at the mercy of the weather. It is always unpredictable. This is true even on a clear, serene day, when you show up on the starting line before dawn and are given the word to go. You climb into your sweltering leathers, pull on your helmet, rehearse the run like mad in your mind and get buckled in. You're fully ready, physically and emotionally. Every fiber of your being is keyed to this one crucial purpose and you've made peace with yourself and with God and told yourself that this is it.

Then a call comes over the field phone to the effect that a twenty-mile-an-hour crosswind has sprung up at the five-mile and that you'll have to wait. That situation can be repeated five or six times in a single day, until you're so emotionally drained that you'd give anything for the nightmare to stop.

And you keep sneaking glances at your wife and wondering about *her* emotions, wondering how she stands it. You know that if *she* were driving that miserable beast and you had nothing to do but sit and wait you'd come unglued. You know that every time she watches the car blurring into the mirage on the horizon it seems to leave the ground, ready to flip and crash. How does she feel when she sees that? How does she stand it? I know she loves me or she wouldn't have put up with all this for all these years. So, loving me, how can she stand it? I'll never know. I just know that she's never hinted that she blames me for these things that I do to her. They also serve who only sit and wait—but their job seems to be the hardest.

Going for a big record is not easy but, if you're lucky, there are all kinds of rewards. There's some money, which I've never really raced for and never will, but you can't race without it and it has to be included in the equation.

There's fame—press, radio, TV, newsreels and so on—and it's a lot of fun for the ego to taste it. The kind I like best is when little kids come up to me and hand me a toy or a scrap of paper to autograph. I'm crazy about kids and these situations remind me of my own speed-struck childhood.

And after we got home in '59 letters began pouring in from all over the country; all over the world. They were from grownups, teenagers and little kids. They were from people who liked what I had done, dared to do, and most of them asked for any little thing as a souvenir. They keep on coming, and so do others, like this one from a gentleman in Detroit.

Dear Mr. Thompson:

What in the world is with you, my dear man? If you want to consider yourself a glorified hot rodder, please do so if it makes you happier. But *don't* claim any World titles. What makes you think that you could even be *compared* with the British, much less run in their league? You have no claim to any title whatsoever. Incidentally, if you are concerned, I am not British.

Such letters usually are unsigned. I wish they weren't. I'd like to shake the hand of each such writer and leave him with my grip as a souvenir. That would be much gentler than Judy's reply or response, which would be withering, if not crushing. She knows what these things take, including the sitting and waiting, the anxiety, the anguish, the personal sacrifice and the cost. Why is it that what is foreign is good and that what is American is bad in the eyes of so many Americans?

I had somehow poured over $40,000 into *Challenger's* 1959 campaign. Where that astronomic sum came from I'll never really know, but I wrung most of it out of thin air. Perhaps this is the time for us to talk about gambling.

29

I HAVE GAMBLED FROM AS FAR BACK AS I CAN REMEMBER, BUT UNTIL recently it was not real gambling. I had an inborn feeling for odds, often backed up by strong hunches, both of which I got from my Dad. I have always enjoyed manipulating odds and usually have come out on the winning end. My sister Colleen has the same gift, but she doesn't use it constantly, as I do.

You know how most little kids are always challenging, "I'll bet you so-and-so." Well, I was always that way. But I was never interested in mere 50-50 odds, like matching coins. That sort of thing just wasn't attractive to me. It gave me no chance to prove and cash in on my own abilities. Actually, I was interested in calculated risks, not in gambling.

Liar's poker is a typical example of the sort of betting contest that I enjoy and I have a reputation for being unbeatable at it. It's a game where each player holds a dollar bill and claims to have a certain poker hand in the serial number. Maybe he's telling the truth and maybe he's not. The man who finally calls the other a liar wins if he's right, loses if he's wrong. In addition to having a good sense for the odds in a situation like that, it gives me a chance to compete psychologically and I get as big a kick out of that as I do out of purely physical competition.

I will bet on just about anything that is a challenge to my ability and on which I can get the right odds. I've never been a brilliant athlete, but determination usually has made up for my shortcomings. I don't always throw out the challenge, but if someone says,

"*You* couldn't do that," he's begging for a bet. In weight lifting, for example, I've out-lifted a lot of stronger men and won lots of bets doing it because I knew that I could count on my determination to give me something that I ordinarily didn't have. And in a situation like that I'll usually bargain for some odds in my favor. But not always. Some months after I'd broken my back Judy and I were at a night club with a group of friends and I got up and danced the twist with Judy, just to show them all that I was anything but crippled.

One of my old needling buddies said, "That's pretty good, Mick, but your days of pushup heroics are a thing of the past."

I bet him $20 that I could do more pushups than he could and we peeled off our coats and had a showdown on the spot. I was very close to passing out when he collapsed on the floor.

I've never been a great runner, but I've made a lot of money and had a lot of fun betting people that I could out-sprint them at the drag strip. Again, I usually wheedle and dicker for odds and/or lull my opponent into thinking that he's whipped me in advance.

My brother-in-law, Gary, is one of the few who has ever out-witted me in that. One night we went tearing down the strip and I stopped at about the three-quarter point while Gary finished the distance.

We strolled toward each other and I said, "Okay, I lost that one. I'll run you for another ten-spot." I was counting on Gary being winded and bashed while I was still fresh. Then I'd really trounce him. But Gary had gotten wise to my ways. He said no.

"What do you mean?" I yelled at him. "You can't quit *now!*"

"Oh yes I can, Mickey," he said. "If there's one thing that I've learned from you it's quit when you're ahead."

I was furious. I'd been out-psyched.

I got back at Gary. He's a very good badminton player and I tried the game with him one time and he whipped me 15 to zero. I came back and played him until midnight every night for two solid weeks until I beat him just once. I've never been near the game since.

At the strip I bet regularly on who's going to win a race and I'll often choose the underdog. Let's say that one car that night is turning about 8.90 while the other is running around 9.50. I'll often take the longer odds and bet on the slower car because I know that the fast one is running faster maybe 50 per cent of the time or less and is being extended hard. Again, I win about 95 per cent of these bets.

As I grew older I came to have stronger and stronger hunches about everything that I had a strong interest in—the drag strip, betting, and anything that has to do with racing. These hunches got to be pretty uncanny.

The night before our crash in Mexico in '54 I had a feeling that I should change the tie rod on the car and I did. The crystal ball was a little bit clouded and I didn't change the tie-rod *ends*, but the hunch was there.

At the strip it got to be downright weird. One night I *knew* that something was wrong in a pitch-dark nearby field. I charged over there and found a man who had been badly beaten and robbed. I could give countless examples like this and there have been plenty of witnesses to them. I came to have the same sure, strong hunches about when I should and should not drive and I try always to respect them.

In house-type gambling these hunches have been invaluable and they have a lot to do with my winning about two out of three house games. Here of course the odds are well on the side of the house but when I play such games I rely heavily on hunches. When I can I play on the house's side, against the other players, while still listening to that silent inner voice. I owe Las Vegas a lot for the financial help it has given me.

There was the time when Judy and I were flying back from Salt Lake City during the '59 *Challenger* campaign. We had a one-hour stopover in Vegas. We grabbed a cab to one of the big casinos and I *knew* that Judy was going to catch a strong lick. I handed a big check to the cashier and Judy rolled seven straight passes at $500 a throw. Then I felt the luck pass to me, grabbed the dice, threw three more passes in a row. That was it. I cashed in, reclaimed my check and gave a cab driver a five-spot to rush us to the plane, which we climbed into seconds before takeoff. The next day I invested those winnings in the land for my manufacturing plant.

There was the time in 1960 when Judy and Colleen were practicing for the Mobilgas Economy Run and Judy called from Vegas to say hello. It was nine in the morning but I had that strong feeling.

"Write a check for $500," I told her. "Put it on the Come Line, pick up your money and walk away."

"Five hundred dollars!" she wailed. "Are you crazy?"

"Just do it," I said.

She did it. The casino was deserted except for the house men at their posts. It must have been rough on their egos when she threw the dice once, picked up her $1,000, paid the cashier, tore up the check and walked out. Judy and Colleen were shaken, too, but it was one of those solid hunches that couldn't be wrong.

Colleen has them. At Bonneville in 1960—at the Stateline Casino in Wendover, on the Nevada side—she was really tuned in. We were playing a quiet game of blackjack when she told the dealer,

"I can call every hand that you deal."

I began betting on her hands and for 17 in a row she called the dealer's score as well as her own without missing once. It became a spooky thing for all of us and I think that Colleen's run stopped because it scared her more and more. But we made a chunk of hard cash that night. There have been many other nights that were the same.

People often ask me if I have premonitions but I prefer to evade the question because there's nothing that I can prove. They ask Fritz the same questions and he also shuts them off. He snorts at intuition. But there's a lot going with him, and his ability to sense trouble at a distance is one of the big reasons that I'd rather not run at Bonneville if Fritz can't be there.

There was the time when the crew had worked all night and Fritz asked, "Did you all put oil in the overdrive units?"

"Sure," the four mechanics answered. But he checked them all anyway and found one bone-dry. It might have killed me, but Fritz happened to catch it.

There was another time when all four engines had been pulled down and reassembled.

"Are all the main bearings in right?" Fritz asked the crew.

Of course they were. But for some reason Fritz decided to pull all the pans again and make another check. He found one engine with its main caps loose. That could have done me in, too.

But Fritz smells these things before they happen. It was the same with my oxygen gear. Twice, for no apparent reason at all, he checked it and found that it wasn't working. For the same unknown reasons he would stop a takeoff to check the parachutes. He'd find that their pins had not been pulled and once again he would casually save my life, never admitting that he'd done anything.

When you live very close to death it doesn't take long to become devoutly superstitious about, or respectful of, the sense of odds and of the hunches that seem to help you to survive. You learn to listen to every whisper of guidance that comes out of nowhere.

When Athol Graham crashed I *knew* how, when and where it would happen. I tried, desperately to warn him but he wouldn't hear me. I sent my son, Danny, far out of the danger zone. Then I set up my movie camera and filmed the tragedy just where I knew it would take place.

This apparent foreknowledge of events makes me think, but it doesn't bother me. I'm grateful for it. But I do think constantly about the odds upon which my life depends. I think that I do my best to keep them in my favor. As Fritz says, "When your number's up, it's up. But why have more than one number?"

I want to quit while I'm ahead, but am determined not to shirk a single challenge that is worthy of my ability and that I feel worthy of. As I've said, my resistance to challenge is very low. I suppose I'll keep on doing what I'm driven to do, while doing my utmost to keep the odds in my favor.

I absolutely do *not* recommend gambling to anyone and I do not feel that I am a gambler. Yes, I am fond of manipulating odds and I have a knack for it and therefore indulge in it. I even have the good fortune to prosper from it. But I would never *gamble*. Pure gambling is a sport for fools.

30

WE CAME BACK FROM THE SALT IN '59 HAVING SCALED FOUR OF THE highest peaks in motor racing history. Of the biggest there were only two left, the flying-start kilometer and the mile. There was plenty of work to be done on *Challenger*. We had to put a stop to clutch slippage and to the wheelspin problems we had been having. And Captain Eyston had come to me after our last run and said,

"Wonderful show, Mickey. Are you going to keep trying for 400?"

"Of course," I told him. "But we have some problems to figure out and I know we'll need more horsepower."

"Exactly," he said. "But I think that another 500 should be quite enough and you should have no trouble getting that with super-chargers."

"That's just the way I plan to go," I told him. "Big GM diesel blowers on all four engines. And Captain, I know how unaerody-namic that body is, even if it did most of what I wanted it to. But it can be cleaned up a lot and drag eliminated. That's horsepower saved."

That plan was to be carried out before the following August, but it left me with loads of time on my hands. Some money came in, I paid off my debts and had some cash left over. My bank credit was good, so I decided to go ahead with something that I'd dreamed of for years: set up my own manufacturing business. I launched it on the small lot in Long Beach that I'd bought with Vegas winnings.

The final impetus to do this had come in '58, when I went to Art Sparks, manufacturer of Forgedtrue pistons, and asked him to make up some pistons for the twin-engine streamliner according to my own design. He refused and when I reminded him that I was *paying* for the job, he still refused; he didn't like my ideas. There were some strong words between us and I told him that I was through with his products but that he would hear from me again.

So, after Bonneville in '59 I finally and sort of wistfully severed relations with the tolerant, ever-patient *Times.* I went right to work designing a building, designing the parts that I wanted to manufacture, and locating the equipment and staff that I would need. I planned to manufacture racing equipment, naturally. This called for a test laboratory and an engine dynamometer and these of course dovetailed right into my personal racing needs.

The first products that I designed and tooled for were forged aluminum pistons. They were very different from anything else available and they got big results in racing. Art Sparks and I had

not spoken to each other for a couple of years when I drove over
to his plant and said,

"Hi. I guess you know that I'm in the piston business now, and
in it big. Well, buddy, I just wanted to rub it in that it's all your
fault. But now that we're real competitors I'd like for us to be
real friends."

We get along okay now and he's a lot less critical of my ideas.

The piston business turned out to fill a long-felt need. The first
ones I tooled were naturally for Pontiacs—engines that I knew
better than any others at the time. They were pistons that *I* could
put to immediate use. These somehow came to the attention of
Bunky Knudsen, then the general manager of GM's Pontiac Division. He gave me tremendous encouragement. Although the automotive industry as a whole was steering clear of racing, plenty of
dealers were up to their armpits taking care of individuals who were
highly active in the sport. They wanted and needed my pistons and
Mr. Knudsen, on his own, helped me to reach them. He is one of
the greatest men I'll ever know. We became very close friends and
the sympathetic help he gave me at a time when I needed it most
desperately never will be forgotten.

If anything, I moved too fast. I had a million ideas for components that I thought the racing world had been waiting for and
I began making most of them.

I wasn't satisfied with the forged aluminum connecting rods that
were available and, working with the Harvey Aluminum Company,
produced my own designs. The demand leaped. I needed more
room, bought the lot next door and put a building on it. Then another lot and another building; we were putting the '62 Indianapolis cars together in it before the roof was on. Then more and more
property, until I've almost lost track.

Today the list of big names in racing that use M/T Equipment
Co. products would fill pages of this book. We make over 1,100
products and are constantly struggling to improve their quality.
They are almost all made of light alloys and include forged connecting rods and pistons, manifolds, pump drives, blower kits, main
bearing supports, timing gear covers, spring retainers, blower end
plates, stroked crankshafts, aluminum hemispherical cylinder heads,
Gilmer pulleys, magnesium final drive units and needle-bearing
forged-aluminum rocker arms. We add about two new products to

the line each month, which keeps my old buddy and general manager of the plant, Kenny Droesbeke, permanently on his toes. At the cost of seeming commercial I might as well mention here that anyone who wants one of our catalogs can get it by sending fifty cents to the company at 1419 Santa Fe Ave., Long Beach, Calif. My wonderful office manager, Fleeta Wasson, sees to it that our every piece of mail gets its prompt and proper reply.

While all this was going on I did not let my racing career stagnate.

Back in 1957 it had come to the attention of drag racer Cal Rice that there were such things as FIA records for acceleration as well as for top speed. He was at the top of the heap at the time and his engine builder, Doug Hartelt, also was one of the very best. They looked at the displacement of their 343-cubic-inch Chrysler mill, looked at the FIA record book and saw that the International Class B (305- to 488-cubic-inch.) record should be within their grasp.

It had been set by Bernd Rosemeyer, driving a Nazi government-subsidized Auto Union way back in 1937 and many experts considered it to be unbreakable. Rice and Hartelt thought that it would be a fine thing for American rodders to topple this record with inexpensive, home-grown equipment. They went to Wally Parks for help and got it.

On February 2, 1958 and running as the *HRM Special,* Rice made racing history at March AFB by boosting the German record for the standing-start kilometer from an average of 117.3 MPH in 19.03 seconds to 123.56 in 18.10. During the same session drag racer Ed Cortopassi in his Chevrolet-engined *Glass Slipper* upped Rosemeyer's Class C kilo record from 21.20 seconds to 19.21.

Not only had I admired Rice's achievement at the time, I was downright jealous of it and wondered how I had failed to think of it, being a drag racer with an appetite for big records. So now I decided to go after Rice's record and, while I was at it, to rewrite most of the FIA record book for standing-start speed. That is how *Assault I* came into being.

I had a good assortment of Pontiac V8 engines on hand. The stock mill had a bore of 4.0625 inches, a stroke of 3.75 and a displacement of 389 cubes. For the World Unlimited Class and for Class A (over 488 cubic inches) I bored one engine out to 4.125

and stroked it .875, for a displacement of 503 cubic inches. For Class B I left the bore alone and stroked the crank .250, getting 415 cubes. And for Class C, I used a '56 Pontiac block with a 3.94 inch bore. For this one I destroked a '55 Pontiac steel crank to an even three-inch throw, which gave me a total of 293 cubes.

I set these engines up with on-top GM 6-71 blowers which I drove by chains off the crankshafts. I machined my own light alloy con rods from billet stock and these served as prototypes for forgings soon to be produced in my little plant. And I tuned the engines on the dyno which was one of my first investments for the plant.

To save time in building a chassis, I bought one from the newly-formed Dragmaster Company, which was in the business of mass-producing slingshot dragsters built of ductile, shock- and vibration-resistant mild steel. I equipped it with Halibrand magnesium wheels, disc brakes and quick-change rear end and with a sixteen-foot ribbon parachute for high-speed braking. I sketched up a slightly lumpy streamlined shell for the machine and Don Borth did his usual perfect job of translating the sketch into an aluminum envelope, which I had painted the same pale blue as *Challenger* was in '59. I set it up to receive the three engines that Fritz and I had tailored for attacks on the three biggest FIA standing-start records.

There are very few courses in the world where standing kilometer runs can be attempted and almost none that are suited to the standing mile. And I wanted them both.

The Salt is out because its relatively irregular and usually moist surface lacks the necessary bite. Long, smooth, wide pavement is essential and Parks had found it at March AFB, near Riverside, California. I applied for the use of the same 13,300-foot runway and, thanks to the Air Force's positive attitude toward hot rodding and to help from Generals Le May and Griswell, red tape finally was hacked through and my request was granted. I had the course surveyed and in the small morning hours of May 14, 1960 the USAC crew set up its equipment and gave me the nod.

An invisible sun dawned through leaden clouds that blanketed the sky all day. In the first dim light I made a southbound run with the Class C engine, but skyrocketing humidity had ruined my carburetion and I backed off, turned out of the course and went

back to the pit area to re-jet. At 6:45 A.M. I burned off the line
and covered the kilo in an ET that was well under the record.
Then I came storming back—two-way averages are required for FIA
standing-start runs too. I was accelerating even more strongly when,
two-thirds of the way down the course, a wrist pin broke, the piston
jammed and the engine locked up. I declutched and coasted through
the traps 1.5 MPH slower than Cortopassi's record. It was a discour-
aging way to start the day.

I had planned to work up to the big engine, but, in the light of
this luck, I decided to alter the plan and make an immediate stab
at the absolute, World record for acceleration. Fritz shared crew
chief duties with Darrell Droke and they were marvelously efficient.
They had rehearsed engine swapping until they had it down to a
smoothly automatic ninety-minute routine. This time they had the
C engine out and the A engine in in eighty-six minutes. Judy gave
me a push start with the same Pontiac Bonneville station wagon
that had been our workhorse with *Challenger* on the Salt. The big
mill thundered massively, leaving very little doubt that we had
horsepower to spare.

At 9:07 I peeled off in a thick, oily blue cloud of tire smoke.
The March AFB course was no billiard table either and I was on
and off the throttle all the way as *Assault* bounced, skittered and
fishtailed over the bumps. I even had to watch out for a well-
drilling crew that was sinking a test hole on the track! Still, I covered that standing-start kilo faster than any man ever had.

This run gave me a pretty clear idea of what I had to cope with
and so I made up my mind to go after the standing mile records
as well as those for the kilo. At 9:41 I hurtled north, chopped the
two-way ET for the kilo from 18.10 to 16.82 and made my first
pass over the mile. At 10: 11 I returned over the mile and knocked
the absolute record for that distance from 25.96 to 24.12 seconds.

This was one of the hairiest driving adventures I ever want to
experience. Observers on the course said that they were able to see
a good foot of daylight under all four of the car's tires at once. I
sheared two sets of rear axle bolts on those runs due to losing bite
and regaining it—a pretty unheard-of thing. Again, it was not just
a case of standing on the throttle and steering straight ahead. It
was hard, desperate work all the way keeping the machine on
course. I salute Rosemeyer, who had the guts to do what he did

on a mere two-lane highway, the Frankfurt-Darmstadt *Autobahn*.

In these three runs I collected eight new records: the World Unlimited record for the kilo and mile, the American Unlimited, the International Class A and the American National Class A for those distances. With those records secured, we pushed the A-frame over *Assault*, snatched the big engine out and lowered the Class B mill into the mounts.

The first run with this engine was a bad one. The clutch facing had begun to let go and a head gasket blew half way down the course. So out came the engine once more. The necessary parts were replaced and the car was ready to run again in 82 minutes. Again I only shot for the kilo on the first pass. But then, having smashed the record decisively, I mopped up the two-way kilo and mile records on the next two runs. USAC's Joe Petrali and I reached the pit almost simultaneously.

"What did I average?" I asked him. "About 150?"

"Your *two-way* average was 149.93 MPH," he said.

Horsepower was the least of my problems on these runs. In fact I went faster quicker in the mile with the Class B engine than I did with the Class A mill, which had 21 per cent greater displacement. The big limiting factors which held back the Class A combination had been a ten-mile-an-hour crosswind and the roughness of the course.

Again, Goodyear and Gene McMannis had met the tire and traction problems magnificently. For *Assault* they built 8.5 inch wide drag slicks (quite wide for that time) that were based on the extreme low profile cross-section of the LSR tire. There was plenty known about the performance of heavy-shouldered slicks over the standing-start quarter-mile. But little was known about how they might hold together over the kilo and *nothing* was known about their stamina over the standing-start mile. Shedding of treads would not have been surprising and a blowout might have been deadly. But the tires held together perfectly in spite of the lack of precedent or information to guide tire engineers and rubber chemists in designing tires for this specific and utterly far-out level of performance.

I broke by over ten miles an hour the World record for acceleration which had been set by Rosemeyer in 1937. I also broke the American National Unlimited and National Class A records, which had stood since Ralph de Palma set them in 1919 with a Packard race car. I smashed the existing International Class A records for the kilo and mile, which had not been touched since John Cobb had set them in 1933. And I took care of Rice's International and National kilo records. This won me almost as much world-wide publicity as the runs with *Challenger* had.

The Motor (London) said:

> Times and speeds are difficult to visualize when they climb to these elite heights. So look at it this way. Thompson and his *Assault* are waiting on the line, ready to start their attempt. You are approaching from the rear (in a suitable car) at 140 MPH. As you pass the dragster to begin your flying mile, Thompson feeds in the clutch. By the end of that mere mile, Thompson has streaked past you and is disappearing into the distance at 230 MPH. Now that is real acceleration.

31

I TOOLED UP TO MANUACTURE THE SUPERCHARGER DRIVES THAT I HAD designed for *Assault*. But the first four were not for sale; they were for *Challenger*. Driving four GM 6-71 Roots blowers, they would raise the total output of the four engines from about 2,000 to about 3,000 horsepower. With the blowers on top of the engines and with sawed-off Hilborn fuel injectors on top of the blowers, a new hood had to be designed and built. I provided it with a pair of inverted troughs to cover the blowers and left the front ends of the troughs open so that they could act as air scoops.

This of course increased *Challenger's* frontal area and wind drag considerably but there was nothing I could do about that. I could make aerodynamic improvements elsewhere to the body, however, and I did. I smoothed, rounded and narrowed the nose and tail, enclosed the wheels and provided openings in the tail and around the exhaust stacks to relieve and vent air that built up under pressure inside the body.

Donald Campbell was due to run in September of '60 and was thinking publicly in terms of speeds up to 500 MPH. With three million dollars to play with, plus a superb engineering staff, plus the active support of a large part of the British automotive industry, I couldn't see that there was much to keep him from achieving this goal. So I reserved a week on the Salt in mid-August and the week preceding Campbell's. In these two weeks I hoped to be able to break Cobb's record, to break it ahead of Campbell and be the fastest man on land in the world. That made it a double-barreled race and challenge.

Even though there is a gap between capability and actual achievement, no one, including me, doubted the potential of the Campbell effort. In spite of the gap the odds were overwhelming that Campbell would go as fast as he hoped to and that he'd do it with ease. After all, he had about 4,250 horsepower to work with.

So I planned to strike back at the record which he almost inevitably would set. I had done a great amount of research on gas turbine engines and knew that Campbell's *Bluebird* would not be driven only through its wheels; that it would get a generous amount of propulsive assist from the exhaust through its engine's tail cone. What's fair for one is fair for all, so I invested in some JATO—jet-assisted takeoff rockets—units to help me challenge Campbell's record if he made it. The few people with whom I confided on this plan raised the objection that once you've turned on a JATO unit, you can't turn it off. I might pull myself into orbit. But naturally I had considered that and come up with a solution.

The year 1960 was the most spectacular and hard-fought year in the whole history of the Land Speed Record, which began in 1898 when Chasseloup-Laubet drove a Jeantaud car at a blinding, officially-timed 39.24 MPH. The only year that approaches 1960 was 1928, when Frank Lockhart, Sir Malcolm Campbell and Ray Keech duelled with each other for the LSR on Florida's narrow and mushy Daytona Beach, the surface of which changes with every tide. But in 1960 there were five of us committed to the same goal. This is who we were and how we were equipped:

Athol Graham, former Mormon missionary from Salt Lake City, Utah. His *City of Salt Lake* was powered by a single-stage supercharged Allison V12 aircraft engine which developed about 3,000 horsepower. The car weighed about 3,800 pounds and was driven through its two rear wheels.

Nathan Ostich, M.D., of Los Angeles, California. His car, the *Flying Caduceus*, was powered by a General Electric J47-19 jet engine, good for about 7,000 horsepower. It was propelled by pure thrust and weighed about 6,000 pounds.

Art Arfons of Akron, Ohio. His *Green Monster* was powered by a two-stage supercharged Allison which delivered about 3,800 horsepower. It weighed about 4,000 pounds and was driven through all four wheels.

Donald Campbell of England. His *Bluebird* was powered by a 4,250 horsepower Bristol-Siddeley *Proteus* aircraft turboprop engine. It had four-wheel drive and weighed about 8,500 pounds.

Finally, there was me. The four blown Pontiacs in *Challenger* delivered about 3,000 horsepower. I had four-wheel drive and a final weight of about 7,000 pounds.

This was the bumper lineup of contenders for the LSR and Graham was the first to run, on August 1. He had turned an effortless 344 MPH the previous December on a highly casual demonstration run and this made him one of the most serious threats to my own objective. Griff had been in constant contact with Graham, offering all the help and counsel that he could. And through Griff, I had offered him all my help. This was not illogical or contradictory to my goal. I work best under pressure, thrive on competition, and prefer victory over an adversary to victory over no competition at all.

I felt that I knew enough about driving at very high speeds to tell that Graham, driving his car through only two wheels, could not hope to deliver enough horsepower to the Salt to go more than about 355 MPH. Still, he was a threat, and I arrived in Wendover on July 31 to see what I was up against.

I got up at the crack of dawn on August 1 and went out to have a look at the course. I had a spooky feeling that morning, which I explained to myself on the grounds that Graham was driving awfully fast for a man who had only made a couple of runs on the Salt. I saw that the telephone pole which stands smack in the middle of the south end of the course was still in place. I felt that Graham was entitled to every possible break in his favor and looked up Roland Portwood, the hard-working foreman of the

Utah Highway Department's local crew. I told him what I thought should be done. He agreed and we unhooked the pole from its wires, lifted it out of its hole in the Salt and stashed it far from the course.

Then I headed down to the north end, where Graham's pit was located, found him and spoke with him for the first time. I offered him any and all the help and advice that I could give and urged him to take it easy for the first few runs and to build up his speed gradually. But he looked at me as though from a remote distance and said. "Look. I've gone 344. I don't have anything to learn below that speed."

I tried to point out that he had changed his car radically since that time and that the surface of the Salt changes almost from hour to hour. But his mind was completely preoccupied with what he was about to do and which he seemed utterly assured of accomplishing. It was at this point that a heavy premonition settled upon me. I gave up talking and drove to where I *knew* it would happen and set up my movie camera. My reasons were not morbid. They were profoundly practical.

Graham took off at 11:02 that morning and 47 seconds later he was doing well over 300 MPH when he got sideways in front of my station. The tail section peeled away from his car; the car leaped high into the air, crashed upside down and then bounced and slid for a good half mile.

I was one of the first at the wreck, hoping to reach Graham in time to do him some good. But it was too late. His roll bar had withstood the impacts but the upper tip of the firewall which was between his back and the engine had somehow bent forward and had chopped his spine just under his crash helmet. I walked back in his tire tracks for a mile, analyzing what had happened. It was crystal clear. He had been accelerating very hard and his car had begun to drift off the black line. If he lifted his foot at all he didn't lift it very much. The tire tracks showed that he just got farther and farther off the course until he apparently got sufficiently sideways to trip over his own wall of air.

I felt profoundly sorry for Graham, particularly since his crash could have been averted so easily. But I wasn't depressed in a personal way by the tragedy. I couldn't identify myself with it because I knew that that was one situation, at least, that I would never let myself get into. Still, it was an ominous way for the season to begin.

Doc Ostich and crew had the Salt from August 5 through 13. I didn't come to observe their efforts because they were meaningless to the FIA, which says that to qualify as an automobile a vehicle must steer through at least two of its wheels and be driven through at least two. Doc's vehicle was the world's first pure-jet contender for high-speed records, whether FIA-valid or not. It had the push to go frantically fast and Firestone had developed gigantic, 48-inch outside diameter tires for it, which had been laboratory tested up to 600 MPH. I felt then and I feel now that—contrary to many people's belief—jet cars can surpass 400 MPH with ease . . . if they can just be steered straight.

The *Flying Caduceus* had its own bounteous share of teething troubles and made its first loafing but successful test run on August 10, registering 228 through Ollie Riley's clocks. On August 12 Doc took off with 90 per cent throttle, but his engine's air ducts collapsed. His crew worked heroically all night and had the ducts rebuilt by the following morning. Doc made another courageous try, the ducts collapsed again and, out of time and in definite trouble, he hauled back to Los Angeles.

Ostich was back on the Salt on September 5 with brand-new, completely redesigned ducts. He got sideways at about 250 MPH, but saved himself with his chute, which straightened the car out. He thought that a crosswind had caused his trouble, waited for still air and ran again. This time he got out of shape at about 330 MPH and again saved himself with the chute.

The trouble turned out to be an excessively wide brake disc which was seizing and pulling the car to one side. It was replaced and Doc made another run under almost full power on September 6. The chute came out again, this time at about 350 MPH. Now the trouble was that the car wouldn't respond to its steering. The steering system had to be completely rebuilt, so Doc packed up after reserving a week on the Salt for the following year.

Art Arfons and his partner Ed Snyder rolled in from Akron on August 26. The design of Art's chassis was clean, efficient and logical and the car was capable of going very fast. It had one glaring fault and Art recognized it on his first run. He sat in the very nose of the vehicle, as he had always done in his Allison-engined dragsters. This never had bothered him over quarter-mile distances but at higher speeds and over a course many miles long he found that he hadn't the faintest inkling of what the mass of the machine was doing behind him. Still, he did his very best.

On August 27, the last day of the Nationals, he made a few shakedown runs in the 190's. On September 5 he was ready to begin working up to speed and made a trial run at 249.57 MPH and looked very steady. But he wiped out a driveshaft bearing and, on top of that, his parachute brake failed. Art had noted about a dozen important changes that he wanted to make in his car and very wisely decided to postpone efforts at higher speeds until the following year.

Donald Campbell's crew began moving into Wendover on August 26. It was like a military invasion. There were roughly a hundred engineers and technicians and they came with twenty or thirty identical Rover sedans, several elaborately equipped Land Rovers, a slew of trucks and a gigantic diesel flat-bed semi with *Bluebird* itself aboard.

The USAF is acutely interested both in speed and in international good will and placed a large hangar at Wendover AFB at the disposal of Campbell's task force. The hangar was none too big. One end was filled entirely just by tires. They were immense Dunlops, fifty-two inches in diameter, and there were eighty of them, each in its own heavy wooden crate. Then there were eighty big bead-separator hoops for these tires. The car itself, thirty feet eight inches long and almost five feet high, occupied the center of the hangar, the rest of which was filled with gear which went with *Bluebird,* such as the motor-generator equipped Land Rover which was its mobile starting unit. This seemed to all of us like carrying preparation pretty far, until we remembered that these people were 5,000 miles from home.

Donald Campbell arrived in Salt Lake City on September 3, held a press conference there and proceeded to Wendover that night. The following morning he was on the Salt when I turned 372 MPH and after that run we met face to face for the first time.

I was disposed to like Campbell in advance. As soon as his crew arrived I had contacted his standby driver and second-in-command, Squadron Leader Peter Carr of the RAF. I offered Pete the benefit of all my experience on the Salt. He accepted it in the open spirit in which I'd intended it and introduced me to the whole crew, including chief designer Ken Norris and chief mechanic Leo Villa. They were all fine, straightforward men without any trace of that snobbery which is not too uncommon among the British.

Pete and I were fast friends by the time Donald arrived. He introduced us—"Mickey: Donald. Donald: Mickey. You chaps are going to get along well."

We did. Donald broke the ice with friendly needling, a language that I understand. Then he asked me all about the 372 run and the condition of the Salt.

"Oh, it's not bad at all," I said. "It's a little choppy and slick here and there. I lost it a few times. At about 350 I got sideways and things looked very bad for an instant but I gave the wheel a snap and horsed the car back onto the course. I've seen the Salt an awful lot better than it is now."

I said this with studied indifference and casualness while watching Donald's reaction with an eagle eye. He laughed at my flippancy but it was nervous laughter and he seemed to blanch a bit.

This was what I wanted, of course. I was trying to psych the man and could see that I was getting through to his emotions. I never told him a word that wasn't the truth but I was careful to feed him all those bits of the truth that might un-nerve him. After all, we were competitors and there was something big at stake. He knew perfectly well what a back yard operation mine was and he knew the magnitude of his advantages over me. He knew that when the time came he could eat me up and spit out the pieces. He was glad to have me around to add drama and conflict and international rivalry to his success-assured effort.

But having the potential for accomplishment and realizing that potential are worlds apart. Until I was beaten I was not going to admit defeat and, whether he knew it or not, Campbell had a long, hard way to go. I had plenty of advantages on my side, and they all fell under the heading of experience, which he totally lacked. So I psyched him like mad, using the techniques I'd mastered during years and years of drag racing, where psyching seems to be more effective and decisive than in any other form of racing.

I pointed out to Donald that from the standpoint of driver safety his car was an atrocity. It had no roll bar, no crash padding and his safety harness was toy-like. He countered that he and his engineers had figured that if the car flipped and landed upside down the high wheel humps in the body would support the car and that the canopy would not be touched. I told him that that wasn't even a half-safe assumption and spelled out the details of accidents on the Salt involving half-safe cars. Whatever he thought of my advice, he made no changes in *Bluebird*. There was one thing I could do and that was replace his poorly-designed, obsolete crash helmet. I had Roy Richter of Bell Helmets mail me one of his newest models and presented it to Donald.

The afternoon of September 5, the incredibly huge *Bluebird* cavalcade made its way from Wendover to the Salt. The car was unloaded and fresh wheel-tire assemblies were mounted. Donald got into the cockpit and Norris and Villa checked him out on the controls. The big turbine engine was started, the chocks pulled from under the tires, and the car began to move. In about 200 feet it stopped abruptly, the canopy flew up and Donald shouted, "What's this red light for?"

It was normal and he made a fresh start, purring down the course at a small, constant throttle setting. It was a mild test run at about 125 MPH and was followed by a similar return run at about 175 MPH, after which the car was taken back to Wendover and torn down completely for inspection. After the first run a BBC interviewer asked Donald if this was the fastest he had ever driven.

"Well, my 300SL *feels* faster," he laughed around his pipe.

On September 15 Donald topped 250 MPH and was to go for 300 the following day. He went north and was pleased to have reached the 300 mark in three miles, but Norris reminded him that he would have to reach 300 in two miles in order to break the record. Each of the five runs up to this point had been made with constant throttle settings but Donald decided to test the machine's acceleration on the next run. Within about 1.7 miles of the start he was turning about 350 MPH. Although *Bluebird* had been yawing more and more off course Donald apparently didn't lift his foot, even though I had done my best to impress him with the danger of this. Suddenly the car got sufficiently sideways to the wind to do a great flip in the air.

The situation was remarkably similar to Graham's, with the difference that *Bluebird* evidently did a complete roll in the air and landed on its wheels. Had it landed upside down Donald almost surely would have been killed. But someone was helping him, too, and he was conscious and not seriously hurt—miraculously—when Norris, Villa and Carr roared up to the scene. They took the wreckage back to England, rebuilt it and, as these words are being written, are on their way to Lake Eyre in Australia for another shot at the LSR.

That's what happened to my competition in 1960 and it all adds up to prove that it takes more than capable equipment and good intentions to do what man never has done before. It takes incredible effort even to attempt it and it can take your life, ever so easily. I wouldn't relive my own ordeal on the Salt that year for all the money in the world.

32

I HAD RESERVED THE SALT FOR AUGUST 14 THROUGH 20, THE WEEK before the Nationals, and for August 28 through September 3, the week following them. I arrived in Wendover on August 12, got settled in and made my first trial run on the 14th. The course was short. There had been no rain all year to smooth the surface by dissolving it and even the scraped portion was not at all up to normal smoothness. When the Salt gets that dry and hard the drag rail tends to bump over the ridges which form over and around the pressure cracks, instead of scraping the ridges away. Plus, which we didn't know at the time, the brine table under the Salt had been pumped away by potash mining operations so that there was little or no percolation of moisture to the surface to help restore it.

The course was rougher than I had ever known a course on the Salt to be. On my first run I backed off in the low 300's. This was very fortunate because during deceleration I was jolted over into the rough shingles of hard crust that littered the whole unscraped portion of the Salt. The pounding I went through was terrible and I don't know what it did to my insides. When Judy and Fritz pulled me out of the car I was vomiting and in a great deal of

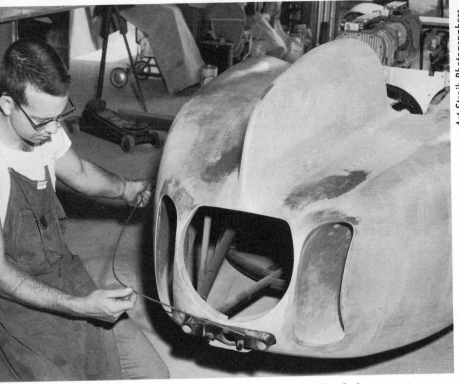

Art Streib Photographers

For 1960 I modified *Challenger* extensively. Here Don Borth demonstrates the old contour of the tail against the reworked body. The vent openings also were new.

Addition of superchargers to the engine required that the hood be redesigned. The big air scoops over the blowers left me with little vision out of the car, but all I was concerned with was seeing the black line on the Salt.

Griffith Borgeson

The Salt was already going bad in August of 1960. This is Athol Graham's pit.

This is Athol Graham's Allison V12-powered streamliner on the occasion of his clocking 344 MPH.

Graham's *City of Salt Lake* immediately after crash.

More competition for me in 1960 came from Art Arfons' *Green Monster*, also Allison-powered.

Dr. Nathan Ostich's *Flying Caduceus* promised to be very fast but was not a threat to me in that it did not conform to the FIA definition of an automobile.

The most serious threat to me came from Donald Campbell's *Bluebird*, shown here making its initial run.

Campbell and I were the friendliest of rivals, spent a great deal of time together.

The *Bluebird* after its crash on September 16, 1960.

Here we are after the 406.6 run, tired but happy.

Bill Burke's *Pumpkin Seed* had clocked 205 in 1960 with a Ford Falcon engine. I bought the car, installed a Pontiac Tempest four-banger, and Bill drove it 234 MPH.

pain. That year I had a doctor and an airplane on hand and the doctor gave me a sedative and I was all right the next day.

USAC's Joe Petrali supervised this run. We talked and he agreed that the course was impossible for my purpose. I got on the phone to Bill Backman, head of the Bonneville Speedway Association, an adjunct of the Salt Lake City Chamber of Commerce, which administers the use of the Salt for racing. I stated the problem and asked him to please have the course in usable shape for the week following the Nationals. I returned to Los Angeles with the impression that all would be taken care of.

I will never know what happened between Backman and me. At that time I had already done as much to bring world fame to Utah as any man ever had, but Backman was already making it clear that he had no fondness for me. Perhaps I had made the mistake of saying for publication that the Salt was rough when the Salt *was* rough. At any rate, I was treated with utter coldness, with downright unfriendliness. This was in contrast to the BSA's almost fawning cooperation with the British. In fact, when Cobb made his LSR runs in '47 he was imported by the state of Utah to add luster to the state's centennial at the state's expense.

But in all my dealings with the BSA I got a runaround that became more incredible as time went on. It was so fantastic that I'd doubt my own sanity if it weren't for the many wise, cool heads who came to me raving about the stark incredibility of the situation. "Are those people trying to *kill* you?" was a standard question. There's logic in any situation, but I'll never be able to understand the logic behind what was done to me on the Salt in 1960. My struggle with machinery and the forces of nature was crushing enough. What I did not need was the human obstruction which kept grinding me down.

I returned to Wendover toward the end of the Nationals' week. I made an easy test run at 354.33 MPH and found the short hot rod course to be not bad.

I was particularly interested in a brand-new car which my old buddy, Bill Burke, had built and brought to the Salt. Burke, now an advertising executive, had invented the belly-tank lakester back in '47 and always could be counted on for exciting new ideas. His new machine was one of the tiniest streamliners ever built in the States and because of its shape he called it the *Pumpkin Seed.*

Although its power was only from a 156-cubic-inch Ford *Falcon* engine, it was so small and slippery that it was bound to show some real speed. It did: 205.95 MPH.

After my 354 run I was working on *Challenger* in the warmup area at the south end and looked up to see the *Pumpkin Seed* coasting toward me but far, far too fast for being so close to the highway dike. In *Sports Cars Illustrated* for January, 1961, Burke described what happened.

"My brakes had failed, I was doing about 100 MPH and was just about out of room as I went whistling by Mickey. He was working on his car and had his own problems but he saw that I was in trouble. He leaped into his pickup, came storming after me, got ahead of me and we flew through the row of phone poles like we were flat out and I guess that he was. Then he led me through a little path that *he* knew of, through the impossible rough stuff and parallel to the highway. When I was down to about 20 MPH, he dashed ahead, jumped out of the truck and as I came by he flung himself on the car, grabbed its canopy and dragged it to a stop. I thanked him and all he said was, 'Congratulations. You broke the record.' Anybody knocks Mickey, I tell them that little story."

This incident was the beginning of an even closer relationship between us and the following year I bought the *Pumpkin Seed* from Bill on the condition that he would drive it for me.

After the 354 run I sat back and waited for my own week to begin. A long course was supposed to be ready for me on August 28 and I was prepared to make my big try on the 29th. This course was in addition to the so-called LSR course, which was utterly miserable and unfit for my use, although The Powers denied this and considered me a troublemaker for taking the stand that I did. They must have thought that I would relent and use the LSR course because they dismissed the road crew, telling it not to report back to work until the 30th.

Talk about psyching, I was almost psyched out of my mind. The weather was very unsettled and rain was falling frequently. Each day of good weather that was lost was almost a catastrophe because bad weather could set in at any time and ruin my hopes for the year. Also, counting USAC's fee and my crew's pay, it was costing me about $1,500 a day just to stand around. I was being crucified financially and my crew, long away from home and jobs, was getting restless.

After endless haggling and on-spot inspection I convinced the BSA that the Nationals' course had the best surface and should be extended to make a better, usable LSR course. I was told, hostilely, "OK, we'll lengthen and smooth it and have it ready for you on the 31st."

Then they turned around and told the road crew to have it ready on September 1, as I learned later.

Roland Portwood's fine crew had to follow its orders to the letter. My crew and I worked all day and well into the night, patching ruts, cracks and rough spots in the miles of Salt. We worked with shovels and even, literally, with putty knives. I designed my own scraper and my crew built it. I mustered my own equipment and worked it at night. My neck was going to be all the way out this time and I was determined to get every tiny break that I could.

August 31 was a perfect day. The Salt was bone dry and the weather sunny and calm. But the course wasn't ready. I was raging. September 1 was the same, perfect. USAC continued to be ready to operate the instant that the road crew finished its dragging operation. But that day, too, was wasted since the work was not completed until close to sundown. Backman and I had ceased speaking to each other long before.

But now we could run and we were ready to at 5 A.M. on the 2nd. But now a high wind was blowing and we just sat there waiting for it to die down. The hours dragged by and it never did die down and then, in the afternoon, the skies turned black and a deluge fell, putting the Salt under about two inches of water. Shot down again, unnecessarily. More frustration and rage. With ideal breaks the Salt might be dry enough to run on on the 4th, but by then my time would have run out and I would have accomplished nothing other than my own impoverishment.

I was saved by the fact that the week of September 4 through 11 had been reserved first by Renault, then by Ecurie Cooper-Climax, but both finally had cancelled, leaving the week wide open for anyone who required it. This was when Ostich returned, Art Arfons made his bold try and Donald Campbell made his first two trial runs.

September 3 was dry and windy and the Salt dried rapidly. But the water had washed away the black line and a new one was to be laid that evening. But when we arrived on the Salt at 5 A.M. on the 4th no line had been put down. More frustration and, to make it worse, there was the oil distributor truck, parked right beside our pit. If it hadn't been locked I would have laid the line myself, but I didn't feel like courting charges of truck theft from the State of Utah.

Weather conditions were absolutely perfect for several hours that morning while we just walked around, kicking at the Salt. USAC had sent messengers in all directions to find the truck crew and get the line laid, but the hours dragged by and the wind began to rise. Around 9 A.M. the crew casually moseyed up, climbed aboard the truck and headed north. I asked them to lay a very narrow line because the fresh oil would remain slippery for days and the less of it there was on the course the better. I stood there watching, waiting to see what sort of stripe they'd put down, but nothing happened. For some unknown reason they elected to drive to the north end and start laying the line from there! That meant another good half hour wasted and the wind kept getting worse.

Okay. Another punch to roll with, so we began sweating out the hour and a half that it would take the truck to complete its job. About forty-five minutes later Reeves Dutton walked over from his field phone. He was on the verge of tears from personal exasperation and from sympathy with what we were going through.

"Mickey," he said, "I can hardly bear to tell you this, but those idiots have gone and driven the truck into the mud at the north end. It's up to its axles. They say they'll have it out in fifteen minutes, but Petrali has gone to investigate."

I leave my reaction to the reader's imagination.

Art Pillsbury had stayed in his High Sierra retreat that year and Joe Petrali was in charge of the show for USAC. He had witnessed the whole fiasco to date and in about twenty minutes he came steaming up, as fierce-looking as any of us. He reported that it would be hours before the truck could be exhumed from the mud. Then he took Griff and Dick Jones aside and said, "What do you think about letting Mickey run without any line at all?"

"If it were any other driver in the world we'd say absolutely not," was the answer. "But Mick knows this course like nobody else in the world. We think he can do it safely."

This confirmed Joe's own opinion and he put it up to me. I grabbed at it even though there were still great ponds of water on the Salt. Joe phoned down the line, ordered a check of the clocks, and Fritz began warming *Challenger's* engines on soft plugs. It was around 11 A.M. when we were ready to go and Judy taped my leathers at the ankles for added fire protection.

I felt terrible. No one who lives close to death and who has escaped from the jaws of death a few times can help being at least a little bit superstitious. This year everything seemed to be against me, seemed to be a foreboding omen. I went to Fritz and the crew and started to make a little speech, trying to tell these guys how much I appreciated their unfailing loyalty and indispensable help, knowing that we might not see each other again. But Fritz saw the tears in my eyes and heard the tremor in my voice and chopped me off.

"Hell, buddy, we know all that stuff," he said. "Just buy us a drink at the Stateline tonight and forget it."

I prayed, climbed aboard, kissed Judy and squeezed her arm hard and then they slapped down the lid and pushed me off. I got on it hard and the added boost of the blowers felt good. I fishtailed badly in first gear, threw the shift to second, lost it a couple of times in that gear, saved it, shifted to top gear and went splashing through the mush. The front wheels began breaking loose, making the whole car wobble sickeningly. Why? Was it the water on the Salt? Clutches slipping again? Aerodynamic lift on the nose of the car? I lost it and saved it, lost it and saved it again. I used all the throttle that I dared to, but I never came close to using full throttle because that would have been certain suicide.

It was a hairy ride, and it was the one that I told Donald Campbell about a few hours later. I didn't have to exaggerate to scare him. The simple facts were disturbing enough.

On that run I had clocked 372.67 MPH. This was ten miles an hour faster than I'd ever gone, but still a long way from my goal. And I still was a long way from finding the combination that would make *Challenger* handle well enough so I could make full use of the power she had available. Nevertheless, I felt much better after that run. I was back in the racing business again and had reached another new height. We all felt much better.

I rushed back to Wendover and called Schiefer in San Diego,

telling him to air-freight me a set of new clutches. I had them the following morning and while Fritz spent the day installing them I went looking for the ballast that I suspected *Challenger* needed in her front end.

Of all unlikely things, in the middle of the Great Salt Desert I found a couple of chunks of yellow bronze bar stock, three inches in diameter, eight feet long and beautifully heavy. I loaded them into the pickup and hauled them out to the Salt, where Fritz and the guys were laboring away.

"Here's our ballast," I said.

"Well why did you bring it here?" Fritz beefed. "That stuff's got to be cut and it's tough as blazes. It'll take half a day to cut through by hand. Why not throw it in the power saw at the Air Base?"

"It takes twenty minutes just to drive over there." I said. "And anybody can saw through one of those bars in twenty minutes."

"You're out of your simple mind," Fritz said disgustedly.

"You want to bet that I can't do it?" I challenged him.

"You're damned right," Fritz said. "Ten bucks' worth!"

"Okay," I said, "Who's going to hold the watch?"

Fritz of course was thinking in terms of eating through that tough metal with an ordinary, fine-toothed hacksaw. But this year I had put together a safety kit that included everything I thought we might need in case of a crash, from blood plasma to a pair of whopping keyhole-type metal saws for chopping through *Challenger's* body and frame.

I laid out these two coarse-toothed saws, pulled on a pair of heavy leather gloves and shouted, "*Now!*" I began sawing away like mad in the desert heat and sun while Fritz even held the bar so it wouldn't vibrate. "Give me water," I kept shouting. "Mop my forehead!" I shed gallons. I sawed so hard that the saw blade jack-knifed. I threw it aside and grabbed the other saw. In about eighteen minutes flat I was through that big bronze bar, and exhausted. But it was good for my soul to take that ten-spot from Fritz and it was relaxing for all our nerves. I was good for nothing for the rest of the day, except dropping by to razz Fritz and the crew.

With the new clutches and ballast aboard—about a thousand

pounds of it—I made another run on September 6. *Challenger* fishtailed horribly but the front tires scarcely lost their bite.

I reduced the ballast, ran again on the 8th, broke a driveshaft and scattered an engine. The front tires, though, were biting as they never had. We seemed to be moving in the right direction at last. I reduced the ballast some more and added a spoiler to *Challenger's* nose in an effort to reduce whatever aerodynamic lift might be contributing to the breaking loose of the front tires.

Again I was running out of time. The open week ended on the 11th and after that the Salt belonged to Campbell. He knew what we were going through, and so did his whole crew. Pete Carr came to our garage one night and saw *Challenger* torn down to the frame.

"When do you think you'll be running again?" he asked sympathetically, consolingly, assuming that we'd been shot down for a week.

"Why at the crack of dawn, like always," Fritz blandly informed him.

Pete and the rest of the Campbell crew never had seen real hot rodders at work and they shook their heads in amused disbelief that soon became awe.

Donald was as impressed and sympathetic as the others and as the open week ran out, he came to me and said,

"Mickey, don't feel that you have to get it done instantly. I have plenty of time reserved on the Salt, as you know. Please know that it's yours whenever you need it."

You'd have a hard time imagining how I loved that man at that moment. *There* was a competitor who was too big to clutch at victory by default and who savored competition all the way.

"You Limeys are pretty good sportsmen after all," I teased, giving him a friendly punch to the shoulder. "And I know it's not just because you think you're going to beat me," I said, a little more seriously. "Thank you, Donald."

The morning of September 9, 1960 I was ready once more. The course was only 10.8 miles long. Going north I had a rough, 4.5 mile approach to the traps but coming back I had a fairly smooth 5.5 mile run before entering the clocks. There was a headwind of about five miles an hour coming from the north and, as usual, I chose to make my first run the hard way. Coming back downhill, so to speak, makes it much easier and lets you extend yourself with more confidence. This day I had every reason to believe that at last the car was perfect.

I blasted off and the car felt wonderful. I waited for tires to break loose and they didn't. The biggest problem always had been getting up to 300 soon enough, which I never had been able to do. But this morning everything clicked and I could bear down and down with my throttle foot.

Through the seat of my pants I sensed the tire diameters and they were all perfectly unifom it seemed, right to the thousandth of an inch. I felt for the clutches and they were locked solid, as they should be. I listened to all the sets of gears and they all sang in one precise key. I felt out for the distribution of weight from front to rear and it was perfect, like a lead brick sailing down a trough of mercury.

I checked the two tachometers that spoke for the fore and aft pairs of engines. I never had been able to get them to follow each other perfectly. This morning they did. At 300 they were indicating identical revs. I stayed on the throttle and at 350 they still were together. *Yes!* At 375 they told me that the front engines and rear engines, front wheels and rear wheels still were turning at the same, identical rate. I *still* stayed on the throttle and *Challenger* went like a dream. No more handling problems at all. The car finally was sorted out and I had the combination that worked. For the first time I didn't have to lift my throttle foot.

Long before I rolled to a stop I knew that I'd broken 400 and while we refuelled and Judy and Fritz and the whole gang were bursting with joy the official time came over the field phone: 406.60 MPH.

I had gone faster than any man in history. It hadn't taken a year or two or three but my whole life and, Dear God, how hard it had been earned . . . not just by me but by all of us. I had an hour within which to make the backup run that would obliterate the last of Cobb's records and bring the LSR finally back to our own country. We worked calmly and deliberately, knowing that we had it made in the shade.

Going back I had the long, smooth approach. To have averaged 406 through the mile trap on the way north I had to have been doing a good 420 MPH as I came out of that trap. With an added mile for acceleration and with the help of the tailwind I should be able to crack 440 with ease. I was just ready to crawl into *Challenger* when Roland Portwood walked up to me, terribly agitated and with tears streaming down his face.

"I've got to tell you something," he blurted.

"What the heck's the matter, man?" I said to this good Mormon. "Spill it."

"Mickey," he said, "I was driving back from Salt Lake last night and I was driving along the highway and the *Lord* stopped me, Mickey. He said to me, 'Roland, don't let Mickey make that return run tomorrow because if he does he'll be *killed.*'"

The tears were really rolling now, but I must have looked incredulous. I hardly knew what to make of the situation. Roland and I had been good friends for two years, during which not a word of a religious nature ever had passed between us. I knew that Roland was no crank and that he had been *for* me as few others had. Yet now he was begging me to quit.

"You're wrong, Roland," I told him. "The car has never been better."

"*Please* don't drive it back," he came on with even stronger force. "You'll never make it. You'll die. The Lord *told* me!"

Now this sort of thing is a little tough to take after you've just survived driving 406 miles an hour. I listened to Roland carefully and tried to weigh what he was saying. I listened to my own intuition but could hear no hint of warning. I thanked Roland very sincerely, told him that everything would be all right and hunched once more into *Challenger's* cramped cockpit. But I don't mind telling you that I was more than a little bit shaken.

Actually, Roland came very close to swaying me all the way. After all, I had accomplished my lifelong ambition. I had been officially clocked at the fastest automotive speed in history and I had the world's fastest car. But my sponsors wanted and deserved a little more than that and I was determined to do my utmost for them.

I wanted to cut a real fat one coming back and used a lot of throttle. I went through the kilometer trap at an average of 392 MPH, accelerating fiercely. And then it happened. A three-dollar driveshaft let go. I declutched soon enough for Roland's revelation not to come true and coasted to the south pit. It was utterly hopeless to repair the damage and storm back north within what was left of the permitted hour. We hauled back to Wendover once more.

We tore *Challenger* down for total inspection while replacing the driveshaft. We were still in the process of restoring the car to perfect condition when Donald Campbell crashed on September 16. This meant that all my competition had fallen by the way and I decided to rest on the laurels that I had won. I was the uncontested fastest man on wheels and really had accomplished all that I had set out to do. I had found the right combination for my machine and could wrap up the two-way LSR during the next season.

I sent the tired and all-but-whipped crew back home with *Challenger*. With Judy I drove the ninety miles east to Tooele, Utah, where Donald was convalescing in the hospital.

He was alert but still hearing bells. He thanked me for dropping by to check on his health and told me that he had a new respect for all my haranguing about safety. Then he showed me a cable that he'd received from Queen Elizabeth. She congratulated him on his gallant effort and prayed for his quick recovery.

"And what have you heard from the President of the United States?" Donald asked me.

That one caught me flat-footed for a moment. In fact I still don't have an answer to it. Donald, no doubt, will be knighted if he makes it.

It was premature, but after that last run on September 9 I blurted to one and all that I was through for the year and that I'd climb back in the saddle when somebody challenged my position. To do so sooner would be stupid. Judy was in that small circle of listeners.

A couple of minutes later Dick Jones spotted her sobbing her heart out on the sidelines.

"What's the matter, kid?" he said. "It's all over now."

Judy mumbled that her sense of relief was too much to bear. But this was only part of what she felt. She had hoped to see the LSR wrapped up, filed away and forgotten. While I was showing a confident, satisfied front to the press she knew what was happening inside of me. Like me, she had yearned for us to stop living for this threatening, insatiable Thing and for life to return to what passes for normal in her world and mine. She knew that we could have done it this year if so many breaks hadn't been against us. Instead, there was a year of the same old suspense, the same old nightmares, to look forward to. That's why she couldn't keep from crying even though cameramen were there.

33

As soon as I returned to Long Beach I committed myself to other racing projects. The first was an attack on water-speed records, for which I built a very fast drag boat, powered by twin Pontiac V8 engines. It was good for about 135 MPH.

Next, I decided to resume my campaign against the major FIA automotive acceleration records and commenced work on two new cars and a whole series of engines.

There was nothing to do with *Challenger* now but wait for the next year's season on the Salt. So I sent her on a tour of car shows all over the United States, in Mel Noriega's care.

Life was very different now that I had turned the 406. From being an unknown punk just a couple of years before I now had access to the private offices of most top executives in the country. This helped my manufacturing business to boom and to get excellent outlets. Except for building a really nice new home for my family I plowed back every penny I made either into racing or into expanding my plant, which also was devoted to racing.

I got along very well with the press and the wire services and they saw good copy in almost every move that I made. They began projecting a new and much more favorable image of hot rodding and hot rodders and I knew that what I had accomplished with *Challenger* and *Assault* had contributed to this. This was the greatest reward I could ask for, and I really mean that. Knighthoods are great, where they count, but my country has its own ways, maybe more subtle, maybe not, of rewarding successful great effort.

I found myself being called upon regularly for local and national

TV appearances. An even more novel experience was when I was called upon to address the Southern California Section of the Society of Automotive Engineers on October 3, 1960. *Me*, a hot rodder!

There were over 200 members present at that meeting. I, who had barely clawed my way out of high school, thought I might panic, but when I took my place on the rostrum I saw eager interest in every face. It was easy to tell them *Challenger's* technical story, explain some of my theories and answer their knowledgeably worded questions. As I warmed to the job, I needled them unmercifully about the professional, text-book approach to creating machinery, rubbed it in that a good hot rodder can solve a design problem and have the new structure in operation in a fraction of the time that it takes a trained engineer to make his calculations and drawings. I still feel that way and I'll never hesitate to express it.

I know that this makes me sound stupid and that it has made me plenty of enemies in Detroit and elsewhere. But I just don't have time for engineers. They're too slow. If I need a special part for a car I'll go into the shop, grab a torch or put a piece of metal in a lathe and create it as I go along. While an engineer is just preparing to cope with the problem I can make the piece and have it on the car and find out whether it works or not. After the engineer has gotten through with all his engineering the piece still has to be made, installed and tested on the car anyway.

I kept running the drag strip and was more active than ever in actual drag racing competition. I became a serious contestant in the Mobilgas Economy Run and so did Judy, in the women's division.

I found time to coach a boys' football team, took it over when it was the local underdog and built it into a consistent winner. I don't care what's happening during football season. When Fleeta tells me it's four o'clock, I'm *gone* to work with those kids. While he was FIA Formula One World Champion, Jack Brabham was sitting in my office one day when that hour rolled around. I told him that he could come and watch practice or come back and see me in the morning. He came and watched practice. I get as much satisfaction from building boys into determined young men as I've ever gotten from any racing activity, and that's saying a lot.

I had scheduled a demonstration run by the drag boat to take place at Lake Mead, Nevada, on November 6, 1960. I've never been particularly interested in driving fast boats, so I had a good handler to look after that chore. But that morning an emergency kept him from showing up. A lot of people had made the trek to see what the twin-engined stormer would do and I didn't want to disappoint them. I decided to drive it myself.

I was doing only about 50 MPH when I hit a low wave from a patrol boat and the dragster kited into the air, me with it, hanging onto the steering wheel. The boat dropped, leaving me still in the air. As I was coming down the boat hit another wave and came slamming up to meet me, crushing something in my spine.

If one has never been paralyzed, it takes a definite span of time for him to realize what's happened. I had no sensation in my legs, but the boat was accelerating and I looked down and saw that my foot was on the throttle. We hit another wave and up and down I went again, my foot landing on the throttle again. I was afraid to cut the ignition switches because the boat would stop so fast that it could be swamped by a wave coming over the transom.

I don't know how many times I banged up and down like that before I got the situation figured out and reached down and lifted my foot off of and well away from the throttle pedal. When I did that the sudden deceleration slammed me into the steering wheel, then around it and against the hull. I couldn't brace myself with my legs. Water coming over the stern filled the hull to within an inch of sinking. I grabbed the wheel and let the boat idle back to shore. By the time I got there I couldn't focus on a thing and the whole world had become a great shimmering blur. The ambulance crew saw the trouble that I was in and rolled the gurney out into the water and pulled me onto it.

They rushed me to a hospital in Boulder City, Nevada, where X-rays were promptly taken and showed that the first and third lumbar vertabrae had been crushed. This was not just disc injury, it was real bone injury. They put me in a plaster cast from hips to toes. They told me not to get my hopes up. They could only guess at the extent of damage to the spinal cord itself, but it seemed certain to them that it would be many months before I walked, *if* I ever walked again. They told me that I definitely would have to spend at least three months in the cast.

I kept trying to move my toes but nothing happened until the third day, when my right big toe moved. I thought that perhaps I wanted it to move so badly that I was imagining it and I called Judy to watch. Sure enough, it moved. I kept working and finally had all of the toes of the right foot moving. Within a couple of days the left toes came to life and gradually I began to get a little sensation in my legs.

On November 15 I phoned Darrell Droke in Long Beach, told him to put a mattress on the bed of the station wagon and come and get me out of there. When he arrived there was a near riot at the hospital.

"We can't force you to stay here," they said, "but there are laws about people committing suicide."

We pushed our way out. During that seven-hour drive back to Long Beach I died many times. But the following morning I felt strong and was hot on the phone, calling orthopedists. I told the first three my problem and told them that I was going to start walking in a couple of days. Each one told me I was mad. Then I remembered to call Doc Schwartz. He had a buddy in that specialty and hustled right over with him.

I told him that I was going to start walking. Instead of telling me that I was crazy he said, "The voice of nature will tell you when the time is right."

"Right!" I said. "You're my doctor. Now let's get me out of this cast!"

On the night of the 17th he was there with a brace-maker, cut me out of the cast and wrapped me in a light aluminum brace.

"This will be just as good as the cast," he told me. "All you have to do is keep it on."

The next day I spent in painfully forcing myself to walk. The evening of the 19th I drove myself over to the Lions' Strip, just to oversee the action. The public address system broke down, nobody could fix it, so I climbed out of the car and fixed it myself.

On the 18th Judy's father died and I drove us to the funeral in Glendale, about twenty-five miles away, after first giving myself a bath. On the 23rd I was up for seven and a half hours, driving around town on errands and working at the shop. Of course after each of these outings I would crawl back into bed weak and wracked with pain. But I wasn't going to just lie down and give in to this thing. People asked me how I did it, which seemed to be a silly question.

"I have faith that won't quit. That's how. Naturally."

The time in bed weighed heavily on me and I was hurting for income. I wondered what I could get going, from my bed, over the telephone, and decided upon a speed-and-power show: hot rods, custom cars, race cars, vintage cars, racing motorcycles and drag boats. I called the Shrine Auditorium in Los Angeles and hired it for the last week in December and had a messenger bring me the building's floor plans. I carved them up and paid for most of the rent by selling space for commercial exhibits. I sold it all in one day, from my bed.

I rounded up about 150 outstanding vehicles and hired Bill Burke to manage the show, a job for which he was well qualified. Gary Campbell rallied round and did a fine job on publicity. Although we had had very little time for preparation or promotion the show was a good money maker. It at least served to establish me in that field and since then my big annual shows have improved in all ways. That first one also served the purpose of keeping me from going stir-crazy.

Even my new doctor told me that I absolutely would have to undergo spinal surgery soon. The extent of nerve damage would have to be determined and surgical measures would have to be taken to keep it from worsening. But I didn't like surgery and I had no time for it. Plus, the operation's success could not be guaranteed and I might *really* be paralyzed for life. So I decided to wait, if only because I had a lot to do. Run the manufacturing business, compete in the Economy Run, knock over the remaining acceleration records, keep the strip going, keep competing in drag racing and finish the LSR job. And I had a few other plans beyond those. The scene at Indianapolis really was beginning to bother me, and I knew just what I wanted to do about it. I began firming up those plans, talking myself into that massive gamble, as the acceleration-record project began to take final shape.

34

IN SPITE OF THE BROAD SCOPE OF MY ATTACK ON MAJOR ACCELER-
ation records I was, for once, excellently prepared for what took
place at March AFB on July 9, 1961.

I had four cars. One was old reliable *Assault*, equipped with a
6-71-blown, 303-cubic-inch Pontiac V8 which belted out 690 BHP
at 7,200 RPM. It had a full body shell, except for open front
wheels, and it was my missile to go against FIA International Class
C, 183 to 305 cubic inches.

For Class D I had a brand-new car, *Attempt*. This was a Dragmaster chassis with full-envelope streamlined body built by Jim
Burrell. Its power source was a four-cylinder Pontiac *Tempest*, 4-71
blown and destroked to a displacement of 180 cubic inches. It
pulled about 460 horsepower at 7,000 RPM. For Class E I had a
similar engine which I had destroked and sleeved to 120 cubic
inches. It used a GM 3-71 blower and was good for about 420
horsepower at 7,400 RPM.

Then, for Class F, I had another Dragmaster, this one without
any body shell at all. To power it I had sawed a *Tempest* four-
banger in two and had destroked the rear half to provide a displacement of ninety cubic inches. It pulled about 300 horsepower
on the dyno at 7,000 RPM. Fritz nick-named it *Little Car*.

All of these engines were equipped with top-mounted GM
blowers and Hilborn fuel injection. All three cars had solid rear
suspension, solid front axles with transverse torsion bars, Halibrand
magnesium wheels, Halibrand disc brakes on the rear wheels
only, parachutes for high-speed braking, Goodyear drag slicks at
the rear and Goodyear Sports Car Special tires at the front. Inside
and out, the engines were loaded with speed equipment of my own
design and manufacture and I knew from endless dynamometer
testing that they would stand up to their job.

I, myself, could have been better prepared when we rolled onto the 2.5 mile strip at March AFB at 2 A.M. on Sunday the 9th. I had worked on the cars all the previous day, run a big meet at Lions' that night and then, without sleep, had made the sixty-mile drive down to Riverside. My back was giving me fits as usual but I had learned long since that if I let that worry me I'd be a cripple.

Petrali had had the course surveyed to the fraction of an inch and we were ready to run as daylight began to break. We fired up *Attempt*, with the Class E engine. It barked strongly for a minute, then konked out. I turned that car over to the crew for inspection and got busy with *Little Car*.

I planned to go after both the kilometer and mile records. First I would run the kilo, in one direction. On the basis of that run I could decide whether changes in gearing, jetting and so on might be necessary and, if so, make them. Then I would make a run back over the full mile distance. If all went well I would turn around and repeat the two distances in the opposite direction. If it didn't I'd just keep trying until I got two-way averages within an hour that exceeded the existing records.

I took off in the two-banger at 6:21 A.M. and cracked the kilo, but missed the mile. I handed it back to the crew for a gear change and they handed me *Attempt*, which had only needed a colder set of spark plugs. I boomed south, breaking both the kilo and mile records, then backed those times up on the return run, with ease and without incident except for the usual bumpiness of the course. So much for Class E. I gave the car back to the crew for installation of the Class D engine.

Now it was *Assault's* turn. The other cars had La Salle three-speed gearboxes but this one I had fitted with an experimental, modified Borg-Warner four-speed automatic transmission. It worked beautifully and I wiped out the Class C records in two exciting runs, hitting terminal speeds of around 240 MPH at the ends of the mile traps. That transmission, incidentally, had been converted to racing use by Bob and Don Spar of B&M Automotive in Van Nuys. They are probably the most inspired automatic transmission engineers outside of The Big Three itself.

Then I went back to *Little Car*, deciding to get it over with by jumping the nitro blend from 25 to 40 per cent. These records, too, tumbled, but barely.

All that was left now was *Attempt*, with its Class D engine. By this time it was about 1 P.M., air temperature had passed 100° F and a stiff wind had come up. We waited and waited for it to die down, but it didn't. I decided to run anyway but was blown all over the course. Then I made up my mind that I'd been lucky enough for such a busy day and decided to file the Class D attempt for future action.

But I managed to work in a couple of more records, even so. I also had brought along a '61 Pontiac *Catalina* with a displacement of 389 cubes and all the high-performance factory options. While the Class D car still was being readied, I blasted south and north in the *Catalina* and demolished the standing-start kilo and mile records for American National Class C.

So, in that busy morning I attacked eight International records and broke eight of them. I attacked ten American National records and broke six of them. My back was killing me and the doctors had warned me that just one good impact would finish me for sure. For the moment I felt that I'd proved enough through racing and that I'd never get close to a fast car again. But of course that feeling blew over in a hurry.

I had witnessed the Indianapolis race again just five weeks before and had come back with clear plans for entering cars there next year. And they would be *different*. Before that, though, I still wanted to be able to hand my sponsors the LSR, although personally I was quite content with just having what was clearly the fastest car in history. And, to be sure of not running out of things to do, I had bought Burke's *Pumpkin Seed* and dropped a hot Pontiac *Tempest* four-banger into it.

I began checking by phone on the condition of the Salt. It was terrible, the locals told me. There had been another year of drought and the Salt's surface had deteriorated to what was probably its worst condition since the last glacial epoch. To help things along, the potash plant, which uses the Salt's brine table for ore, had been running out of brine. So a ditch had been dug, about twenty feet deep and wide, to recover brine from that depth. It paralleled the course for about ten miles. This seemed to mean that no brine would be drawn to the surface by the sun's heat, where it could evaporate, constantly renewing the surface with fresh mineral deposits.

I couldn't believe what I heard and Griff and I drove to Wendover. There it was! What had been the world's most beautiful desert, the most perfect speedway, was being turned into a choppy, shingle-ridden mud flat, a vast, ugly, useless badland. The change from 1960 to 1961 was hard to believe. But now that we were looking at it, it was easy to recall the annual stages which had led up to its present condition.

Many of the locals agreed with us that the time was overdue for drastic action. I delegated that to Griff, who organized and launched a really tremendous press, radio and TV campaign in the western United States, which most of the media supported eagerly. After all, the Salt had always been a good source of news for them. But *nobody* else seemed to care and the public was uniformly apathetic. Griff wrote a long open letter to the Secretary of the Interior, detailing exactly what was happening to the Salt and urging that this unique national treasure be given National Monument status, so it would be protected and preserved. The letter was published and parts of it quoted nationally. But the only result of all this struggle was an eventual statement from Washington that the matter had been given due investigation and the conclusion had been reached that the potash industry was important to the economy of Utah. Period.

Everyone in the speed fraternity prayed for rain that year and the healing effect it would have on the Salt. But only drizzles came. For a long time it seemed that the Nationals would have to be called off because even a five-mile course would not be available. In the end it was, and it was a good one in the sense that it was bone dry and traction never had been better. But the situation boded ill for the future.

I kept in touch with Wendover until the last days before the Nationals and when conditions failed to improve I had no choice but to leave *Challenger* at home. Nobody else went for big speed that year; they couldn't.

Burke and I took the *Pumpkin Seed* to the Salt, powered this time by the 180-cube *Tempest* that had powered *Attempt* in its unfulfilled Class D standing-start runs. Bill hurled the tiny streamliner over the choppy course at 234.22 MPH but this was still 14 MPH under the old record, which Caracciola had set in a Mercedes-Benz in 1939. Again we told each other, "Well, maybe next year," packed up and went home.

Before taking *Assault* to March Air Force Base, we prepared ourselves thoroughly. We could, for instance, swap engines in under 90 minutes.

On a 13,300 foot runway at March AFB, *Assault* set new absolute records for the standing start kilometer and mile.

Wayne Thoms

Here, with Fritz standing by, is *Attempt* without her streamlined shell. Goodyear again came up with a winning tire combination.

Wayne Thoms

On September 18, 1962 I went after International and American National Class C records at Bonneville, running a Chevrolet engine in the Harvey Aluminum Special. Except for one or two things (above, Fritz solders a penny over a radiator leak), the car performed beautifully and I really re-wrote the record books.

One small corner of the shop at Mickey Thompson Enterprises in Long Beach. This was when I was preparing for the big attack on FIA acceleration records.

Here I am, shaking down the machine that I hope to win with at Indianapolis in '63. Note the nearly non-existent frontal area; also the tires, which I designed and which Firestone built for me exclusively.

Most of us were heartbroken over the state of the Salt. I reported to Art Pillsbury on all this and showed him photos of the colossal drainage ditch.

The old man—he was about eighty—whose life had been so much devoted to the Salt and to making history on it, just shook his head.

"That's it," he said with weary sadnesss. "That's the end."

35

At this time there were two racing challenges left that still pulled at me hard. The Class D acceleration record still was not mine, leaving a gap in a list that otherwise was neatly complete. And I wanted to get a car of my own in the Indianapolis 500-mile race. It would be unlike anything seen before and its power plant would, of course, be based on American mass-production components.

I believe that the last time a car with a production-block engine had gotten into the 500 was 1946, when Andy and Joe Granatelli showed up at the Speedway with an eleven-year-old Miller-Ford, which they really made run. A silly fluke put it out in the fifty-second lap. Since then many costly efforts had been made with modified production engines to challenge the domination of the heavy, ancient Offenhauser four-banger, but every one had failed. So, naturally, whenever I spoke of my own production engine plans for Indy the usual reaction was that there are fools in this world who just refuse to learn.

But the design of our passenger car engines was getting more sophisticated by the year and Buick had recently introduced an "all aluminum" V8 that was unprecedentedly light, relative to the power it produced. This obviously was an ideal base for the development of a racing engine, provided it could be made to yield power enough and also would stay together for a reasonable number of flat-out hours.

So, when I got back from Bonneville at the end of August, I invested in a couple of these Buick aluminum engines and began wringing them out on the dynamometer, checking their reliability and their responsiveness to performance modifications. There was no point in taking steps to design and build a chassis until I had a fairly thoroughly developed and proven engine. It took a long time to reach this point, even though I had some very competent help on that project from Bob Bubenik. Also, I had to keep the business going and make a whole lot of money. Building Indy race cars and racing them really is a pastime for millionaires and I, just a budding, small-scale industrialist, really had no business trying to move in that league.

It was not until early February that I had the 255-cubic-inch engine developed to the point where it was belting out a steady 330 horsepower for hours on end, and I was able to feel that I had the power source that I needed. It was not until then, less than four months before the biggest race on this side of the Atlantic, that I was ready to build the car to receive the engine. And to make the time-bind even more agonizing, I decided that the odds would be much better if I built three identical cars instead of just one.

While watching the action at Indianapolis over the years I had long since decided that the classic, bulky Indianapolis roadster, with all the heavy parts that are dictated by the heavy Offy engine, belonged entirely to the past. There had to be something a great deal better and my idea of it was a car that would be smaller and lighter in every way. Its frontal area in particular should be much smaller. Unlike those solid-axle, wagon-sprung roadsters it should have independent springing of all four wheels. The recent evolution of the European Grand Prix car had shown that the ideal location for the engine in such a car is at the rear. So why not profit from that lesson? The old sleds at Indy were still running locked rear ends with no differential action to keep both driving tires biting in the turns and that, too, had to go.

These were some of the characteristics that I wanted in my car when I started looking for help in building it. I made the rounds of nearly every race-car builder in Southern California and told each one what I wanted to get done. But they all thought in traditional, tried-and-true terms, told me that I was all wrong, that I was throwing my money away and that if I'd just listen to them they'd show me how an Indy car *should* be built. I was very discouraged and time was running out fast.

Then, in early February, I had the luck to hear about John Crosthwaite. He had been with Cooper and Lotus in England and had been one of the pioneers in the adaptation of the Coventry Climax engine for racing purposes. In addition he was an expert on modern road-racing chassis. He had come to the States for the Sebring twelve-hour race a couple of years before, liked the country and stayed. He eventually landed in San Diego, where he designed and helped to build the Dolphin Formula Junior cars. He was still there and I blasted down to interview him.

"Yes," he said to all my ideas. "Yes, I think you're quite right on each of these features. Now, if I were doing it I would add a few more," and he spelled them out.

They all dovetailed with what I had in mind. He thought like a sophisticated European race-car designer and he could also think realistically in American oval-track terms, but without creaking, ancient preconceptions. He could think like no one else I had been able to find. We clicked. John moved to Long Beach and went to work for me.

He was and is tremendous. Like Fritz, he refuses to yes me. When he knows he's right he argues his point until he's won it or been proved wrong and we've had some fine struggles. He took over on the job quietly but masterfully. Every car I had ever built had been "engineered" solely by guess and experience and chalk marks on the garage floor. John made engineering drawings for every part of the Indy cars and when each part was cut, machined, ground, finished, it fit perfectly where it was supposed to fit without rubbing any other part. This for me was a novel and lint-picking approach, but John insisted upon it and, since we were building three identical cars, it did pay off.

Of course the project was utter madness. It was much more chaotic than the *Challenger* project ever had been, which should be impossible. But Voigt, Bubenik, Crosthwaite, Don Borth, Jack Sutton and all the other race-hardened—and therefore used to making supreme efforts—members of the team slaved magnificently and it began to look as though we might do the impossible and be at the Speedway when they opened the gates on May 1.

As the cars took shape they looked awfully good, so good that tycoon Jim Kimberly bought one on sight before it was half finished. He signed Jack Fairman of England to drive it for him in the 500. Early in the game I borrowed Chuck Daigh from Reventlow Automobiles to serve as chief test driver on the Indy project. He was to work on the cars and drive one in the race. I still needed another driver and although many Big Names began hitting me for a ride, I held out for one who had never driven at the Speedway.

Years before, during the second race ever held on the Willow Springs course in California, I had had a lap-after-lap battle with one of the most determined drivers I have ever encountered. He was in a big, ill-handling Ferrari and it was beautiful to see how his smooth handling skill overcame the car's vices. I sat on his tail and pushed him mercilessly for a lap but he would not move over and let me by. Then another lap, and he showed no sign of being bothered, although the average driver would have been a nervous wreck by this time. This went on for five laps and he never gave an inch nor made a move that wasn't perfectly calculated. As I finally squeaked past him I thought,

"Man!" That kid is going to be a great driver!"

I found out that his name was Dan Gurney and watched his career over the years as he became one of the world's most polished and perfect road racing drivers. Most of his experience in the Big Time had been gained in cars that had the general configuration of my own. He had had outstanding experience with light-weight, rear-engined, independently-sprung race cars. I wanted him.

He was booked to drive one of the John Zink entries: a standard Offy, or else a roadster powered by a gas turbine. I arranged with Gurney that if neither of those cars qualified, he would drive for me. Again the old heads called me a fool for choosing a driver without a shred of Speedway experience.

Our departure for Indianapolis was much more frantic than most of our photo finishes with race dates. We left six hours after what was supposed to be the latest possible deadline. We were still loading our vehicles as we pulled out of Long Beach at 5 a.m., literally shovelling parts into the cars and trucks. Naturally there was no packing list, but by a miracle most of the mechanics remembered and managed to bring most of the parts that they were supposed to bring. Getting that jumble sorted out at the Speedway was another madhouse, but we got there for the start of the qualifying round.

There were seventy-one other cars trying to get into that race. Did we rank rookies stand a chance of being among the thirty-three starters? The odds were rough.

First we had to run the gauntlet of technical inspection. The Indianapolis 500, with its almost half-million dollar purse, is organized around one of the world's tightest, most exclusive cliques. I was a newcomer, an outsider, an interloper, trying to enter a set of machines that were in violent rebellion against all that was secure and sacred at the hallowed Speedway.

That keel-hauling was rough. They were only doing their job, screening every entry to make sure that nothing about it was unsafe. My cars were absolute freaks and they got the super-suspicious scrutiny that they deserved as such.

They picked the first car to pieces, looking for faults.

"Your bumper is too close to the car's tail," they told me. "You've got to have better fuel tank protection."

"Would the bumper be all right if the fuel weren't in the tail?" I asked, like a real bumpkin.

"Well naturally," they shot back.

"That's really definite?" I asked.

"That's what we said," they said.

"Well the fuel tanks are in the car's sides, not in its tail," I told them. "Now what else is wrong?"

That's how it went, a point-by-point battle from the car's tip to tail. Finally there was just one more hurdle: no leakage of oil onto the track would be tolerated. Daigh took the car around for several laps and the car didn't ooze a drop. Plenty of the Offies were squirting the stuff. So my cars finally were pronounced race-worthy and OK'd for practice and for qualifying attempts.

The reaction of the public at large to my cars was uniformly one of excitement, approval and hearty wishes for our success. Our garage was constantly hemmed in by crowds of onlookers and every time we pushed a car to the track, it was followed by a large crowd. We were smothered with well-wishers and it was wonderful how people volunteered their help. Journalist Jack Brady, for example— a sort of amateur Alfred Neubauer—just attached himself to our crew and for the whole month provided us with absolutely invaluable records of our cars' lap times, ambient temperature, humid-

ity, track temperature, tire temperature and pressure and all those
data that there never seems to be time to record.

One morning Brady didn't show up until around noon. I had
gotten so used to him and to leaning on him that I yelled,

"Where have *you* been? Who do you think's paying you?"

Then I did a slow double-take, and said, sheepishly,

"Gee. That's right. I'm *not* paying you, am I?"

Reactions to the cars by drivers, mechanics and car owners fell
into two sharply defined classes. The non-thinkers who are mere
imitators grumbled and criticized.

"Eleven hundred and fifty pounds ready to go! Why, those things
are so flimsy that they'll never finish the grind. They're a menace.
They ought to be banned!"

The real thinkers at the Speedway—men like Watson, Bignotti,
Brauner and Hirashima—were different. They came to my garage
and looked hard and long. They respected the possible break-
through that they saw and asked intelligent questions. I appreciated this and took the time to answer all of them in detail, just
as Clay Smith always did. I also hoped that they would adopt some
of my ideas. This was because I already had my next year's cars
designed in my head and they were full of innovations that made
these obsolete.

Kimberly's outfit ran into no end of bad breaks and his car was
grounded. We had trouble sorting out the combination that would
let Daigh's Harvey Aluminum Special go as fast as it should and
that car also failed to qualify. But our luck with Gurney was something else.

Gurney was at the Speedway when they opened the gates. He
got into the Zink Offy, turned some effortless practice laps and
asked to take his driver's test. He was the first rookie in history to
complete those tests within the first two days that the track was
open. That certainly vindicated my faith in Gurney and I tensely
followed every run by the two Zink cars. Neither would go fast
enough to qualify and they gave me the driver that I wanted most.

Dan practiced in the other Harvey Aluminum Special and ana-
lyzed the chassis as only a highly intelligent driver with his special-
ized experience could. He dictated change after change in its
adjustments and each one made for quicker lap times. Finally he
told Crosthwaithe,

"Now it's perfect. Do not lay a wrench on this car. Is that clear?"

He gave the impression that he'd break the neck of anyone who tampered with the combination that he had developed. On the first day of qualifying he took a couple of laps, then raised his hand— the signal that he was ready for the crucial test. He turned four smooth laps, all within a few hundredths of a second of each other, for an average speed of 147.886 MPH over the ten miles. Parnelli Jones, in the pole position, had qualified at 150.370. Gurney gave us a starting position in the middle of the third row, just eight positions behind Jones. This was far more than I had dared to hope for. We were faster than 64 other cars—one little Buick against the mighty Novis and that horde of torquing Offies.

Gurney packed his helmet and goggles and said goodbye to us for a few days. He flew to Europe, drove a Porsche Formula One car in the French Grand Prix and won his and Porsche's first World Championship race. And then he zoomed back to Indianapolis for our own little go.

In the meanwhile we kept working, trying to get the other Harvey car squared away. I have no desire to drive fast any more except when my cars aren't going as fast as I am convinced they should and will go. I had to see why our second car wouldn't go faster, so I went to Chief Steward Harlan Fengler and told him what I wanted.

"Well okay," he said. "Just keep it under 125 MPH."

I took off and the car went wonderfully. That old fearless feeling was with me and I began to feel the car out. Naturally, I hadn't taken a driver's test and hadn't ever driven on the track before, although I had put the car through its paces at Riverside Raceway. When I got away from the front straightaway with all its observers, I just naturally stepped harder on the throttle and was having the time of my life. Everything would have been fine if a spotter in the northwest turn hadn't put a watch on me and phoned ahead to Fengler. I was timed through that turn at 137 MPH and Fengler did everything short of banishing me from the track for life. I'd like to have driven the car in the race but I knew better than to ask for a driver's test after having asked for and gotten the full wrath of top authority.

When we first arrived at the Speedway one of the more hip

mechanics had greeted me with, "Welcome to the antique automobile club."

He was referring of course to the traditional, 1,600 pound sleds.
After Gurney's qualifying run, however, the few seeds of doubt
about the Old Order turned into an unexpected harvest. Even before the race, one of the pillars of the inner clique stated, "Thompson has busted this thing wide open. It's the end of an era. Buyers
are clamoring for his cars and they haven't even raced yet. The
writing is on the wall. Every last Offy must be up for sale."

Came race day and, according to our strategy, Gurney drove to
last. He lay in about tenth place almost to the half-way point.
Then, just past 232 miles, a miserable, two-bit grease seal failed in
the car's transaxle, the rear end locked up and ended our effort for
the year. It was all right with me. I had done much more than
I had hoped to do and I had learned those things that can only be
learned in the crucible of speed, through actual participation. I had
learned much about what it takes to compete at Indianapolis and
I could hardly wait for 1963.

We all went to the big victory dinner after the race. Fritz and
I were hatching plans over the Chicken *à la* King and canned peas
when a voice jolted me:

"Will Mickey Thompson please step to the rostrum!"

"Now what have I done?" I thought. I clambered up in front
of the elite of American professional racing and placed myself at
the mercy of USAC director Don Cummins of diesel-engine fame.

"Mickey," he said, "It is my pleasure to present you with the
coveted D-A Lubricant annual award for Mechanical Achievement.
Sixty-seven sharp men voted on who should receive it. Fifty-nine
named you."

Can you imagine what that meant to me? Me, Mechanic of the
Year in the eyes of the Indianapolis crowd? To me, this was as
precious as a knighthood and it was more precious than winning
the race. Along with the honor went a trophy and a handsome
ring that will always be among my most cherished possessions.

Now let me backtrack to an important incident in my '62 Indianapolis campaign.

My cars weighed approximately 450 pounds, about 30 per cent
less than the conventional Speedway cars. Because of this, I knew

that I could run successfully on tires with a much softer tread compound than was standard for the heavier cars.

So, early in the project—if you can call February early—I had gone to Firestone and asked for such tires, which would give me a sharper bite and therefore would add whole miles per hour to my cars' lap times. Because of the much lighter loading of the tires they should wear no faster than much harder tires on much heavier cars. Soft-compound tires were a major factor in the whole concept on which my '62 Indy cars were based.

Firestone agreed to accommodate me, in view of the radical nature of my cars. They made a firm provision that the soft-compound tires would have to be track-tested at the Speedway in prototype form long enough before the race so that absolutely safe and reasonably durable tires of this type could be put into production.

Of course we barely made our timetable at all. I asked for the special tires anyway.

"We can't do it, man. You know that. You know that we can't release any product that hasn't been thoroughly tested."

I wanted my cars to go faster and they were holding back the key. I was under a million tons of pressure and I became livid. And just at that time Raymond Firestone, president of the company, looked in at my garage.

"Mr. Firestone," I said, "your company has probably just lost me a qualifier and it may have lost me the race. I designed these cars to run on a specific type of rubber. Your company promised me that rubber and now it refuses to give it to me. I just want you to know that I'll never use a Firestone product again except in the direst emergency."

Mr. Firestone tried to explain his company's position, but I could only think of the two or more MPH that were being withheld from me. It was months before I cooled off.

36

As SOON AS I RETURNED TO LONG BEACH THERE WERE OTHER THINGS
to do. There was that Class D acceleration record, which left a
gap in an otherwise perfect score. Again I contacted General Le
May, got the use of March AFB and got *Attempt* and its 180-cubic-
inch Pontiac engine into shape. On July 15, 1962 I bumped the
average for the standing-start kilo from Caracciola's 110.2 to
112.088, which also counted as an American National record. I
wanted the mile in the worst way, but my engine seized on the
return run and I slid for the last 500 feet. Good enough. Let someone else have a shot at absolute acceleration records now.

Again I took along a new passenger car, a Pontiac *Catalina*
loaded with all the factory high-performance options. My plan for
it was to raise my own American National standing kilo and mile
records and then to set new *flying*-start kilo and mile records. Everyone said that this couldn't be done on so short a course. But I took
care of that by backing off into the fields and charging and bouncing through high grass at 100 MPH or so before reaching the strip.
But the pessimists were right for once and I got standing-start
records only with the *Catalina*.

Meanwhile, the drought in Utah had broken during the previous winter and astronomic amounts of precipitation had flooded
the Great Salt Desert. The Salt promised to be in better condition
than it had been in for several years. Bill Backman and I had overcome our differences, had actually become very good friends, and
he and his board couldn't do enough to be helpful. I kept in constant touch with Wendover and right after the March AFB runs I
received word that the Salt was almost dry and ready. Back again
I went with *Challenger*, hoping at last to get this LSR ordeal over
with. I also took the *Catalina* along for a little run on the ten-mile
circle.

Late in the afternoon of July 23 Fritz, as usual, shoe-horned me into *Challenger's* cockpit. This normally calls for him to push down on my shoulders and head and squeeze me back under the car's roll cage. Well, we had rehearsed this of course before leaving Long Beach and it was *tough*. It seems that three of my vertebrae had fused and my back just didn't want to bend to follow the seat's contour. But we made it anyway. Before this run I announced to the press that as of July 27 I was through with LSR driving, win or lose.

The Salt looked fairly rough when I took off from the extreme south end of the course, but I didn't mind that. I was used to rough courses. But from the start *Challenger* began oscillating violently, dribbling far worse than she ever had before. When I began seeing triple images and thought my innards would never unscramble themselves, I backed off. It wasn't the roughness of the course this year, but rather a washboard quality which it had at the south end. It made about two miles of runway useless, leaving only 9.6 miles that were fit to run on.

Challenger shook so badly that I had to make sure that something wasn't seriously wrong with the car. After all, she hadn't been run for two years. So I took off on the good surface after first removing the canopy, the better to observe what was happening to various parts of the car. It felt wonderful, just like the 406 run. I went through first cog, then second and then, at about 325 MPH, into high.

At that point the pressure of the wind split my goggles at the center hinge and threatened to blow the eyeballs right out of my head. I instinctively raised a hand to deflect the wind and it was slammed into my face, almost breaking my nose. I ducked, got off the throttle and popped the chute, at least having found out that the dribbling had been no fault of the car.

I was too tired and shaken to say anything to the press at that time or even to decide what to say to them later. I overheard one newsman say,

"Well, it looks like Thompson's lost his nerve."

I ignored that and headed back to Wendover. That evening, after I had rested and reflected on the situation, I got together with a good friend, author Wayne Thoms.

"You know," I said to him, "getting the big record on that short course is a total impossibility. Cobb had fourteen miles! I don't want to do it, but I'm just going to have to throw in the towel. And those news guys are already saying I'm chicken."

"Why don't you do this?" Wayne said. "One by one, put them in *Challenger* and give them a push-ride over that washboard. Let them see and feel for themselves what you're up against. Count me out because I can already imagine it and want none of it. Then, after you've shaken the paperboys apart, ask them if they think you ought to try driving 400 out there."

And that's what I did. I pushed them up to only 50 MPH but that was plenty. When the last man climbed out wet, limp and shattered I said,

"OK, boys, you're my witnesses. Would you consider driving a *passenger* car over that stuff?"

They laughed at the ridiculous suggestion. I told them that four years of fighting for the LSR against worsening course conditions was enough for me, and that as of that instant *Challenger* was a museum piece.

Judy cried again. This time the tears were from pure happiness.

Before dawn on the 24th I was back on the Salt, this time in the *Catalina*. The ten-mile circle—in the best area of the Salt—was in splendid condition and at 5:45 A.M. I took off for attacks on American National Unlimited and Class B (closed car division) records. The Pontiac ran strongly at 153 plus. This was quite a sensation because even on that huge circle you are in a constant slide with the rear end of the car hanging out at least a foot and a half beyond the front tire tracks.

One of the hazards of driving on the Salt is the prevalence of loose nails there. The courses must be resurveyed every season and the surveyors drive spikes into the surface to mark their stations. Then, when the surface is dragged, nails occasionally become uprooted inadvertently and are left lying on the course. A team that is careful will first go over the course looking for nails and other bits of flotsam and jetsam such as pieces of broken flywheels. But finding every loose nail in that vastness is a pretty hard thing to do.

We made fuel stops at intervals of about 100 miles and Lloyd Cox of El Monte and I took turns at the wheel. Once when I came in Fritz heard a hissing tire and, sure enough, it had picked up a nail. Thank God we caught it at that time. And then, incredibly enough, when Cox came in at the end of his turn at the wheel, the same thing happened again. A blowout at that speed and with that centrifugal force acting on the car could have been very serious. Somebody was still looking out for us, it seemed.

At the 100-mile distance our speed had dropped to 139 MPH, Fritz pulled the plugs, found a dead hole, pulled the rocker cover on that bank of cylinders and found one rocker lying there loose. Due to the steady and high centrifugal force it had been starved for oil and had broken its stud. Fritz removed the pushrod and other loose parts and I went out again, on seven barrels. We managed to run quite steadily at around 143 MPH until the 500-kilometer point. Then we began to bog down once more. Another check showed that two more rockers in that starved bank had broken, so we cut back to five cylinders. Knowing that it was just a matter of time until we lost the last barrel in that bank, we kept going until the 1,000-kilo and three-hour marks were behind us and called it a day. We had picked up 94 new USAC records in spite of our little mechanical problems

I had been working on the design of my 1963 Indianapolis cars and the Harvey Aluminum Company had agreed to sponsor them all. I had no great, burning desire to drive at the Speedway, but I planned to have four, maybe five entries there and was not sure that I could find that many drivers who could get the cars around the track as fast as the cars were capable of going. I knew that I could do the job and decided that I had better get some experience driving a vehicle of this type at real speed. Also, having decided to switch to Chevrolet engines, I wanted to test one under those conditions. Finally, there were many American National Class C records waiting to be plucked. Some had stood since as far back as 1933; many had been set by that great old record breaker, Ab Jenkins.

So we dropped a Chev V8, destroked to 301.5 cubic inches, into one of the '62 Harvey Aluminum Specials and headed back to Bonneville, where we turned out to practice on September 17. There had been a great deal of speculation about how fast the car could go on the ten-mile circle. I said that I thought that 180 MPH was possible, but most people said I'd never get near that. The car would slide right off the circle because it was so light, they said.

The Salt was wet and slippery in several areas and I just tooled around between 150 and 155, feeling the whole situation out. After a few laps of carefully studying the car and the course I came in and said to Fritz,

"Why don't you take it around a few times and let me know what you think about it?"

Fritz was delighted to get a ride. He'd never driven one of our Indy cars and he wanted to. He charged off and everything seemed so easy. He knew that 5,000 RPM was 150 MPH and he zoomed right up to that. Real easy.

"What's he afraid of?" Fritz thought. "I'll show these guys some nice fat times."

He was still on his first lap and not yet familiar with the course, but he came wailing toward our pit area at about 165. Right in front of it was a big slick expanse which he hit. He spun and looped about seven times.

When we got through razzing him Fritz said, "Well, at least it didn't scare me. It was only like being on an ice rink."

It wasn't my plan that Fritz would be the one to prove the point, but now we knew that the car had no tendency to flip in a slide or spin but instead wanted to stay solidly on its four wheels.

I went back out and worked my speed up to a comfortable 170, when the engine's water temperature approached the danger point. That told us that the radiator which had been adequate for the smaller aluminum Buick mill was not up to the cast-iron Chevvy's requirements. So we went into Wendover, bought an old radiator in a wrecking yard, cut it in half and made up the connections necessary to couple it to the car's existing cooling system. It looked pretty untidy but it made a big difference. I turned a couple of laps at 180 and we seemed to be in business.

USAC was on the job bright and early, as usual, and I began record runs at 6:05 A.M. My first lap—standing start—was 164 MPH. The next one jumped to 177 and the next to 178.9. Then, three-quarters of the way around the fourth lap the engine blubbered and quit, the car went sideways, the engine caught again, the exhaust indicated an extreme over-rich condition. I pulled into the pit, disgusted with having just thrown away almost an hour. The cause turned out to be a scrap of note paper which had been sucked out of my pocket by the slipstream and plastered to the Chev fuel injector's single inlet in the side of the hood.

So I took off again, making a fresh start at 7:15. My first six flying laps were between 176 and 179 MPH with the car feeling ideal. But then the coolant temperature drove me back down to about 165. Then steam began jetting from one of the radiator cores and I headed for the pit.

"Stay in the car!" Fritz shouted.

The crew tipped the car on its side; Fritz deftly and quickly soldered a penny over the leak, the car was dropped, the cooling system topped off, and I was on my way again.

Finally, after having driven at nearly full throttle for 725 miles, a couple of connecting rods let go, the engine locked up and the car looped, spun about fifteen times and slid for a good half-mile. Away from the scraped course the Salt was rough enough to gouge out the underside of the body. During all this action the car slammed against one of the flimsy little lath course-markers which hit me full in the face, cracking right through the bubble shield that I was wearing. Thank God I also had goggles on under the shield. Without them I would have been hurt badly.

Although the ride ended too soon I had learned a great deal about cornering to the left in an independently sprung vehicle at high speed. If I had to take a driver's test at the Speedway this experience would help. And, having driven almost one and a half times the 500's distance, I satisfied myself that I could do that too, stiff back or not.

Also, I had racked up forty-two new records, eight of them FIA International ones. Most of those had been set at Monza by J. B. Baillie in a Jaguar. I topped them by about 37 MPH—on gasoline.

This brought my list of FIA International and American National records up to 182. I'll never defend one of them and I don't care who comes along and breaks them. That's what records are for. Once I've broken a record I forget it. Once I've accomplished any far-out goal I have no interest in going over that ground again.

1962 was an awfully busy year, like all the rest. One of my rails, driven for me by Jack Chrisman, won the annual NHRA National Championship and two of my stock car entries won their classes in that important event. Tom McEwen, driving another of my rails, took low ET at the annual American Hot Rod Association Championship meet. Doug Hooper drove my *Sting Ray* in the Riverside Raceway three-hour Enduro and won against terrific competition.

In the Economy Run, Judy won her class and I won mine—the first time in the history of the Run that a husband and wife had done that. The year is full of such memories.

And one of the proudest moments of my life came in July when our son, Danny, an ardent Little Leaguer, was one of 28 chosen from 267 twelve-year-olds to try out for the local Area Championship. He made that. Then our Rolling Hills All Stars moved up to the Sectional Championship, which they won. And then they won the Southern California Championship. And then, all expenses paid, the Little Leaguers were flown to Vancouver, B. C., for the big, annual, international showdown. Judy and Lyndy and I tagged along of course and even though our team lost two to three, I couldn't have been a happier father.

37

I NEVER EXPECT TO WIN ANYTHING THE FIRST TIME OUT, BUT ONCE I've experienced a challenging situation I expect myself to have sense enough to figure out what it takes to win the next time.

Indianapolis in '62 was strictly a reconnaissance operation for me. I felt that I had learned from it what it would take to win the next time around. However, the machines that I wanted to build for '63 were such a wild departure from those we had in '62 that it would be almost a fresh start. Maybe it would take until '64 for me to really prove my point at Indianapolis. But of course, with my '63 cars still under construction, I was already full of new ideas for '64. So I'll just say that my hopes for '64 are high.

Tires are always basic, even though this is generally overlooked. A vehicle either is designed to fit available tires or—almost unheard of—the tires are designed to fit the vehicle. This happens so rarely because it is very expensive for tire companies; plus, they don't like being told their own business; plus, hardly anyone outside of the industry knows anything about the black art of tire engineering.

There is not an educational institution in the country that teaches a first-class course in that subject.

The experience I had with the '62 cars convinced me that I was on the right track and that brute horsepower, torque and structure had been emphasized to a ridiculous extent. The new emphasis had to be on smaller frontal area, lighter weight, lower center of gravity, lower unsprung weight and greater traction. Each of these is inseparably linked with tire design. If I wanted to build a better race car I could not do it without building a better tire. So, as I designed the new car I simultaneously designed tires that were an integrated part of it. They, too, were wild.

I designed everything about them: bead structure, casing, cord angle, tread pattern and approximate hardness of tread compound. And then I designed the cast iron molds in which to make them. Naturally I had a little help.

With these drawings and specifications in my briefcase I went to Akron and told the people at Goodyear what I wanted to do. They were astonished, first, because no one in the history of the American tire industry ever had been known to come in from the outside with such detailed tire requirements and with the engineering already highly completed. Second, there was the tire itself.

Its bead diameter was just twelve inches, the rim width was nine inches and its cross section was eleven inches at the widest point and terrifically low and squatty. It smacked of drag slicks and of the LSR tire.

"What on earth are you trying to do here?" they wanted to know.

I explained it point by point.

"Tires are part of a car's frontal area; this design will help to reduce the area. They are part of its weight, unsprung and over-all; these will help to reduce weight. They very largely determine center of gravity; these will help to lower it. Being smaller, they exert less leverage on running gear, so those parts can be made lighter. Because they are small and I still want good tread life, I just widen the tread. I lose some of the savings on frontal area, but I gain traction. Now I know that such a small tire will have very high surface speed and that its extreme width will contribute to centrifugal throwout. But that's the only real problem and we all know of a certain new molding technique that can probably eliminate it. What do you say?"

There was definite interest in the proposal, but Racing Director Tony Webner did not endorse it. The company felt that it was not quite ready to invade Indianapolis and did not see fit to go along.

This was devastating. Without the tires I couldn't build the car. Therefore I would have to build the tires. All right. I began organizing my own tire company. But as its financial demands grew along with all the other problems it entailed, I decided to leave it dormant for a while and try the one possible alternative.

I went back to Akron and went straight to Raymond Firestone.

"You remember what I said about your products and dire emergencies at the Speedway last May?" I asked him.

Yes, indeed he did.

"Well, I've come smack up against one already," I told him, "and I'm very sorry for having been so hot-headed. I need some very special tires built and if you don't build them for me I'll be driven into the tire business, which I really don't need right now."

"It's nice to have you back, Mickey," the big man said. "Now let's hear about what you have in mind."

Mr. Firestone was startled not so much by the type of tire— ultra-wide single tires are being made to replace duals on big trucks —as he was by the application: for Indianapolis. We sat down with his development engineers and he told them, "You tell me if you think you can control the centrifugal growth of this design at Indianapolis speeds. If you can, I say go ahead."

Engineer Steve Petrasek would not, could not promise success without a great deal of development and testing. But he said, "Mickey tells us he's convinced that this is *the* racing tire of the future. He's had a couple of good ideas before and this one just might be another. We can control the growth, but the extent to which we can do it in terms of performance can only be discovered on the track. I'd say it's a good gamble, though."

That did it I gave Steve the drawings and he began ordering cast iron for the molds immediately. There were a few conditions to the deal. Firestone would not release the tires to me for actual racing until they had been proved 100 per cent safe through actual track testing. Therefore I had to place one of the new cars at their disposal in ample time for such testing. I insisted upon the strictest secrecy for this project and insisted that the tires be available for the '63 Indianapolis race, providing I paid much of the development cost. After that Firestone could sell them to others as they saw fit. Raymond Firestone himself okayed the project and I owe him a great deal at this time for his confidence in my ideas.

It would be many months before tires could be built and tested, before it would even be known if Firestone would release the tires to me at all. And my '63 Speedway car was such a tightly integrated design that it could run on no other tires. If it was a gamble for Firestone it was a much bigger one for me. But I thought the odds were pretty good and rushed ahead with the construction of the first chassis.

Crosthwaite gave me a lot of argument over the design but finally resigned himself to it and built it my way, becoming steadily more enthusiastic. I decided to build three cars, all powered by 255-cubic-inch Chrevolet engines modified to give about 335 horsepower. The blocks and heads are aluminum, chopping about 125 pounds from the weight of the engine in cast-iron form. One engine will have dual overhead camshaft heads if we can complete them in time and don't run completely out of money. Two of the cars will have steel tube frames and should weight about 1,050 pounds dry and 1,400 wringing wet. One will have a titanium frame, a very strong metal that is about 40 per cent lighter than steel. This is the first such use of titanium in automotive history and should make for a saving in weight of about sixty pounds.

The cars will be 21.5 inches high at the base of the windscreen, meaning just about knee-high. They will be the lowest, lightest and most aerodynamically slippery cars ever seen at the Speedway and I expect that the first time they are rolled onto the track the agonized screams of Offy roadster owners will be heard from coast to coast.

Rumors about my plans were running wild in January, when word reached me that USAC's technical and safety committee was having a major rules meeting in Indianapolis and they were gunning for me and things like super-light cars and teeny-weenie tires.

I flew to that meeting, was admitted and soon was asked to state the reason for my presence. I stood up and said, "Gentlemen, I came here expecting to meet a group that is opposed to advanced thinking. I don't know how true that is. But I have spent $150,000 on this project so far and if you shut me out that's what I'll be

losing. I think that for $150,000 invested in the sport I deserve five
minutes of your time."

I told them that I felt like Daniel in the lion's den but to please
tell me what their worries were about my project and that I would
do my best to explain how and why I was handling these problems.
They kept asking and I kept talking until the first thing I knew
president Tom Binford was saying, "Mickey, it looks like you're the
lion and I'm Daniel. We are *not* enemies of advanced thinking; we
are impressed by what you've told us and find no fault with it. In
fact, we could use a man like you on our technical committee."

I was dumbfounded. I had gone there expecting to be slain and
was honored instead. I stammered my appreciation, declined the
honor because I was too impossibly busy to do it justice and went
home a happy man.

Things began shaping up fast. Firestone forged ahead with its
side of the project. I signed Bill Krause, whom I consider to be
one of the best drivers in the States today, to drive one of the new
cars. Then I contacted Britain's Graham Hill, World Champion
of Formula One Grand Prix racing for 1962, told him of my plans
and asked if he would drive for me. He would! And I wanted Gurney again in the very worst way, but so did Ford Motor Company.
Having more money than me, they got him.

On February 18 we were due to run the first tests of the new tires
at Riverside Raceway. Hill flew in for the occasion and, cramming
months of work into days, as usual, we got the first car completed
and ready for him to try. I'll just say at this point that no one was
disappointed.

When this book is off the press the 1963 Indianapolis 500 will
be history and we will all know what Thompson & Co. did there.
There is always the possibility that we might win, in which case I
will be through at Indianapolis. However, my guess right now is
that it will probably be another year before I win that race. And
if I don't then I'll keep right on trying until I do.

I was tremendously lucky in getting Dan Gurney to drive the Harvey Aluminum Special at Indianapolis in 1962. Although a rookie, he got seventh fastest qualifying time, at 147.886 MPH.

Firestone Tire & Rubber Company

Here is Gurney at speed. His performance in the Buick aluminum V8-powered, rear-engined, all-independently-sprung car had a revolutionizing effect upon Speedway engineering.

Wayne Thoms

Here is a good, clear view of my 1962 chassis layout. That's famous mechanic Harry Stephens leaning on the tire.

Here we are, pushing Dan off to qualify. Crowds like this followed us wherever we went.

This was our second pit stop and it was slow. It's one lesson I won't have to learn twice.

It was a great shock to Dan Gurney not to be able to finish the '62 Indianapolis 500.

A fine shot. Poor Dan getting shouted at from both sides.

The first test of our '63 car and tires at Riverside. Bending over making adjustments is John Crosthwaite, who has played a vital role in the building of the Indianapolis cars. Graham Hill behind the wheel.

A shot of Griff and me as we shook down our Sting Rays at Daytona in February of '62.

Graham Hill takes his first long look at his mount in the 1963 Indianapolis 500.

38

THOSE ARE THE HIGH POINTS OF MY LIFE SO FAR. I'M AWFULLY happy to have them behind me and to have little else in the realm of speed to feel I must do in this short and precious life.

Of course there's the old dream of taking an all-American road racing team to Europe and doing well for the USA. We have done magnificently in providing the world with excellent drivers, but our home-grown road racing machinery has been pretty pitiful. *There* is a challenge that could tempt me and it would not be incompatible with my manufacturing business, which keeps right on growing. We'll see.

I would like for this concluding chapter to be entirely positive but there is a negative note that fits best here.

Psychologists tell us that small children are capable of being the most heartlessly sadistic creatures on earth. Next to them, I say, come spectators. Our modern ones often are no better than those human beasts who flocked to the bloody games in the arenas of Rome. I am very serious about this. And, of course, I'm still speaking autobiographically—about myself.

When I was nobody, nobody else cared what I did or did not do. When I was just a little bit successful, people showed a little interest in what I would do next. But the more successful I've become, the more I've been knocked and the more I've been booed by the mob.

I realize that the mob tends to love the underdog. But what I find hard to accept is that I spent many long, lean years being an underdog myself. Where is the incentive for self-improvement, for accomplishment, if all it gets for you is jeers and catcalls from the very fraternity to which you've devoted your all?

I have lived for racing. It happens to be my best vehicle for expression and achievement. It is true that in very recent years I have made a good amount of money out of racing, which still is no crime. But beyond that, except for providing for my family, I have plowed every cent back into racing. My house is safe and my life insurance is paid up. But beyond that my every last asset is tied up in my Indianapolis effort for 1963. I have made money out of racing so that I could support racing.

Many people who follow racing are rebels against authority so that when a given individual dominates his sphere of racing he becomes an authority to be rebelled against. If this is true, and it probably is, it's bad for the sport and bad for all concerned.

It hurts me to my heart when all I have to do is drive out on a drag strip to have the crowd boo and lust for my defeat. What is infinitely worse is when a gentleman, a sportsman and a fine competitor such as Jack Chrisman, who has never offended a human being in his life, gets the same treatment when he appears in one of my cars. That is cruelly wrong and I hope and pray that by speaking out bluntly and honestly on this sad aspect of racing that a few will hear and think and encourage behavior that is more fair, humane and mature within our ranks. End of sermon.

A couple of years ago I did my utter best to get the Soviet government's permission to bring *Challenger* and/or *Assault* to the USSR for exhibition. I sent a personal representative to Moscow, but permission was denied. The story that I wanted to tell would not have been flattering to the Soviet system.

The story that I wanted to tell in that part of the world was what an almost penniless kid can achieve in our part of the world. I had no intention of shouting it blatantly. I only intended to state the facts: my background and what I had been able to accomplish because of and in spite of it. At least I can tell it here and I hope that the lesson means something to a few people. In our part of the world almost anything can be achieved through determination, imagination and effort. Money is not the absolute thing that it's cracked up to be.

I always say this: that what I have done anyone could do because it certainly hasn't been done on a basis of money or privilege. I can honestly say that every cent I've ever made has been made the hard way, and anyone who knows me at all can vouch for that, in spades.

I also say that no one, myself above all, ever has achieved anything important without the help of others. I mean that with all my heart and in this book I've tried at all times to emphasize the importance of that help.

Anyone who is trying to climb upward should never forget for an instant that the ladder of success is not self-supporting. It takes many hands to steady it and to keep it from toppling. It is all-important to learn to move up the ladder without stepping on those important hands, so that they let go.

When you're in a driven hurry, as I've always been, that is not always easy to remember. I have forgotten, often enough. But if there is a lesson I've learned that seems important to pass on, it's this: Don't step on those essential hands. And if you should happen to in your haste, take the time to forget your destination long enough to see that they are healed appreciatively and restored to strength.

Thank you, Judy. Your hands have been the strongest of all. I know they've taken the worst of it, yet you have complained the least.

Appendix

NOTE: As used hereafter, K is kilometer; M is mile. (F) is flying start; (S) is standing start.

WORLD'S UNLIMITED SPEED RECORDS

5 K (F)	10/6/59	Bonneville, Utah	Challenger I (Pontiac)		345.33
5 M (F)	"	" "	" " "		340.70
10 K (F)	"	" "	" " "		327.59
10 M (F)	"	" "	" " "		286.16
1 K (S)	5/14/60	March AFB, Calif.	Assault I (Pontiac)		132.94
1 M (S)	"	" " "	" " "		149.93

INTERNATIONAL CLASS A
8000 cc. and over (488 cu. ins. and over)

5 K (F)	10/6/59	Bonneville, Utah	Challenger I (Pontiac)		345.33
5 M (F)	"	" "	" " "		340.70
10 K (F)	"	" "	" " "		327.59
10 M (F)	"	" "	" " "		286.16
1 K (S)	5/14/60	March AFB, Calif.	Assault I (Pontiac)		132.71
1 M (S)	"	" " "	" " "		149.23

INTERNATIONAL CLASS B
5000 to 8000 cc. (305 to 488 cu. ins.)

1 K (S)	5/14/60	March AFB, Calif.	Assault II (Pontiac)		132.71
1 M (S)	"	" " "	" " "		149.93

INTERNATIONAL CLASS C
3000 to 5000 cc. (183 to 305 cu. ins.)

1 K (S)	7/9/61	March AFB, Calif.	Pontiac V-8		123.90
1 M (S)	"	" " "	" "		138.93
50 K (S)	9/18/62	Bonneville, Utah	Harvey Alum. Spl. (Buick)		172.53
50 M (S)	"	" "	" " " "		174.08
100 K (S)	"	" "	" " " "		174.87
100 M (S)	"	" "	" " " "		174.52
200 K (S)	"	" "	" " " "		172.65
200 M (S)	"	" "	" " " "		168.76
500 K (S)	"	" "	" " " "		162.35
1 Hour (S)	"	" "	" " " "		170.04

International Class D
2000 to 3000 cc. (122 to 183 cu. ins.)

1 K (S)	7/15/62	March AFB, Calif.	Attempt (Pontiac)	112.088

International Class E
1500 to 2000 cc. (91.5 to 122 cu. ins.)

1 K (S)	7/9/61	March AFB, Calif.	Pontiac Tempest	96.37
1 M (S)	"	" " "	" "	114.35

International Class F
1100 to 1500 cc. (67 to 91.5 cu. ins.)

1 K (S)	7/9/61	March AFB, Calif.	Pontiac Tempest	91.37
1 M (S)	"	" " "	" "	106.78

National Class—Unlimited

1 K (S)	5/14/60	March AFB, Calif.	Assault I (Pontiac)	132.94
1 M (S)	"	" " "	Assault II (Pontiac)	149.93
5 K (F)	10/6/59	Bonneville, Utah	Challenger I (Pontiac)	345.33
5 M (F)	"	" "	" " "	340.70
10 K (F)	"	" "	" " "	327.59
10 M (F)	"	" "	" " "	286.16

National Class A
488 cubic inches and over (8000 cc. & over)

1 K (S)	5/14/60	March AFB, Calif.	Assault I (Pontiac)	132.94
1 M (S)	"	" " "	" " "	149.23
5 K (F)	10/6/59	Bonneville, Utah	Challenger I (Pontiac)	345.33
5 M (F)	"	" "	" " "	340.70
10 K (F)	"	" "	" " "	327.59
10 M (F)	"	" "	" " "	286.16

National Class B
305 to 488 cubic inches (5000 to 8000 cc.)

1 K (S)	5/14/60	March AFB, Calif.	Assault II (Pontiac)	132.71
1 M (S)	"	" " "	" " "	149.93
5 K (S)	7/24/62	Bonneville, Utah	Pontiac Catalina	124.20
5 M (S)	"	" "	" "	134.69
10 K (S)	"	" "	" "	137.80
10 M (S)	"	" "	" "	143.56

National Class C
183 to 305 cubic inches (3000 to 5000 cc.)

25 K (F)	9/18/62	Bonneville, Utah		Harvey Alum. Spl. (Buick)					177.90
25 M (F)	"	"	"	"	"	"	"		177.02
50 K (F)	"	"	"	"	"	"	"		177.05
50 M (F)	"	"	"	"	"	"	"		177.11
75 K (F)	"	"	"	"	"	"	"		177.03
75 M (F)	"	"	"	"	"	"	"		176.79
100 K (F)	"	"	"	"	"	"	"		177.21
100 M (F)	"	"	"	"	"	"	"		174.77
200 K (F)	"	"	"	"	"	"	"		172.75
200 M (F)	"	"	"	"	"	"	"		169.05
250 K (F)	"	"	"	"	"	"	"		170.81
250 M (F)	"	"	"	"	"	"	"		168.96
300 K (F)	"	"	"	"	"	"	"		169.06
300 M (F)	"	"	"	"	"	"	"		162.29
400 K (F)	"	"	"	"	"	"	"		168.98
500 K (F)	"	"	"	"	"	"	"		162.39
1 Hour (F)	"	"	"	"	"	"	"		169.73
1 K (S)	7/9/61	March AFB, Calif.		Pontiac V-8					123.90
1 M (S)	"	"	"	"	"	"			138.93
25 K (S)	9/18/62	Bonneville, Utah		Harvey Alum. Spl. (Buick)					168.94
25 M (S)	"	"	"	"	"	"	"		172.23
50 K (S)	"	"	"	"	"	"	"		172.53
50 M (S)	"	"	"	"	"	"	"		174.08
75 K (S)	"	"	"	"	"	"	"		173.93
75 M (S)	"	"	"	"	"	"	"		175.26
100 K (S)	"	"	"	"	"	"	"		174.87
100 M (S)	"	"	"	"	"	"	"		174.52
200 K (S)	"	"	"	"	"	"	"		172.65
200 M (S)	"	"	"	"	"	"	"		168.76
250 K (S)	"	"	"	"	"	"	"		170.88
250 M (S)	"	"	"	"	"	"	"		168.93
300 K (S)	"	"	"	"	"	"	"		169.02
300 M (S)	"	"	"	"	"	"	"		167.55
400 K (S)	"	"	"	"	"	"	"		168.94
500 K (S)	"	"	"	"	"	"	"		162.35
1 Hour (S)	"	"	"	"	"	"	"		170.04

National Class D
122 to 183 cubic inches (2000 to 3000 cc.)

1 K (S)	7/15/62	March AFB, Calif.	Attempt (Pontiac)		112.09

NATIONAL CLASS E
91.5 to 122 cubic inches (1500 to 2000 cc.)

1 K (S)	7/9/61	March AFB, Calif.	Pontiac Tempest	96.37
1 M (S)	"	" " "	" "	114.35

NATIONAL CLASS F
67 to 91.5 cubic inches (1100 to 1500 cc.)

1 K (S)	7/9/61	March AFB, Calif.	Pontiac Tempest	91.37
1 M (S)	"	" " "	" "	106.782

AMERICAN STOCK CAR—UNLIMITED CLASS—CLOSED CAR DIVISION

1 K (S)	7/15/62	March AFB, Calif.	Pontiac Catalina	90.55
1 M (S)	"	" " "	" "	105.14
25 K (F)	7/25/62	Bonneville, Utah	Pontiac Catalina	149.28
25 M (F)	"	" "	" "	149.25
50 K (F)	"	" "	" "	149.24
50 M (F)	"	" "	" "	149.27
75 K (F)	"	" "	" "	149.27
75 M (F)	"	" "	" "	148.96
100 K (F)	"	" "	" "	149.27
100 M (F)	"	" "	" "	139.38
200 K (F)	"	" "	" "	141.23
200 M (F)	"	" "	" "	143.22
250 K (F)	"	" "	" "	142.57
250 M (F)	"	" "	" "	142.37
300 K (F)	"	" "	" "	143.11
300 M (F)	"	" "	" "	143.44
400 K (F)	"	" "	" "	142.31
400 M (F)	"	" "	" "	142.94
500 K (F)	"	" "	" "	143.42
500 M (F)	"	" "	" "	140.64
1000 K (F)	"	" "	" "	137.78
1 Hour (F)	"	" "	" "	142.09
3 Hour (F)	"	" "	" "	143.12
25 K (S)	"	" "	" "	142.37
25 M (S)	"	" "	" "	144.92
50 K (S)	"	" "	" "	145.75
50 M (S)	"	" "	" "	147.07
75 K (S)	"	" "	" "	146.90
75 M (S)	"	" "	" "	147.77
100 K (S)	"	" "	" "	147.49
100 M (S)	"	" "	" "	146.78
200 K (S)	"	" "	" "	140.42
200 M (S)	"	" "	" "	142.93
250 K (S)	"	" "	" "	141.99
250 M (S)	"	" "	" "	142.01

300 K (S)	"	"	"	"	"		142.75
300 M (S)	"	"	"	"	"		143.07
400 K (S)	"	"	"	"	"		141.98
400 M (S)	"	"	"	"	"		142.67
500 K (S)	"	"	"	"	"		143.30
500 M (S)	"	"	"	"	"		140.70
1000 K (S)	"	"	"	"	"		138.18
1 Hour (S)	"	"	"	"	"		141.47
3 Hour (S)	"	"	"	"	"		143.11

AMERICAN CLASS "B"—CLOSED CAR DIVISION—
305 to 488 cubic inches (5000 to 8000 cc.)

1 K (S)	7/15/62	March AFB, Calif.	Pontiac Catalina			90.55
1 M (S)	"	" " "	" "			105.14
5 K (S)	7/24/62	Bonneville, Utah	Pontiac Catalina			124.20
5 M (S)	"	" "	" "			134.69
10 K (S)	"	" "	" "			137.80
10 M (S)	"	" "	" "			143.56
1 K (F)	"	" "	" "			153.64
1 M (F)	"	" "	" "			153.67
5 K (F)	"	" "	" "			153.52
5 M (F)	"	" "	" "			153.45
10 K (F)	"	" "	" "			153.42
10 M (F)	"	" "	" "			153.47
25 K (F)	7/25/62	" "	" "			149.28
25 M (F)	"	" "	" "			149.25
50 K (F)	"	" "	" "			149.24
50 M (F)	"	" "	" "			149.27
75 K (F)	"	" "	" "			149.27
75 M (F)	"	" "	" "			148.96
100 K (F)	"	" "	" "			149.27
100 M (F)	"	" "	" "			139.38
200 K (F)	"	" "	" "			141.23
200 M (F)	"	" "	" "			143.22
250 K (F)	"	" "	" "			142.57
250 M (F)	"	" "	" "			142.37
300 K (F)	"	" "	" "			143.11
300 M (F)	"	" "	" "			143.44
400 K (F)	"	" "	" "			142.31
400 M (F)	"	" "	" "			142.94
500 K (F)	"	" "	" "			143.42
500 M (F)	"	" "	" "			140.64
1000 K (F)	"	" "	" "			137.78
1 Hour (F)	"	" "	" "			142.09
3 Hour (F)	"	" "	" "			143.12

25 K (S)	"	"	"	"	"	142.37
25 M (S)	"	"	"	"	"	144.92
50 K (S)	"	"	"	"	"	145.75
50 M (S)	"	"	"	"	"	147.07
75 K (S)	"	"	"	"	"	146.90
75 M (S)	"	"	"	"	"	147.77
100 K (S)	"	"	"	"	"	147.49
100 M (S)	"	"	"	"	"	146.78
200 K (S)	"	"	"	"	"	140.42
200 M (S)	"	"	"	"	"	142.93
250 K (S)	"	"	"	"	"	141.99
250 M (S)	"	"	"	"	"	142.01
300 K (S)	"	"	"	"	"	142.75
300 M (S)	"	"	"	"	"	143.07
400 K (S)	"	"	"	"	"	141.98
400 M (S)	"	"	"	"	"	142.67
500 K (S)	"	"	"	"	"	143.30
500 M (S)	"	"	"	"	"	140.70
1000 K (S)	"	"	"	"	"	138.18
1 Hour (S)	"	"	"	"	"	141.47
3 Hour (S)	"	"	"	"	"	143.11

NOTE: Records for 25 K and above set on 10-mile circle at Bonneville in several classes with Pontiac stock car are shared by Mickey Thompson and Lloyd Cox, who co-drove after the first 100 miles. This applies to both the Unlimited Class and Class B stock car records.